S0-BZN-810

Jewish
Radicalism

Jewish Radicalism:
A Selected Anthology

Edited and with an Introduction by

Jack Nusan Porter
and Peter Dreier

Grove Press, Inc., New York

Copyright © 1973 by Jack Nusan Porter and Peter Dreier

All Rights Reserved

No part of this book may be reproduced, for any reason, by any means, including any method of photographic reproduction, without the permission of the publisher.

ISBN: 0-394-48125-9

Library of Congress Catalog Card Number: 72-3714

First Printing

Manufactured in the United States of America
by The Book Press, Brattleboro, Vermont

Distributed by Random House, Inc., New York

Dedicated to the men and women of the radical movement, both here in the United States and abroad.

"If I am not for myself, who will be for me? And if I am only for myself, what am I? And if not now, when?"

(Talmudic Saying, Hillel the Elder, *Ethics of the Fathers*, I, 14)

Contents

Preface

As we write this, another new Jewish student newspaper has reached our desks. There are others underway. It is impossible to say whether the next will be the 50th, 55th, 60th, or perhaps the 70th to have appeared in the past few years.

Since the 1967 Israeli-Arab Six-Day War, there has emerged a political and cultural renaissance among young Jews, young in spirit or in age, and not only in the United States and Canada, but in Europe, Israel, Australia, and South America.

All over the world, groups are publishing a Jewish "underground" press—an exciting alternative to the staid and lifeless weeklies and bi-weeklies which pass for the "establishment" press. They may not even know that they are part of a movement. What they do know is that they are angry and restless over the condition of world Jewry. And unlike the vast majority of their peers, they are willing to do something about it.

The genesis of this anthology was our fear that some of the best writings from this movement would be lost. Several of the Jewish student papers lasted for only one or two issues; others publish irregularly, often uncertain where the funds for the printer are coming from. To the majority of the American Jewish community, this Jewish student press is invisible, the radical Jewish movement ephemeral.

It was our idea to make at least some of the anguish and

outcry of young radical Jews available to a wider audience. This book is written for future generations. It is a collection of manifestos, articles, poems, and cartoons selected from movement journals and newspapers. It is a literary "snapshot" of an ongoing process.

These pieces represent a small patch of thought on a much wider landscape. There has been a resurgence of ethnic, racial, sexual and religious pride in the middle of 20th-century America. Catholic and Protestant radical theologians and rebels like Father James Groppi, the Berrigan brothers, and Bishop Pike; "Jesus freaks," "Polish power," "black power," "Indian power," gay and women's liberation, the Italian-American Anti-Defamation League, these are all manifestations and nuances of a multifaceted quest for historical roots, personal identity, and intimate community amidst a mad, technocratic, and antiseptic society.

We believe that these thirty-eight pieces will stimulate the reader—the committed liberal, the skeptical radical, the anxious parent, and the full-time professional—to recognize that something is happening among Jewish youth.

Ultimately, our debt for this anthology is to the thousands of young people who are challenging the way things are.

We ask our readers to get in touch with the local Jewish student groups in their area—or to start one if none exists— if the ideas in this volume provoke, interest, anger, or outrage you. To aid the reader to do so, we have added a bibliography on Jewish radicalism and Jewish youth, plus a listing of presently existing movement groups and journals.

This has been a difficult book to collect because of the preponderance of material. We are sorry we could not include many other excellent articles. Our thanks to all the contributors and editorial boards of the journals involved.

We also acknowledge the support of the following people: Bernard Beck, Leonard Fein, Morris U. Schappes; David Kaufman of the Jewish Student Press Service; Rabbi Oscar Groner of the B'nai B'rith Hillel Foundation; Maralee Gordon, Myron Pearlman, Bob Loeb, Bob Frankel, Marc Gellman,

Robert Siegel; Ellen Koblitz for her detached disinterest; Sheldon Bankier, Golden and Kseil Wolf Stundel for too much; the Twerski family; Esther and Richard Press; Sylvia and Allan, Sol and Bella Porter; and finally Elie Wiesel. They generated much energy in all of us. Thanks must also go to Gladys Greenman for her secretarial help.

We are especially grateful to our editor at Grove Press, Fred Jordan. He is not only a fine editor, but a warm and generous friend.

And finally, we express our appreciation to our parents; this book is a gift of *naches* and joy.

Jack Nusan Porter
Peter Dreier

Introduction

The Roots of Jewish Radicalism

In an essay on Jewish youth written in 1961, David Boroff lamented the retreat from radicalism among young, third-generation Jews. Their parents' generation, he wrote, "was characterized by a restless groping for meaning and identity . . . [but] as the doors of American society swing open hospitably to talented Jews, the impulse to castigate and criticize becomes attenuated."

Only a year before the beginnings of the New Left, Boroff predicted, with regret, that "as Jews increasingly become part of the 'Establishment,' intellectual teenagers will merely see themselves as apprentices rather than critics."[1]

In retrospect, of course, we all know better. Jewish participation in the New Left was the Jewish Establishment's worst-kept secret. The visibility of the Mark Rudds, Jerry Rubins, and Abbie Hoffmans only underscored what observers of the new radicalism knew all along—that Jews were greatly over-represented among the leadership and activists of the student movement.

Nor would Boroff have expected a movement of young Jews directed at specifically Jewish issues. Yet, as the New Left began to wane, and in the aftermath of the Arab-Israeli Six-Day War of 1967, an upsurge of Jewish consciousness hit the campuses, and a new voice—what we call the "Jewish Left"—appeared.[2] Young Jews began to make demands for

"Jewish studies" programs, to publish Jewish underground newspapers, to criticize Israeli policies while defending Zionism against Arab and pro-Arab attacks, to protest on behalf of Soviet Jewry, and to confront the Jewish Establishment for "selling out" to the "American dream" while ignoring the needs of the Jewish community.*

The focus of this anthology is the Jewish Left. It did not emerge in a vacuum. It is crucial to understand the experiences of these young Jews in the context of trends within the New Left, the American Jewish community and American society in general. So we shall discuss the participation of young Jews in the student movement and also the reaction within American Jewry to the radical activity of the past decade.

Most adult Jews are considered—and consider themselves —to be liberals and Democrats. Still, there has been a noticeable shift in recent years; not to the far right, but to a less vocal liberalism, a cautiousness when discussing "Jewish interests" and what are "liberal interests." Especially on local issues—such as the mayoralty elections in New York and Philadelphia—Jews have split along class lines. Crime in the streets, open admissions to college, community control in black neighborhoods threaten those working class and lower-middle class Jews who remain in our cities' transitional neighborhoods, in civil service and blue-collar occupations. Many Jews see the demands of the New Left and black militants as direct challenges to their own liberalism; others as threats to their neighborhoods or job security. At the same time that many Jews have begun to feel secure as Americans, accepting a mode of accommodation to middle-class life, many of their children are challenging the very foundations of this experience.

Thus, the American Jewish community now finds itself under attack by both Jewish radicals and radical Jews—each

---

* Throughout this introduction we shall refer to the "Jewish community." The term is shorthand for six million American Jews. As we shall discuss below, however, we believe that little sense of "community" exists among American Jewry. Indeed, this belief is the point of the book.

group a small but outspoken minority among Jewish college students and young adults. In both the political and ethnic arenas, Jewish parents and the Jewish Establishment spokesmen are increasingly at odds with their sons and daughters.

* * *

Between 1881 and 1914, the grandparents of many of today's Jewish students brought with them from Eastern Europe a variety of radical ideologies. In America, predominantly working-class, having left behind many relatives and friends in the oppressive Old World, they retained their radicalism and internationalism. The early part of this century saw the simultaneous rise of two mass movements among Jews—a Jewish labor movement and a Jewish radical political movement.

In the midst of the formative period of the American labor movement, the Jews found work in the sweatshops of the "needle trades" in New York's Lower East Side and other large ghettos. Often as not, their employers were German Jews of an earlier wave of immigration. Many elements of the labor union movement were extremely nativistic, excluding Jews and dividing the working class. Also, as Louis Ruchames has pointed out:

> The motivation for a separate Jewish organization was neither religious nor nationalistic, but linguistic. Yiddish was the mother tongue of the masses of East European Jews who constituted the vast majority of Jewish immigrant workers and who, by and large, knew no other language. The idea of separate trade unions based on language was hardly new in the United States. German- and Russian-speaking union locals already existed and the formation of Yiddish-speaking unions therefore followed an established precedent.[3]

In 1907 the United Hebrew Trades comprised 74 affiliated unions and 50,000 members; by 1914 the numbers had soared to 104 and 250,000, respectively. The Jewish unions were the backbone of the Socialist Party, which had its own Yiddish-speaking wing. The radical Yiddish press—anarchist, communist, socialist, religious and secular, Zionist and anti-Zionist—was widely-read and influential. The largest and longest-lasting example, Abraham Cahan's *Jewish Daily Forward,* reached a circulation of over 200,000 in 1916. The radicalism of Yiddish-language playwrights, novelists, and poets also dramatized the plight of the Jewish masses.

Nathan Glazer has estimated that perhaps one-third of the American Communist Party membership was Jewish. And although the number of dues-paying C.P. members only briefly exceeded 50,000, "the turnover was so rapid that perhaps ten times that number or more were party members."[4] And, of course, there were a great many nonmember party sympathizers among the Jews. Hal Draper* found that support for the 1934 "Student Strike for Peace" was strongest in New York City, especially at the three city colleges—C.C.N.Y., Brooklyn College, and Hunter College—each with high Jewish enrollments at that time.

We thus find a mixed bag of radical activity among the grandparents and parents of today's Jewish students. They were, unlike today's New Left activists, acutely aware of their Jewishness. Although they divided over issues of Zionism, religion, and assimilation, they united on issues of anti-Semitism, discrimination against Jews in colleges and employment, and encroaching fascism in Europe. They were, for better or worse, part of a Jewish milieu—outsiders looking in.

All that changed after World War II. The Ribbentrop-Molotov Pact and the hard line of the American Communist Party caused the desertion of many Jews from the radical ranks. Disenchanted with Stalinism and the cold war, and relentlessly upwardly mobile into the free professions, small businesses, the service bureaucracies, and the intellectual

---

* Hal Draper, "The Student Movement in the Thirties," in Rita James Simon, ed., *As We Saw the Thirties.* University of Illinois Press, Urbana, Illinois, 1967.

world, the Old Left dissolved, only to spawn, in time, a different breed of radical—the New Left.

In the 1950's and early 1960's, spokesmen for the Jewish Establishment—that network of overlapping philanthropies, research and defense agencies, social clubs, religious and educational institutions and community centers—focused on two concerns. One was the changing occupational and residential character of American Jewry, into the middle-class and urban fringes and suburbs. The other was the fight against anti-Semitic and anti-Zionist attacks, especially from the right. The right-wing equations which peaked in the mid-1930's—international "Jewish" conspiracies, fierce isolationism and jingoism, and overt anti-Semitism—reemerged during the dark days of McCarthyism. In its pursuit of civil liberties and rights for Jews, the Jewish Establishment found a natural ally among blacks. The rhetoric and activities of liberalism won substantive gains.

While Jews built temples in the suburbs, fought restrictive clauses and quotas, and polemicized for Israel and against the John Birch Society, the Jewish Establishment attempted to wash out the stain of the label "commie Jews." To some extent, they were successful. Charles Stember reports that 32 percent of Americans surveyed in 1938 believed Jews to be more radical than others. Only 17 percent held this view in 1962.[5] It is ironic, then, that the beginnings of the New Left that year (the S.D.S. "Port Huron Statement") coincided with a time in American history when anti-Jewish prejudice and overt discrimination were at a low ebb. With the coming of the New Left, the Jewish Establishment saw a threat to the Jews' new and hard-fought respectability—the threat of many of their own children challenging the very ladders of Jewish success, and the threat that the "stigma" of the Jew-as-radical would reappear.

Unable to ignore the obvious fact of Jewish visibility in the New Left, the Jewish Establishment addressed the question by whitewashing it.

Afraid of a backlash of anti-Semitism, they attempted to assure non-Jews that the Jew-as-radical picture was overblown; that while a good many New Left activists may be Jews, only a small number of Jews are New Leftists. They pointed out that over 80 percent—or approximately 350,000 —of eligible college-age Jews are enrolled on campuses, and that the vast majority of them are, like their non-Jewish peers, apolitical or apathetic, but not active New Leftists. A recent example of this mentality is Norman Podhoretz's reminder in the American Jewish Committee's *Commentary* that:

> David Dellinger is not Jewish; Tom Hayden is not Jewish; Staughton Lynd is not Jewish; Carl Oglesby is not Jewish; Timothy Leary is not Jewish; Kate Millett is not Jewish; and neither, it somehow seems necessary to add, is Stokely Carmichael Jewish, nor Huey Newton, nor Angela Davis.[6]

To their Jewish constituency they tried to explain the alleged turn of the New Left toward a posture of anti-Zionism and, they alleged, anti-Semitism.[7] Many Jews had shared and supported the concerns of their sons and daughters—and some rabbis—in the civil rights movement (indeed, the names of the martyred Goodman and Schwerner remain symbols of that period) and their progression into the peace movement. But they were puzzled and angered by this new breed of militant radicals-who-happen-to-be-Jewish, who support the Black Panthers, the Palestinian guerrillas and other anti-Zionist groups. The Jewish Establishment's initial response was to label them "self-hating" Jews, outcasts, the offsprings of over-permissive parents, spiteful, and self-indulgent.

* * *

Still, they failed to answer the question: Why were so many young Jews attracted to the New Left?

Kenneth Keniston, Richard Flacks, and others believe that the "continuity hypothesis" helps to explain New Left activism.[8] Basically, it suggests that radicals share, rather than repudiate, the basic value commitments of their left-liberal parents. As Keniston writes:

. . . it may be that protesters receive both covert and overt support from their parents because the latter are secretly proud of the children's eagerness to implement the ideas that they as parents have only given lip service to. But whatever the ambivalences that bind parents with their activist children, it would be wrong to overemphasize them; what is most impressive is the solidarity of older and younger generations.

The basic formulas used to explain New Leftism correspond well with the American Jewish experience. Many Jewish parents are highly educated, urbanized, and cosmopolitan professionals, service workers (teachers and social workers, for example), or intellectuals. In rearing their children they stressed sensitivity to injustice and discrimination, distrust of irrational and bureaucratic authority, and urged their offspring to question, to make their own decisions, and to challenge the *status quo.*

The initial period of the New Left, that associated with the early Students for a Democratic Society (1962), was a predominantly WASP undertaking. Beginning with the Berkeley Free Speech Movement (1964), the Freedom Rides in the South, S.D.S.' community organizing projects in city ghettos, and later in the anti-war movement, resistance and mass protest, the New Left saw a large influx of Jews, centered on the selective elite and urban campuses with high Jewish enrollments.

If by New Leftist we mean one who participates in mass demonstrations, sit-ins, and picket lines, planning and organizing and publishing newspapers and ideological manifestos, then it is safe to say that Jews constituted at least 30 to 50 percent of the Movement's ranks. A study of Free Speech Movement advocates at Berkeley found that although only one-fifth of the student body was Jewish, 32 percent of the demonstrators were Jews.[9] Flacks found that 45 percent of the University of Chicago students who took part in a sit-in against the Selective Service System in 1966 were Jews.[10] Lucy Dawidowicz, in the *American Jewish Yearbook* for 1965, suggested that between one-

third and one-half of the student volunteers on the Mississippi
Freedom Summer Project in 1964 were Jews. The first two
high school S.D.S. chapters grew out of the Zionist youth
group Habonim in 1965. Jewish students are also more likely
to express "radical" attitudes about civil disobedience, the
draft, racism, abortion, and other issues.[11]

During the late 1960's, as militant activity spread from the
urban and elite campuses (such as Oberlin, Cornell, Harvard,
Chicago, Michigan, and Berkeley) to the less select colleges
and universities, the *percentage* of Jews in the New Left de-
creased, but the *number* of Jews drawn into the radical whirlpool
certainly increased. Put another way, Jews were disproportionately found among the "prophetic minority"[12] who built the
New Left from the ashes of liberalism. But as the movement
spread, it attracted students from a wide social base and more
conventional backgrounds.[13]

* * *

In facing these facts, one wonders if there is anything
specifically Jewish about these young Jews' radicalism. Talking to them, one does not get that impression. Few radicals
deny their Jewish roots, but they do not see them as a de-
terminant of their political activism. Still, there seems to be a
vague understanding that, as Jews, they identify with oppressed peoples, despite their own affluence.[14]

Said one early S.D.S. community organizer:

> We've all been messed over, but I feel its been more sharp
> for American Jews. What we detest about the lives of our
> parents, what we would talk about as emptiness, hypocrisy,
> and . . . materialism is the behavior that comes out of those
> insecurities, plus our own experiences of those insecurities.
> We see a way of getting beyond that . . . a possibility of the
> liberation from that.

The label of "self-hating" Jew—by that we mean a conscious attempt to escape one's Jewishness, to change one's
name, or leave the neighborhood, and to "pass" as a non-Jew

—seems decidedly inappropriate and misleading.* Most radicals are what Isaac Deutscher called "non-Jewish Jews," singularly unself-conscious about their Jewishness. Among them there is scant knowledge of Jewish history—even the radical tradition of the prophets, the Maccabees' struggle for liberation or their Jewish counterparts in Eastern Europe and the Old Left. Their view of the Jewish community, if they articulate one at all, is ahistorical; all they perceive is the status-striving and middle-class entrenchment of their parents' generation, which they identify with the Establishment. Whatever Jewish education they received did not expose them to any alternative Jewish way of life.

Why do they turn their backs on their Jewishness? "Universalism"—the customary response—is not the answer, for it does not explain their support for national and racial liberation movements. The answer is far more subtle. In their view, the oppressed peoples of the Third World are attempting to overcome years of colonialism, including the negative stereotypes imposed on them by the colonialists. The cultural and political nationalism of these groups—blacks, Vietnamese, Quebec French, American Indians, and others—is seen as an essential ingredient toward liberation and self-determination. The important difference is that while the Third World peoples struggle to survive, to exist as self-conscious and autonomous entities, American Jews are passively, quietly watching their culture (Yiddish, for example) drift away, with only a trace of anguish or outrage. At the same time, they note the Jews' concentration in particularly visible middle-man occupations. Their estrangement is not unlike Jerry Rubin's:

> I personally feel very torn about being Jewish. I know it made me feel like a minority or outsider in Amerika from my birth and helped me become a revolutionary. I am shocked at Julius Hoffman and Richard Schultz [Chicago 7 prosecutor] 'cause they try to be so Amerikan. Don't they know they're

---

* These tendencies were more characteristic of second-generation Jews.

still "Jewish" no matter how much "power" or "security" in Amerika they have? . . .

But despite this . . . Judaism no longer means much to us because the Judeo-Christian tradition has died of hypocrisy, Jews have become landlords, businessmen, and prosecutors in Amerika.[15]

In fact, among radical and non-radical Jews alike, positive Jewish identity is not particularly salient. The modal pattern among Jewish youth is not hostility, but indifference. The trend among third-generation Jews is away from ethnically-stigmatized occupations and into the salaried professions and out of ethnically segregated neighborhoods.*

A number of observers have characterized the campus as a "disaster area" for Jewish identity.[17] In the early and mid-1960's, concerned articles on the "vanishing American Jew" and "our alienated Jewish youth" repeatedly appeared in the Jewish press. The traditional strongholds of Jewish activities— the Jewish fraternities and sororities and the Hillel Foundations—began to lose their effectiveness as deterrents to inter-dating and intermarriage. Many barriers were breaking down and the Jewish students were not looking to construct barriers of their own.

* * *

Beginning in 1967, however, several factors contributed to the emergence of the Jewish Left and a Jewish youth culture. In that year, the first signs of fragmentation within the New Left appeared. The cries of black power sprang up as Stokely Carmichael crusaded in the South and the consequences surfaced at the August, 1967, Conference on New Politics in

---

* For example, a study of college freshmen in the fall of 1969 showed that the fathers of 54.3 percent of the Jewish students, but only 28.6 percent of the non-Jewish students, were self-employed businessmen. When asked about their career intentions, only 9.2 percent of the Jews, but 11.3 percent of the non-Jews, said business.[16]

Chicago. This convention of leftist groups crystallized the black-white tensions within the movement. This event was a landmark in the history of American radicalism and an important crisis for many white—and Jewish—radicals. A number of Jews walked out when the black caucus demanded acceptance of an anti-Zionist platform. But it was significant in another respect. The blacks' advice to whites was to "organize among your own."

Another factor, the Six-Day War, awakened an entire generation to the possibility that Israel could be destroyed. One must remember that the present generation of young Jews had never known what it was like *not* to have a Jewish state. Israel was born in 1948. It had "always" existed. Many young Jews surprised even themselves by the extent of their sympathy for and identification with Israel during the crisis. One radical, a former S.D.S. leader at Michigan, told us he was "frightened" by his own "chauvinism." The Israelis' victory also effected the ambivalence toward militancy among many young Jews. It is unlikely that many of the present Jewish generation were even familiar with the Jewish partisans of the Warsaw Ghetto or the underground Haganah. The sudden Israeli triumph altered the stereotype of the Jew as the passive, book-loving scholar or economic hustler.

About the same time, the New Left was beginning to experience the strains of co-optation and repression. The Johnson Administration had pushed through a flurry of civil rights legislation. The violence during the 1968 Democratic Convention in Chicago, despite the official finding that it was a "police riot," turned public opinion even more sharply against the radicals. Students began to question the wisdom of mass protest. Later answers would come from S. I. Hayakawa, who ordered a crackdown on dissent at San Francisco State College, and the National Guardsmen at Kent State and Jackson State. The election of Richard Nixon on the promise to end the war in Vietnam further took the initiative away from the New Left. During the November, 1969 moratorium, while more than half a million Americans protested the war outside the White House, Nixon promised that he would ignore their peaceful dissent. The changing technological nature of the American presence in Indochina—sending troops home while continuing the impersonal, but more destructive, bombing— calls for a new era of teach-ins to a people who want to think of the war as past history.

In 1969, S.D.S. split and the Weathermen, a small, hard- core group of radicals who romanticized violence and terrorism, emerged. Following the "Days of Rage" protest in Chicago and the indictment of twelve radicals (eight of them Jews) by a Federal Grand Jury, the Weatherpeople went underground to avoid arrest. Most radicals reject the Weathermen's violence though they understand the futility and desperation which led to this terrorism. Indeed, the 1970–71 academic year was notable for its absence of violence—or organized mass activism at all. The Movement for a New Congress—a within-the-system effort to elect anti-war Congressmen and Senators in November, 1970—attracted relatively few veteran radicals; most of those involved were first-time left-liberal activists. Many radicals re- luctantly supported the Presidential candidacy of George Mc- Govern, though few actively worked on his behalf.

It was this sense of chaos and lack of direction which caused a number of activists to seek other targets. Israel, the underdog, emerged from the Six-Day War as the "oppressor" and the "tool of Amerikan imperialism." For some, a desperate attempt to "out-radicalize" each other led to glorifying the Palestinian terrorists as the Viet Cong of the Middle East in- stead of searching for a just plan to allow both the Jews and Palestinians self-determination.

Nevertheless, there is no monolithic New Left position toward Israel, as a reading of *Ramparts, The Guardian, Chal- lenge, New Left Notes, New University Thought, Monthly Re- view,* and the *New Left Review* makes clear. Rather than labeling the entire New Left "anti-Zionist" or "anti-Semitic," a more realistic appraisal might suggest that most radicals are not themselves opposed to Israel, but are unwilling to criticize the anti-Zionist statements of the Black Panthers and the

Progressive Labor Party. In truth, their silence and ambivalence is often due to uncertainty and the lack of reliable information, from the Jewish Establishment on one side and the supporters of Al Fatah (such as the Liberation News Service, which provided extremely biased reports to the influential underground press) on the other. To the former, almost any criticism of Israel is unwarranted and threatens American support for the Jewish state; all radicals are thus labeled "anti-Zionist." On the other hand, Al Fatah and its supporters threaten to drive the Jews into the sea and anyone who suggests that Jews, too, have the right of self-determination is called a "Zionist." In their uncertainty, and over fear of further fragmenting the left, many radicals said nothing, while a few, such as Noam Chomsky and Paul Jacobs (through the Committee on New Alternatives in the Middle East), began to formulate alternatives to the pictures painted by the immutable extremes.

*　*　*

The sense of futility, frustration, and isolation caused by the black-white split and Establishment co-optation and repression made the movement particularly vulnerable to internal strains. As Demerath, Marwell, and Aiken suggest, "radical movements under duress and in close quarters have a tendency to convert minor interpersonal abrasions into major interpersonal sores."[18] Political weariness and despair often accompanied personal struggle and anxiety. Many committed radicals came to feel that the New Left failed to deal with personal adjustment and to provide support for their identities. Women often found themselves relegated to routine office chores. And many Jews began to feel uneasy about openly discussing their Jewishness. Both were made to believe that such private "hang ups" were superfluous to radical politics. In other words, the movement not only failed to deal with the oppression of women, Jews, and others, it actually reinforced it. This process undoubtedly raised the consciousness of these groups regarding the various forms of oppression within American society.

Underlying all this was the failure to achieve and sustain within the movement a sense of "community"—a dominant theme of New Left politics. By "community" the New Left meant the merging of politics and life style, the creation of a society based on cooperation rather than competition; the desire for intimate human relationships and the expression of emotion; the breakdown of impersonal bureaucracies* and support for personal fulfilment and creativity. The early New Left, those who built the movement, shared an optimism that "community" was possible.[19] But the strains of movement work, and the recruitment of a new variety of young radicals with different backgrounds and motivations, caused many of the strong personal bonds to disintegrate.

Thus the desperation of the late 1960's led some to the senseless violence of the Weathermen. But others found new directions in their effort to build a viable radical community. Some turned inward—to encounter groups, experiments with Eastern religion and the occult,[20] or heavy use of drugs.[21] Some, however, looked toward developing radical communities "with their own kind"—women, Catholics like Father Dan Berrigan, homosexuals, lawyers, Chicanos, teachers, and Jews. This development is an affirmation as well as a protest. Its implications are cultural as well as political. It emphasizes spiritual as well as material needs and suggests that a mass movement has to find room for primary bonds within which individuals feel comfortable. A radical strategy based on self-conscious group identities would orient itself to the basic needs of its constituents. It challenges the passive, socially-assigned roles with which so many Americans feel dissatisfied. It would also attract a great many people who previously felt unable to channel their discontent with American society into the politics of the New Left.

It was thus a convergence of several factors—the shifting politics and institutions of American Jews, the rise of black

---

* Recall the slogan: "I am a college student. Do not fold, bend or mutilate."

separatism as a legitimate expression of protest, the Six-Day War and the anti-Zionism which followed among segments of the New Left, and the fragmentation of the student movement leading to a realignment based on small scale communities—which led to the emergence of the Jewish Left.

* * *

The Jewish Left is not a cohesive, overarching movement with prominent charismatic leaders (such as a Martin Luther King, a Tom Hayden, or a Gloria Steinem) nor does it have an official organization. It is, rather, an amalgam of local, indigenous groups with varied ideologies and appeals. It shares with the adult Jewish community the pluralism of Jewish experience—religious and secular, cultural and political, Israel- and Diaspora-oriented. Our discussion focuses only on the *collective* expressions of Jewish consciousness which have emerged among young Jews. In doing so, we are forced to overlook the no doubt thousands of young Jews who are dealing privately with their Jewishness but who have not found it necessary—or possible—to articulate their feelings publicly. Unlike their elders, however, the Jewish Left attaches no stigma to the unaffiliated and unattached.

Just when and where the movement began is difficult to pinpoint. Jewish youth movements existed long before the Six-Day War,[22] but almost all of them—Young Judea, National Federation of Temple Youth, Student Zionist Organization, Hillel Foundations, United Synagogue Youth, Habonim, B'nai B'rith Youth Organization, and Hashomer Hatzair—were and are the "youth divisions" of large, adult organizations in America and Israel. And while we should not be surprised to find that much of the leadership of the Jewish liberation movement grew out of these groups, it differs in that the impetus and momentum came from the young Jews themselves.

During the early 1960's isolated incidents by radical Jews foreshadowed this new movement. For example, during a Free Speech Movement sit-in at Berkeley on Channukah eve in 1964, young Jewish demonstrators brought a menorah with them, and in the midst of Sproul Plaza lit the candles and recited the traditional prayer. However, the first stirrings of a self-conscious movement and youth-initiated activities occurred in the academic year 1967-68, following the Six-Day War. That Yom Kippur, a group of civil rights and anti-war activists, calling themselves Jews for Urban Justice, demonstrated in front of a prestigious Washington, D.C., synagogue, protesting the involvement of individual Jews in the black community and the "insensitivity of Jewish organizations to social problems" such as open housing, welfare rights, and migrant workers.[23] *Response* magazine first opened its pages to a growing body of Jewish arts and letters that year. About the same time, a group of discontented, restless rabbinical students and their friends conceived the idea of an unstructured, experimental Jewish seminary; the Havurat Shalom opened its doors in Somerville, Massachusetts, during the fall of 1968. And that winter (1968–69), the first three Jewish "underground" student papers—*The Jewish Radical* in Berkeley, the *Otherstand* in Montreal, and *The Jewish Liberation Journal* in New York—issued their first numbers.

The number of groups has spiralled since then, spreading the movement to more than 100 campuses and cities in the United States and Canada. Rather than attempt to catalogue each group, we prefer to outline the major themes and activities around which the Jewish Left is organized. For the sake of simplicity, we shall divide the movement into its political and cultural focuses.

On the political side, the Jewish Left concerns itself primarily with four basic issues: Israel, Soviet Jewry, the Jewish Establishment, and Jewish oppression in America.

A conspicuous phenomenon is the revival of Zionist ideology on campus. Early in 1970, at a conference of local student Zionist groups, the Radical Zionist Alliance was founded. Claiming affiliates on 75 campuses, R.Z.A. aligns itself ideologically with Siach (ironically, Israel's "New Left") and other Israeli critics of the present government in Tel Aviv. Their heroes are the early Socialist-Zionists, such as Ber

Borochov (1881–1917) and Nachman Syrkin (1867–1924), whose classic works they reprint, study, and quote with enthusiasm. The R.Z.A. is critical of "checkbook Zionists"—those whose commitment to a Jewish state only goes so far as an annual contribution and an occasional trip to Israel—and their stranglehold on all matters related to Israel. R.Z.A.'s continuation is unclear, however. Its leadership seems unable to decide whether it should concentrate on "Judaizing" radicals or "radicalizing" young Zionists. While its official membership list claims 700 persons scattered on about 75 campuses, it is difficult to assess its impact in raising Jewish or Zionist consciousness among young Jews. Yet in an ironic way, R.Z.A. finds that it may have been too successful, for many of its most dynamic leaders have already settled in Israel.

The impetus for a new radical Zionism was, of course, the desire for counterattacks on Israel from the student left and the increasingly sophisticated Arab propaganda.[24] The first organized efforts were confrontations with Arab and anti-Israel spokesmen, in debates, symposia, and letters-to-the-editor. In doing so, they insisted that one can legitimately be both radical and Zionist. Zionism, they argued, is nothing less than the national liberation movement of the Jewish people. Critical of Israel's treatment of the Israeli-Arab minority and Palestinian refugees, R.Z.A. promotes the idea of changing Israeli society from within: "Be a Zionist in the revolution and a revolutionary in Zion."

A number of campus groups have organized the *irbutz* and the *garin**—Jewish collectives, both urban and rural—which they hope to transplant to Israel, as several have already. The number of young American Jews, visiting, studying, and settling in Israel has increased dramatically since the Six-Day War.[25]

---

* An *irbutz* is an urban collective of professionals and workers; a *garin* is a collective of American Jews living and working together in the United States. The *garin* members expect to settle in Israel.

A growing interest in Israeli culture—what one R.Z.A. leader calls "Israelism"—is seen in the increasing numbers of Israeli coffee houses, Hebrew classes, discussions of Middle East politics, and folk dancing clubs around campuses. Yet we should, not overlook a decidedly nonradical approach which has attracted growing numbers of young Jews, particularly in working-class areas of New York. This is the other side of the ideological coin, the right-wing Zionism of the Jewish Defense League and Betar, and their own hero, Zev Jabotinsky. Their counterpart in Israel is the Gahal Party whose leader, Menachem Begin, a disciple of Jabotinsky and a member of the underground Irgun during the 1948 war, was ousted from the cabinet for his "Greater Israel" sentiments (he desired the annexation of the occupied territories).

The Jewish Left is ambivalent toward Rabbi Meir Kahane and his followers. Most radical Jews are critical of the J.D.L.'s strategy—harassing Russian diplomats, its symbolic alliance with Joseph Colombo's Italian-American Civil Rights League, and its appeals to anticommunist sentiment. On the other hand, some view the J.D.L. as misguided "brothers" and "sisters," as victims entrapped in transitional neighborhoods, isolated from the Jewish Establishment, symbols of the "forgotten Jews" in the lower and working classes. The Jewish Left's confusion over the J.D.L. is reflected in the comment by one activist: "I like their style, but abhor their politics."

Although the J.D.L. has attracted the most publicity in its protests on behalf of Soviet Jewry, it has no monopoly on the issue. The Student Struggle for Soviet Jewry, organized in 1964, has intensified its efforts during the past four years in coordinating activities in behalf of the three million Russian Jews. S.S.S.J. conducted teach-ins and letter-writing campaigns to American and Russian officials and several leaders were personally responsible for the release of Leonid Rigerman of Moscow. S.S.S.J. was the major force behind the Passover Exodus March to the United Nations in New York (which attracted 25,000 participants) and in other cities in 1971. It has organized all-night vigils at the Soviet Embassy in Washington and the U.S.S.R. Mission to the United Nations in New York (where several activists chained themselves to the gate and were arrested). Soviet artists performing in the United States are confronted by young Jewish dissenters. At the opening of the Moscow Ice Circus in Madison Square Garden, S.S.S.J. staged a "counter-circus" with Soviet Jewry exhibits called "Judaism Under Ice." During a performance of the Moiseyev Dance Company in Washington in September, 1970, several activists disrupted the Soviet national anthem by sounding the shofar (ram's horn). The Soviet news agency Tass and the airline Aeroflot have been targets of pickets, and violence as well (though no one will claim credit for the latter). From October to December, 1971, a Soviet Jewry Freedom Bus carrying three American students and two young Russian Jewish *émigrés* toured the country. It stopped in 34 cities to bring the message of the growing resistance movement among Russian Jews, who risk the loss of their jobs and university student status, separation from their families, and imprisonment as alleged "Zionist spies" for demanding the right to leave. The Leningrad Trials in the spring of 1971 mobilized protests at Soviet embassies around the world. Elie Wiesel's moving book, *The Jews of Silence,* has had an important impact on many young Jews and motivated many to join the movement to dramatize the Soviet Jews' plight.

Early efforts focused on the "cultural genocide" of Soviet Jews by demanding the publication of Yiddish books and plays, opening of training schools for rabbis and Hebrew teachers and synagogues, and permission to manufacture or import religious articles. More recent protests have called for the mass exodus of all Soviet Jews who wish to leave.

Despite the urgent pleas to American policy makers to take diplomatic initiatives to help Rusian Jews, few radicals have much faith in America's interest in broaching the issue at the risk of threatening the U.S.–Soviet détente. Often they cite Arthur Morse's *While Six Million Died,* which documents the reluctance of the Roosevelt Administration to save European Jews from the Nazi solution, as proof of an underlying anti-

Semitism, or indifference to the fate of Jews, in American
society.

More salient than their ambivalence toward the J.D.L. is
their condemnation of the Jewish Establishment's overreaction
to Kahane's publicity. They see in the Establishment's attacks
on J.D.L.[26] signs of "*galut* (Diaspora) mentality"—hyper-
sensitivity, fear of what the *goyim* will think, and class
snobbery. In February, 1971, the World Conference of Jewish
Communities on Soviet Jewry, a prestigious *ad hoc* meeting
in Brussels, refused to admit Kahane, or do more than pass
resolutions. That, wrote Robert Goldman in *The Jewish Liberation Journal*, "was the most telling evidence of the moral
bankruptcy of world Jewish leadership." Goldman further accused the representatives at the meeting of "organizational
self-aggrandizement, bureaucratic buck-passing, cowardice,
and cynicism" (see page 195).

Such indictments of the Jewish Establishment are standard
fare among the Jewish Left. Judaism, they say, has been
turned into a voluntary association rather than a community
with cultural, political, or moral autonomy. And WASHs
(White Anglo-Saxon Hebrews), who appoint themselves
leaders, wrote Sherman Rosenfeld in Berkeley's *Jewish Radical*, "are chosen on the basis of their bank accounts, not integrity; the causes they discuss are overwhelmingly financial."*

They accuse spokesmen for the Jewish Establishment of
lacking any knowledge of Jewish history and religion, and, as
a result, of shortchanging Jewish education. An article in *The
Jewish Liberation Journal* pointed out that in 1969–70, less

---

* This situation has its precedents. Discussing 17th-century Polish Jews,
David Rudavsky has written: "The wealthier Jews and the intellectuals,
who formed the ruling oligarchy in the self-governing *kahal*, did not
distribute the tax burdens fairly, but favored their richer friends at the
expense of the poor. Unfortunately, not all rabbis protested against this
injustice. In fact, some were even parties to the evil, thereby losing their
prestige among the common folk." (*Modern Jewish Religious Movements*,
Behrman House, New York, 1967).

than 5 percent of the local New York City philanthropies' budget went toward education. To make their point, they occupied the offices of the Federation of Jewish Philanthropies of New York and called for the "democratization" of the Jewish community. A group was arrested—and soon labeled the "Federation 45."

By far the most dramatic confrontation took place at the annual meeting of the Council of Jewish Federations and Welfare Funds in November, 1969, in Boston. Afraid that the young rebels would disrupt the meetings, the leaders permitted Hillel Levine, a young rabbi, to address the assembly.* And throughout the meetings, the students pressed their demands: increased subsidies for Jewish day schools, improved curriculum and teacher-training in Hebrew and religious schools, chairs, and departments of Jewish studies on college campuses, scholarship programs for students of Judaica, more dramatic efforts—political and educational—on behalf of Soviet Jews, student participation in Federation policy-making, and subsidies for student-initiated projects. While some of the Federation leaders at the Boston meeting looked at the students as ungrateful heretics, most took their demands seriously.[27]

With or without adult support, the Jewish Left has lobbied for Jewish studies programs—courses in Hebrew, Yiddish, Middle Eastern politics and history, Jewish history, and theology—on their campuses and have been successful beyond expectations. By late 1971, 185 colleges and universities in the U.S. and Canada sponsored credit courses in some area of Jewish studies. At Oberlin, for example, Hebrew House— a living center set up for and by Jewish students—was incorporated into the credit curriculum. Students have also established Jewish "free universities" with such courses as "Judaism and Conscientious Objection," "Jewish Mysticism, Chassidism, and Radical Theology," "Zionism and World Lib-

* See page 183.

eration," "The *Shtetl* Culture," "The Oppression of Jewish Women," "Marxism, Anarchism, and Judaism," and "Jewish
Cooking," taught by professors, local Jewish professionals, and
the students themselves.[28]

A central theme of the Jewish Left is the entanglement of
the Jewish community with America's power structure. The
obsequiousness of the Jewish Establishment is a sign of the
Jews' marginality and ultimate vulnerability. Despite popular
stereotypes, studies show that few Jews are to be found
among the corporate elite.* Rather, where Jews are involved
at all, it is as technocrats; they may oil and run the machine,
but they don't own it. Jewish success was bought at a price.
It destroyed Jewish culture† and ethnic solidarity, forced Jews
to rely on others' goodwill, and alienated masses of young
Jews. It is a price the Jewish Left is unwilling to pay. A number of campus groups offer an "Uncle Jake" award to "the
Jews who have outdistanced all competitors in the imagination
and creativity with which they have ass-licked the Establishment." The "Uncle Jake" syndrome is reminiscent of the advice "enlightenment" poet Yehuda Leib Gordon gave to
Russian Jews, to "be a Jew at home and a human being on
the street." Confronting the "Uncle Jake" syndrome means
challenging the legitimacy of wealthy Jews such as Max
Fisher (a major Republican Party fund-raiser and President
Nixon's advisor on Jewish affairs) and Henry Crown (a major
shareholder in General Dynamics Corporation, which manu-
factures war machinery; the Crown family name is attached to
many Jewish institutions in the Chicago area) to speak on be-

---

* The stereotypes persist, which perhaps explains why in a bookshop near
the University of Chicago, Ferdinand Lundberg's book on the WASP
corporate elite, *The Rich and the SuperRich,* was found in a section labeled
"Jewish studies."

† For example, early in the century before the five-day work week, Jews
had to choose between working on the Sabbath (Saturday) or keeping the
tradition by becoming their own bosses—one reason for the concentration
of Jews in self-employed business, especially among Orthodox Jews.

half of the Jewish community. It also means castigating Jews such as Henry Kissinger, whose positions in the American power structure are more obvious, even if their Jewish commitments are negligible.

When Jacques Torczyner, President of the Zionist Organization of America, publicly adopted a hawkish position on Vietnam, he did so, he announced, to guarantee the support of the Nixon Administration for Israel. *The Jewish Liberation Journal* called him "Nixon's hatchet man in the Jewish community," while the Jewish Liberation Project picketed the Z.O.A. building in New York.

A "Trees for Vietnam" campaign was organized to rally support within the Jewish community for a symbolic pledge of solidarity with the Vietnamese people by helping to rebuild the defoliated countryside destroyed by war. According to one radical Jew: "As long as there are 'gooks' there will be 'kikes.' " The Jewish Peace Fellowship encourages young Jews to learn the pacifist tradition within Judaism and to seek conscientious objector status on these grounds. In Chicago, the young Jews organized a Jewish draft counseling center and received enough support from the local Board of Rabbis to employ a full-time counselor.

The involvement of Jewish landlords and businessmen in black ghettos is another target. And in the San Fernando Valley, radical Jews picketed a Jewish-owned supermarket for selling nonunion California grapes and carried placards in English and Yiddish, quoting Isaiah: "Thou shalt not eat the fruit of the oppressed." Many young Jews resent their exposure to racism within Yiddish culture and object, for example, to the word "*schvartze*" when one means "black."

More than 500 radical Jews demonstrated outside a Los Angeles hotel in September, 1971, while Israel's Foreign Minister Abba Eban presented his country's Medallion of Valor to California Governor Ronald Reagan. A leaflet charged that "through his welfare and education program Ronald Reagan has consistently ignored the desperate needs of the poor and minorities of this state. . . . It is time for the Jewish community to cease linking the Jewish homeland to the names and actions of men who perpetrate injustice in the United States."

In November, 1970, the Philadelphia Histadrut campaign, a Labor-Zionist organization, honored then Police Chief Frank Rizzo. Na'aseh, a group of Reconstructionist rabbinical students and other Jewish activists, demonstrated outside the dinner. The following year, following a "law and order" campaign, Rizzo was elected mayor with substantial Jewish support.

In May of 1969, the Oakland chapter of B'nai B'rith bestowed its Man of the Year award to S. I. Hayakawa, the President of San Francisco State College. "We honor men whose exemplary conduct manifests the true spirit of America in its finest hour," said the local lodge president of the man who ordered National Guard troops to quash a student protest. The Berkeley Radical Jewish Union picketed the "affair."

In other ways, the responses of Jews and the Jewish Establishment to the social problems of today have enraged the Jewish Left.

In 1969, Los Angeles Mayor Sam Yorty conjured up images of black militants running city hall if his opponent, black moderate Thomas Bradley, overcame Yorty's reelection bid. Yorty's histrionics increased his support among Jews from 18 percent in the four-way primary (which Bradley won) to 48 percent in the two-way run-off against Bradley.[29]

During the New York City school strike of 1968–69, Jewish spokesmen fanned the flames of racism and turned an essentially class and educational conflict into an ethnic and racial one.[30] Lower-class blacks demanded community control of the schools, while the predominantly Jewish United Federation of Teachers, feeling its job security threatened, resisted. Several anti-Semitic remarks by black leaders were seized upon by the U.F.T. head, Albert Shanker, who began a campaign against "Gestapo tactics" and "Nazis." Local rabbis created hysteria by preaching sermons about alleged arson of synagogues by blacks. And the Anti-Defamation League of B'nai B'rith issued a report which warned that "raw, undisguised anti-Semitism is at a crisis level" in New York. The tensions created by that event are still being felt within the Jewish community. For example, in Forest Hills, the Queens Jewish Community Council clashed with Mayor Lindsay and the Department of Housing and Urban Development over a proposed low-income housing project in the predominantly middle-class Jewish neighborhood in late 1971.

During the spring of 1971, the A.D.L. mounted a campaign against a number of groups—Physicians for Social Responsibility, the Medical Committee for Human Rights, and the Student Health Organization—which called for better medical service in ghettos and the restructuring of the "health industry." The A.D.L. implied these groups were anti-Semitic.[31] The Jewish Left responded that rather than combatting anti-Semitism, the A.D.L. was creating it where there was none. "The A.D.L.'s preconception of what's good for the Jews is what's good for the established Jewish doctors," said one Jewish activist.

Major Jewish organizations attempted to boycott the speaking tour of Uri Avneri, a member of the Israeli Knesset and outspoken opponent of Israel's power structure, to American campuses in the fall of 1970. Local groups were urged not to sponsor or promote appearances by Avneri, a popular figure within the Jewish Left.

A particularly stinging criticism centers on the Jewish Establishment's attempt to gather statistics on American Jews. Each year various Jewish communities undertake population surveys, usually for the purposes of identifying potential contributors to Jewish philanthropies. Despite enormous sums involved, major Jewish organizations (particularly the American Jewish Congress) have consistently fought against the inclusion of questions on religion in the U.S. Census which could provide sophisticated—and free— information. Many radical Jews see in this the persistence of the Jewish Establishment to define Jews as a religious, rather than an ethnic, group to insure their assimilation into what Will Herberg termed the "triple melting pot" of Protestants, Catholics, and

Jews. (The early Reform Jews called themselves "Americans of the Mosaic persuasion.") When the philanthropies launched the National Jewish Population Study (cost: $650,000), Shelley Schreter, then a sociology student at Berkeley, scolded the Jewish Establishment's "reluctance to be collectively conspicuous"— that is, their fear that non-Jews might have access to figures on Jewish income, education, and residences.

The examples cited are symbolic rather than systematic evidence of a political realignment within the Jewish community, a shift in which Jews identify the interests and values of the American elite as their own. For most young Jews, such evidence is enough to "write off" Judaism and the Jewish community as hopelessly irrelevant to their central concerns. To the small, but growing, Jewish Left there is a faith that the Jewish community can be "saved" if confronted openly. Such confrontations are motivated by mixed emotions of love and hate, hope and despair. It suggests both an intense identification with, and deep estrangement from, the present condition of American Jewry.

As we noted earlier, the search for "community" is fundamentally an attempt to link radical politics and life style. A number of the more visible innovators of the past decade— Allen Ginsberg, Paul Goodman, Bob Dylan,[32] Fritz Perls, Julian Beck, and Leonard Cohen—are Jews. And yet young Jews are more likely to be found among the political than the cultural radicals. Among the nonconformist "street people" around Berkeley in the mid-1960's, only 17 percent had Jewish parents, while 32 percent of the political radicals had Jewish parents. These early hippies were less likely to be drawn from the prototypical Jewish family. Rather, they tended to come from Protestant and Republican households, with little social consciousness or political involvement. Their parents' occupational and leisure concerns were more with status and materialism rather than with service or ideas. These parents were less supportive of their children's nonconformity. By dropping out of college, the hippies were repudiating the basic goals of their parents.[33]

And just as the New Left widened its social base, so did the counterculture. Today, more young Jews are involved—living in communes, working on underground newspapers, performing with street theaters, and organizing free schools. The counterculture, however, cannot be so neatly labeled. It is unclear just who and what the counterculture is. The breakdown of traditional mores regarding sex, drugs, and dress is widespread, among all classes, religions, and ethnic groups. What was "underground" yesterday may be in *The New York Times* or Saks-Fifth Avenue tomorrow. Tie-dyed shirts are mass-produced and *The Los Angeles Free Press* recently installed a time clock for its staff. Or put another way, the counterculture has been co-opted, exploited, and robbed of its critical function. It points out America's capacity to absorb that which threatens its stability.

Like the radicals-who-happen-to-be-Jewish, the Jews within the counterculture do not see their estrangement as a particularly Jewish one. Yet others do, and among them a Jewish counterculture has emerged, an effort to translate the ethnic and religious distinctiveness of the Jewish experience into current relevance—an attempt at "creative Jewing."*

Jews, in particular, embody the tension between politics and life style. For many Jews, liberal ideology accompanies their preoccupations with bourgeois status-striving. What do their children identify as Jewish from the wasteland of American culture? Only, perhaps, the world popularized by Phillip Roth and symbolized by the Miami Beach and Catskill scenes.

To a young Jew like Sherman Rosenfeld, writing in *The Jewish Radical*, American Jewish life means "extravagant buildings, Friday night fashion shows, *bar mitzvah* exhibitions, and weddings smothered in wealth" (see page 222).

Offered no Jewish alternatives, they have had to create their own. They have rejected the prevailing Jewish life style without rejecting Judaism and Jewish culture.

---

* "Creative Jewing" was the theme of a World Union of Jewish Students conference near Philadelphia in the summer of 1971.

Among the most exciting experiments is the Havurat Shalom ("Fellowship of Peace") seminary in Somerville, Massachusetts, a religious "community" organized as an alternative to the standard, highly-structured institutions of Jewish higher learning.

Founded by young rabbis, disenchanted rabbinical students, and graduate students from Boston area colleges, the *havurah* is a self-conscious attempt to challenge the rigidity of structure and dogma within the rabbinical schools while retaining the "spirit" of Jewish tradition. At the *havurah*, as at the Fabrangen* in Washington, Jewish tradition is a creative, on-going process. In trying to come to terms with *halakhah* (legal) problems in Judaism—such as blatant sexism—the members are developing their own midrash or commentary, on the traditional texts. There exist no course credits, no teacher-student relationships, no strict rules about riding on Sabbath. Instead, the *havurah* emphasizes learning together, sharing meals, and providing communal support for members' own explorations of Judaism. The Boston-area *havurah* has inspired other experimental Jewish communities (some real communes, some community centers) in New York City, Chicago, Ithaca, Philadelphia, and elsewhere. Chicago has HaMasmid, a "free *yeshivah*" where young Jews help each other to study Jewish sources.

Related to the *havurot* is the growing interest in neo-Chassidism and Jewish mysticism among many young Jews. Perhaps the principle living source of inspiration is Shlomo Carlebach, a striking figure with his beard, earlocks, and love

---

* The Fabrangen is an outgrowth of the Jews for Urban Justice in Washington, D.C. Around 1969 the members of the group began to feel the need for more Jewish religious and cultural activities, more study, and more religious celebration to supplement their political activities. The Fabrangen (literally, "to pass the time") is a rented house where young Jews come to study, pray, dance, plan political activities, etc. The members do not live in the house. But in the summer of 1972, several members were living on a Maryland farm owned by one of the group. They called it Kibbutz Micah.

beads. In 1968 he set up the House of Love and Prayer in San Francisco, a community center for hippies and drop-outs.[34] Carlebach tries to bring the messianic message of the Jewish mystics to a generation already involved with Eastern religion, psychedelics, and astrology. A scholar himself, Carlebach comes from a renowned family of European rabbis. But for the past ten years, beginning with his exploits around New York's Greenwich Village, Shlomo has "turned on" young Jews all over the world with his concerts, recordings, and Sabbath happenings of Chassidic prayer, songs, and dances. Another "guru" of modern neo-Chassidism, Rabbi Zalman Schachter of Winnepeg, is a Lubavitcher Chassid and was an early advocate of the religious use of L.S.D.; he now espouses a "post-drug" ideology. But by far the most influential figure in this Chassidic revival is Martin Buber, the German scholar who interpreted the Chassidic tales to generations, the Zionist whose *Paths in Utopia* analyzed the roots of kibbutz socialism, the radical who called for a bi-national Jewish-Palestinian state. But more important was his vision of a personal "I-Thou" dialogue between man and God, and man and his fellow man. Buber's prolific writings are increasingly popular, while more recent books—such as *9½ Mystics* by Eugene Weiner, a Reform rabbi—indicate the burgeoning interest in Chassidism among even scholars within the rationalist tradition.

Another example of this encounter with tradition is the "Freedom Seder" by Arthur Waskow, a radical historian and guiding spirit of the early New Left. Waskow's service draws parallels between the Exodus from Egypt and contemporary liberation movements. More than 10,000 students, Jews and non-Jews, celebrated the Passover with Waskow at Cornell University in the spring of 1970, which included an appearance by Father Daniel Berrigan, then a fugitive from the F.B.I. In small groups, on campuses across the country, students are using the Waskow Seder or creating ones of their own.

During the past year, young Jews have begun to challenge the rigid sex roles within the Jewish tradition. Young Jewish women, objecting to the stereotypic "Jewish mother," "Jewish princess," or "Hadassah lady" image, have organized "consciousness raising" groups to discuss their experiences. Some enter the Jewish movement through women's liberation. *Off Our Backs,* a radical feminist paper, recently devoted an entire issue to the position and problems of Jewish women. Orthodox women, while more hesitant to challenge the separation of the sexes in Judaism, are beginning to talk about reinterpreting, within the tradition, the role of single women, access of women to the rabbinate and to *yeshivahs* and Jewish education in general, and the participation of women in Jewish institutions. A group of Orthodox and Conservative Jewish women, Ezrat Nashim in New York City, recently presented a manifesto to the Rabbinical Assembly calling for equal status.

Gay Jews have until recently been "in the closet" in regard to Jewish issues. Now small groups of Jewish homosexuals have begun to express their Jewish identities. A few months after Robbie Skeist published his article, "Coming Out Jewish" (see page 314) in Chicago's underground paper the *Seed,* gay Jews held a gay Passover seder.

Finally, we see a renewed interest in Yiddish culture and Jewish arts and letters. Many second generation Jews ignored Yiddish, refusing to teach it to their children, but third generation Jews have created a renaissance of Yiddish theater, literature, and poetry. Several colleges, including Columbia and McGill, have added courses in Yiddish. Yuguntruf— "Youth for Yiddish"—publishes a journal with a circulation of 2,500. A Jewish arts festival at Brandeis University included readings by young Jewish poets, a Jewish choral group, a dance ensemble, production of original plays in Yiddish and Hebrew, and exhibits by Jewish photographers, filmmakers, sculptors, and artists. *Response* magazine, along with *Davka* (in Los Angeles) and *Strobe* (Montreal) are the major outlets for this body of poetry, essays, and other arts and letters.

* * *

Like all movements of dissent, the Jewish Left must confront a skeptical and often hostile Establishment, for it poses a symbolic threat and challenge to the Jewish leaders. *Commentary* magazine, once the flagship of Jewish liberalism, has in recent years turned full-steam-ahead to the right with bitter attacks on women's liberation, the counterculture, the New Left, black nationalism, and the Jewish Left. Editor Norman Podhoretz stigmatized Waskow as a "wicked son" and his Freedom Seder as a "document of self-loathing and self-abasement masquerading as a document of self-affirmation."[35]

In Washington, the United Jewish Appeal withdrew its financial support of the Fabrangen community center following a vicious hate-campaign by the local Jewish press. In its short three-year existence, Fabrangen has managed to bring scores of alienated young Jews back to Judaism with its communal (kosher) meals, Sabbath services, study retreats and Jewish free school, and its free-wheeling spirit. But its support of radical politics and its attacks on the Jewish Establishment's stand on Israel, Soviet Jewry, and racism, spearheaded by Waskow and others, has created tensions with local Jewish leaders. Following an article in a local Jewish paper headed "Al Fatah in *Shul*," a completely misleading epithet concerning criticism of Israel by some Fabrangen members, the U.J.A. voted to discontinue its support. At this writing, its members were preparing to abandon the three-story frame house.

Nathan Glazer, writing in the Zionist monthly *Midstream*, talked about "Jewish interests" which he identified with lawyers, stockbrokers, businessmen, New York teachers, and students in elite colleges—categories "in which Jews are prominent." Radicalism, he suggested, threatens these interests, and thus threatens Jewish survival. To the Jewish community, Glazer wrote, "capitalism is not an enemy—it is a benign environment. When radicalism conquers, even if there is not a trace of anti-Semitism in it, the classic Jewish occupations suffer and individual Jews come upon hard times." Speaking of the Jewish Left, he wrote, "[I] find it inconceivable that it can become the dominant sentiment among American Jews."[36] And certainly not if influential Jewish intellectuals continue to ignore the Jewish role as both oppressor and oppressed in the "classic Jewish occupations."

This is not to say that among the Jewish Establishment some members have not been hospitable to the Jewish student movement. More than fifty Jewish student newspapers are now being published, and many receive funds and encouragement from the local Jewish federation. Various projects, like the Jewish Student Press Service and several Jewish free universities, exist on support from sympathetic Establishmentarians. Nor do we claim that no parents have changed along with their children during the last, volatile decade. Indeed, it may be that some parents are adopting the political and ethnic perspectives of their offspring—a "continuity hypothesis" in reverse.

But despite this, the Jewish student movement has had to go it alone. They have learned to negotiate their way amid the hostility or indifference of their Jewish elders and student peers. As one young radical Jew remarked at a recent conference in Madison, Wisconsin: "Between us and our 100 members or so, and the 4,000 Jewish students on campus, there's a tremendous gap. I've begun to realize what a marginal phenomenon we are." And another explained: "In Bloomington, I'm sort of caught in the middle. I'm caught between the radicals I'm involved with and the Jewish Hillel kids."

Thus, only a special kind of young Jew can survive and persist in this situation, a Jew who is willing to endure intense scrutiny from his peers and the Jewish Establishment, and to continually justify his stance without apology. He has had to create a role where none existed before.

Who are these radical Jews? Our recent survey of Jewish student leaders found that they are not drawn from any one segment of the Jewish community. Like many New Leftists, most had been brought up on what one leader called *"New York Post* liberalism." Still others had parents in the Old Left

—one actually fought in Spain with the Abraham Lincoln Brigade—and at an early age accompanied their parents on ban-the-bomb marches and open housing demonstrations. Some are the sons and daughters of Jewish Establishment professionals. Many are from Zionist, but secular and unaffiliated homes, and were active in Zionist youth movements such as Habonim and Hashomer Hatzair. A significant number are what might be called "enlightened Orthodox," with Jewish day school educations (*yeshivahs*) and from traditional homes whose ritualism they reject but whose spirit they retain. But not surprisingly, a plurality rediscovered Jewishness and Judaism on their own. They grew up in acculturated middle-class (and some working-class) homes where Judaism was a revolving door—in Rosh Hashana and out Yom Kippur. Their Jewish education lasted until *bar mitzvah* age at thirteen. Most, however, retain warm memories of close family occasions such as Passover. What was missing was some substance to their Jewish experience. For this last group, commitment to things Jewish was a process of changing identity—following a year or a summer living in a kibbutz or study at an Israeli university, a job as a counselor at a Jewish camp, disillusionment with the New Left, or being turned off by the Hillels and Jewish fraternities and sororities.

Relatively few have had direct experience with overt anti-Semitism, but almost all believe that the Jewish position in American society is a tenuous one—especially if he (or she) wants to live a Jewish life. Almost all were involved in civil rights, anti-war, and college protests. Along the way, they began to think about what it means to be a Jew. James Sleeper has written with insight:

> Perhaps it begins as a curiosity. Jewishness becomes intriguing when you try to make sense out of the fact that as a Jew on the current scene you are a slumlord to blacks, a civil rights worker to Southern whites, a well-heeled business school opportunist to hippies, a student radical to WASP conservatives, an Old Testament witness to Vermont

Yankees, an atheist to Midwestern crusaders, a capitalist to leftists, a communist to rednecks.[37]

Unlike the majority of American Jews, the Jewish Left sees this marginality as predisposing them toward a special kind of radicalism—Jewish radicalism. In "My Evolution as a Jew," M. J. Rosenberg writes:

> I had a problem. How could I reconcile my leftist procliv-
> ities with my now admittedly Zionist ones? Did I have to
> choose between the Fatah-supporting S.D.S. and the ultra-
> middle-class lox-and-bagel breakfast club Hillel society?
> There could be no doubt but that the most interesting Jewish
> kids were on the left. The Jews of the anti-war movement
> were infinitely more intellectually exciting than the business
> majors of State's Hillel. The choice was an impossible one. I
> felt that there had to be a third route.[38]

This third route, of course, is Jewish radicalism. Numerically, it cannot be considered a major force among Jewish students. It is the effort of a small group of Jews to synthesize their radical and Jewish identities, to create alternatives to the transient student culture and the intransigent Jewish Establishment.

What is the fate of the movement? Cynics predict that in ten years the bulk of the Jewish Left will be the next presidents of B'nai B'rith lodges and Hadassah chapters, watered-down radicals who copped out. For a host of reasons, this is unlikely.

What is more possible is that the hard-core leadership of the Jewish liberation movement might give up on America and settle in Israel, leaving behind the "checkbook Zionists" and "bagel and lox" Jews to lead the Jewish community. If this happens, then the future direction of the American Jewish community is uncertain.

What is more important, however, is that right now the role of the Jew in modern America is being seriously questioned by the young. The New Left and members of the counterculture excluded their Jewishness from their identities. Segments of the

Jewish Left and the Jewish counterculture are attempting to remake American Jewish life within a pluralistic framework; while to still others, like the Radical Zionists, the "Jewish question" can only be answered by living in Israel.

Jews define themselves in many ways. But also, as Sartre has pointed out in *Anti-Semite and Jew*, they are defined by others as well.[39] A group's survival depends, to some extent, on its willingness to be unique, to emphasize its distinctiveness. The Jewish Left is warning that if the Jews do not assert their own uniqueness, then others will ultimately define the Jews' uniqueness for them.

They fear America's capacity to absorb its minorities, whether political or cultural. They fear the spiritual poverty of the so-called affluent society. They fear being overwhelmed by the grinding machine of technology, consumption, and bureaucratic impersonality. In their search for community, they are saying "No!" to the machine—what Herbert Marcuse calls the "Great Refusal."

America must change, they are saying. It must reassess its priorities, its role in the world, its myths, its racism—indeed, its national character. Jews must change. Liberalism and assimilation are dead ends. America is *not* different. It is only bigger, and therefore more overwhelming, more dangerous, more destructive.

The message is clear: Be Jews at home AND Jews in the street.

References

1. David Boroff, "Jewish Teenage Culture," *The Annals*, November, 1961, p. 90.
2. The term "Jewish Left" may be something of a misnomer. "Activist" rather than "radical" is perhaps more appropriate, for the movement includes a broad spectrum of political perspectives. Many participants

have only vague notions rather than well-defined ideologies for programmatic social and political change. In this, however, they are no different from participants in other social movements. (In his book *Theory of Collective Behavior*, N.J. Smelser calls these notions "generalized beliefs.") Nevertheless, their "instincts"—about the distribution of wealth, political participation, the existence of a ruling elite, advocacy of extralegal channels to achieve change—as well as their self-images are radical. Except for the Jewish Defense League, there is a noticeable absence of "charismatic" leaders who define the ideologies and directions; this, in fact, is a healthy sign that the Jewish Left is built on grass-roots interests rather than the blind following of "true believers." With this in mind, we feel safe in referring to a "Jewish Left."

3. Louis Ruchames' excellent historical survey, "Jewish Radicalism in the United States," is found in Peter I. Rose, *The Ghetto and Beyond*, Random House, New York, 1969.

4. See two articles by Nathan Glazer, "The New Left and the Jews," *Jewish Journal of Sociology*, December, 1969, and "The Jewish Role in Student Activism," *Fortune*, January, 1969.

5. Charles Stember (ed.), *Jews in the Mind of America*, Basic Books, New York, 1966.

6. Norman Podhoretz, "The Tribe of the Wicked Son," *Commentary*, February, 1971.

7. It would be virtually impossible to document all the cases of this. One might look at the following: Geraldine Rosenfield, "Interim Report on the New Left and Alienated Youth," American Jewish Committee, December, 1967; Richard L. Rubenstein, "Israel, Zionism, and the New Left," Public Affairs Department, Zionist Organization of America, 1969; and the articles by Howe, Kahn, Lipset, Fein, Glazer, Chertoff, Rosenstreich, and Milstein in Mordechai S. Chertoff, (ed.), *The New Left and the Jews*, Pitman, New York, 1971.

8. The first statements can be found in Kenneth Keniston, "The Sources of Student Dissent," and Richard Flacks, "The Liberated Generation: An Exploration of the Roots of Student Protest," in the *Journal of Social Issues*, July, 1967. See also Keniston's *Young Radicals*, Harcourt, Brace and World, New York, 1968; and Flacks' "Who Protests: A Study of Student Activists," in Julian Foster and Durwood Long (eds.), *Protest: Student Activism in America*, Morrow, New York, 1970, and bibliography therein.

9. William Watts and David Whittaker, "Free Speech Advocates at Berkeley," *Journal of Applied Behavioral Science*, January–March, 1966.

10. Flacks, "The Liberated Generation," *loc. cit.*

11. See David Drew, "A Profile of Jewish Freshmen," *Research Reports, American Council on Education,* Vol. 5, No. 4, 1970.

12. See Jack Newfield, *A Prophetic Minority,* Signet, New York, 1970, for an excellent report on the early New Left.

13. For these changes, see Milton Mankoff and Richard Flacks, "The Changing Social Base of the American Student Movement," *The Annals,* May, 1971; and Riley Dunlap, "Radicals and Conservative Student Activists," *Pacific Sociological Review,* Summer, 1970.

14. For a psychoanalytic interpretation, see Robert Liebert, *Radical and Militant Youth,* Praeger, New York, 1971, especially p. 233.

15. Jerry Rubin, *We Are Everywhere,* Harper and Row, New York, 1971, pp. 74–76.

16. See Drew, *op. cit.*

17. See Irving Greenberg, "Jewish Survival and the College Campus," *Judaism,* Summer, 1968.

18. N. J. Demerath, Gerald Marwell, and Michael T. Aiken, "Criteria and Contingencies of Success in a Radical Political Movement," *Journal of Social Issues,* No. 1, 1971.

19. See Rick Margolies, "On Community Building," in Priscilla Long (ed.), *The New Left,* Porter Sargent, Publisher, Boston, 1969; and Gerald Rosenfield, "Generational Revolt and the Free Speech Movement," in Paul Jacobs and Saul Landau (eds.), *The New Radicals,* Vintage, New York, 1966. One should explore other themes of the New Left in Massimo Teodori (ed.), *The New Left: A Documentary History,* Bobbs-Merrill, Indianapolis, 1969; Michael Goodman (ed.), *The Movement Toward a New America,* Knopf, New York, 1970; and James P. O'Brien, "The Development of the New Left," *The Annals,* May, 1971. Also Paul Cowan's political autobiography, *The Making of an Unamerican,* Viking, New York, 1970.

20. See Andrew Greeley, "Implications for the Sociology of Religion of Occult Behavior in the Youth Culture," *Youth and Society,* December, 1970; and a forthcoming book edited by Irving I. Zaretsky on new marginal religious movements to be published by Princeton University Press.

21. See a good collection of articles on the subject, without moralisms, in John McGrath and Frank R. Scarpitti (eds.), *Youth and Drugs,* Scott, Foresman and Co., Glenview, Ill., 1970.

22. See Alfred Jospe, "Jewish College Students in the U.S.," in the 1964 *American Jewish Yearbook;* and Leonard Fein's excellent "Dilemmas of Jewish Identity on the College Campus," *Judaism,* Winter, 1968.

23. From an internal document of Jews for Urban Justice called "An Abbreviated History of Jews for Urban Justice, 1966–69." See also the book by Arthur Waskow, *The Bush Is Burning,* Macmillan, New York, 1971.

24. See the report by Mel Galun, "The New Tone of Arab Propaganda on Campus," American Zionist Youth Foundation, 515 Park Ave., New York, 10022, and, from a different point-of-view, Michael Lerner, "Jewish New Leftism at Berkeley," *Judaism,* Fall, 1969.

25. There are no exact figures on immigration to Israel from the U.S. and Canada by age. Some overall figures are available, although they do not give percentages of those who eventually returned.

Immigration from U.S. and Canada to Israel

1965	1,879		1968	5,599
1966	2,041		1969	6,831
1967	2,402		1970	8,014

Source: Israeli Ministry of Immigrant Absorption. Planning and Research Division; personal letter to Peter Dreier from S. Adler, Director.

Another index is the growth of the One Year Program at Hebrew University in Jerusalem among American college students, most of whom spend their junior year in Israel. Note increase in 1968.

	Applications	Participants in One Year Program
1965/66	not available	87
1966/67	not available	135
1967/68	238	177
1968/69	536	478
1969/70	738	529
1970/71	773	612
1971/72	824	624

Source: Personal letter from Mrs. Johanna Schlobohm, Office of Academic Affairs, American Friends of Hebrew University, December 3, 1971.

Further evidence is the number of participants in American Zionist Youth Foundation programs. For example, its Volunteers for Israel program, begun following the war:

1968	1,400
1969	1,700
1970	3,000
1971	4,200

26. Every major Jewish organization and publication has issued a statement or article on the Jewish Defense League. Check the Jewish press since 1968, especially *Commentary, Jewish Currents, American Zionist, Congress Bi-Weekly, Jewish Frontier*, and in particular, *Facts*, published by the Anti-Defamation League of B'nai B'rith, February, 1971, called "The Jewish Defense League: Exploiter of Fear"; a controversy arose within the Jewish community early in 1971 when the ADL provided information on the Jewish Defense League to the FBI. See Mel Ziegler, "The Jewish Defense League and Its Invisible Constituency," *New York*, April 19, 1971.

27. "Hillel vs. the Elders," *Newsweek*, December 8, 1969.

28. See two reports by Alfred Jospe of the B'nai B'rith Hillel Foundation: "Free Jewish University: An Experiment in Jewish Study" and "Jewish Studies in American Colleges and Universities," revised edition. See also Arnold Band, "Jewish Studies in American Universities," in the *American Jewish Yearbook*, Vol. 67. All of these reports, however, are by now outdated as the number of free universities and Jewish studies courses increases every month.

29. Richard L. Maullin, "Los Angeles Liberalism," *Trans-action*, May, 1971.

30. For several perspectives on the school strike in New York, see Nat Hentoff (ed.), *Black Anti-Semitism and Jewish Racism*, Schocken, New York, 1970. Also, Herbert Gans, "Negro-Jewish Conflict in New York," *Midstream*, March, 1969.

31. See Nat Hentoff's column in *The Village Voice*, February 18, 1971.

32. Rumors of Bob Dylan's "coming back" to Judaism have circulated for over a year. See Anthony Scaduto, "Won't You Listen to the Lambs, Bob Dylan?" *The New York Times Magazine*, November 28, 1971; and Jonathan Braun, "The Bob Dylan Rumor Machine," *The Flame* (New York Union of Jewish Students), March, 1971, which was reprinted in *Rolling Stone* several weeks later. One of Ginsberg's most popular works, of course, is his poem, *Kaddish*. For an excellent study of the roots of the counterculture, see Theodore Roszak, *The Making of a Counter Culture*, Doubleday, Garden City, 1969.

33. William Watts and David Whittaker, "Profile of a Non-Conformist Youth Culture: A Study of Berkeley Non-Students," *Sociology of Education*, Spring, 1968.

34. A provocative article on the House of Love and Prayer is Leo Skir, "Shlomo Carlebach and the House of Love and Prayer," *Midstream*, May, 1970, and Carlebach's reply in the same issue.

35. Podhoretz, *op. cit.*

36. Nathan Glazer, "The Crisis in American Jewry," *Midstream*, November, 1970, and Glazer's article in Chertoff, *op. cit.*

37. Sleeper's comments are to be found in an excellent book he co-edited with Alan Mintz, *The New Jews*, Vintage, New York, 1971.

38. M. J. Rosenberg, "My Evolution as a Jew," *Midstream*, August/September, 1970. See also the articles by Mintz, Danny Siegel, Kenneth Braiterman, Jonathan Braun, and Benjamin Ross in *Midstream*, March, 1970.

39. Jean-Paul Sartre, *Anti-Semite and Jew*, Schocken, New York, 1965.

Part One

Voices of the Movement—I

History is seldom changed by mass movements, but rather by angry and persistent minorities—people with visions of a better world. Manifestos are the written attempts to record those visions: a movement's "statement of purpose." History has been profoundly altered by these authors and their followers: Lenin's *What Is To Be Done?* sparked the Russian Revolution; Theodore Herzl's *The Jewish State* inaugurated the modern Zionist movement.

Thus, we should not ignore the early attempts to map out a strategy, an ideology, and a set of goals. Often these efforts are crude. Many, if they are not totally banished to obscurity (as most undoubtedly are), are met with derision, condemnation, and skepticism by the Establishment of the day.

But the mixture of pragmatic *Realpolitik* and Utopian idealism which accompany these manifestos often surface at later periods of history as a rallying point for progress and change.

We begin this anthology with the Jewish Left's own visions. Written as the "old" New Left began to lose its idealism and influence, they speak to a generation of restless and searching young Jews. Unlike their parents' generation, they are not afraid of social change and are ready to face its consequences. These statements are the gropings of a new movement. They are the beginnings. Their authors are honest and disarmingly self-critical. They look to the past to explain and understand the failures and achievement of Jewish history; they look at the present and see the anger and rootlessness of an entire generation; they look toward the future seeking direction for their visions.

No two of these authors completely agree with each other. The Jewish Left makes no claim to unanimity. There exists no "orthodox" doctrine and no "revisionist" challenges. Their premises and their conclusions vary—from Zuckoff's and Rosenberg's forthright Zionism to Waskow's Diaspora-orientation, and yet none excludes or denies the other their place in the Jewish Left or the Jewish people.

These pieces reflect the difficult art of transforming a vision into a movement.

To Uncle Tom and Other Jews

M. J. Rosenberg

It has become fashionable in certain liberal (and predominantly Jewish) circles to scoff at anything that smacks of Jewishness. The Jew, the classic bumbling liberal, is today subject to scorn by virtually every left-wing spokesman. And the young American Jew is falling into line. He sees nothing inconsistent in his support of black "leaders" who warn of "Zionist conspiracies," and he can fit, albeit uncomfortably, into political organizations that advocate the liquidation of Israel. At one time such a Jew would be ridiculed and perhaps referred to a competent psychotherapist. Today he is respected and is, at the very least, considered legitimate. His more rational Jewish peers avoid the subject of the "Jewish question" with him while his gentile allies rejoice at the sight of this "liberated" Jew.

It is about time that this intellectual misfit be challenged. One must make clear that not all Jewish leftists subscribe to the militantly pro-Arab and anti-Jewish line of such organizations, popular on campus, as the Al Fatah-supporting Socialist Workers Party. But it must also be said that any Jew, regard-

M. J. Rosenberg is a graduate of the State University of New York at Albany and Brandeis University and is presently Hillel director at Temple University. This article first appeared in *The Village Voice* (February 13, 1969) and is reprinted by permission of the author and *The Village Voice*. Copyrighted by The Village Voice, Inc., 1969.

less of how pro-Israel he might personally be, who remains in one of these organizations, supports it financially or merely helps distribute its literature under the pretense that there are more important issues than the Middle East, is guilty of the greatest crime. And he will be dealt with.

It is most ironic. The self-hating Jew should have died with the creation of Israel. If the drama enacted in Cyprus, Europe, and Palestine between 1945 and 1948 did not convince him of the blood and guts of his own people then I am not sure that anything would. But in this time of exploding nationalism we should be less than tolerant of any Jew who chooses the route of self-denial and submission. One can sympathize with an individual who feels such self-hatred and yet we are also entitled to condemn him.

In the context of America, 1968, it is all the more amazing. The black American is the first to openly abjure the idea of assimilation, to recognize the inherent lie in the concept of the melting pot. Through black nationalism he has developed a new black pride and hence the ticket to liberalism.

The young American Jew is a good deal slower. He desperately craves assimilation; the very idea of "Jewishness" embarrasses him. If you tell him that he doesn't "look Jewish," he will invariably take it as a compliment. The concept of Jewish nationalism, Israel notwithstanding, he finds laughable. The leftist Jewish student—and this also applies to such apolitical college-age Jews as the fraternity boys, although to a far lesser degree—is today's "Uncle Tom." He scrapes along ashamed of his identity and yet is obsessed with it. He goes so far as to join black nationalist organizations, not as a Jew, but as a white. He does not and will not understand that his relevance is as a Jew, a fellow victim, and that his only effectiveness is as such. His destiny is that of the Jews but he denies what is apparent to the rest of us; he wants to be an "American," a leftist American talking liberation and an aspiring WASP. In relating to blacks, he will not come on as a Jew but as a white; he is hardly ready to relegate his precious whiteness to a secondary position. The potential Jewish

WASP is a ludicrous figure. If certain black spokesmen have been sounding anti-Semitic, we can attribute part of this feeling to the inherently racist attitude of the leftist Jew. The black militant comes into contact only with these self-hating Jews; it is not hard for him to realize that any man who cannot accept his own national identity is hardly likely to honestly accept any other man's. He can only see the self-abnegating Jewish leftist as the hypocrite that he is.

If he accepts the most basic tenets of the black nationalist movement, he should get himself out of it. Blacks don't want his "leadership" and they certainly don't need it. They realize the need for autoemancipation even if he doesn't. The sad fact is that the Jewish "Tom," so desirous of flagellation, is an inevitable product of American civilization. But it is time that he realizes that he is truly the invisible man. He, not today's black, is wandering in a no-man's land.

The Jew can be an ally of the black liberation movement and he should be. But first he must find himself. He must realize that his own struggle for liberation is a continuing one, that he also has much to fear and also much to take pride in. The miracle of Israel, a national liberation deferred for two thousand years, should be his inspiration. As the late Robert F. Kennedy said, "Israel's creation . . . has written a new chapter in the annals of freedom and courage—a story that my children and yours will tell their descendants to the end of time." This is recognized by free men everywhere. In Biafra, the struggling Ibo looks to Israel as a symbol of man's never-ending fight for survival and freedom. It would be doubly tragic if the young American Jew does not see clearly what is so apparent to a Biafran, a Czech, a free Irishman, or a West Berliner. The miracle of 1948 was that the Jew did it alone, with the guns he could smuggle and the iron will that is the legacy of Auschwitz. The Jew prevailed and he did it without a single ally. This makes it so imperative that we ensure that which was won by Jewish heroes on the fields of Palestine will not be lost with the aid and connivance of Jewish moral cowards here at home.

Therefore it is as a Jew that I must accept black nationalism. The black nationalists may or may not be the equivalents of the militants of the early Zionist organizations, and Malcolm X may or may not be a black Vladimir (Zev) Jabotinsky, but surely the parallel is there. The Jewish war of liberation differs from that of the black American or of the Viet Cong only in that the Jewish struggle has seen its greatest aim realized, however tenuously. So will the black revolution succeed. And yet I know that when the black man wins his freedom, he will lose all his white "friends." He will be called "antiprogressive." We will be labeled an "aggressor." If he wins again and again, he will be called an "oppressor." The black in America will then realize that he stands completely alone, as he, in fact, does now.

He can learn this much from the Jewish experience. When they slaughtered six million Jews, the good people muttered sympathetic noises. But the gates of America and Britain remained closed. And when the war ended, these good people wanted to help the few remaining Jews. They told them that they would help them return "home"—to Germany, to Poland, and to Rumania. But the Jews wanted more. It was only when the fighting Jew arose from the blood and ashes of Europe, when the pitiful skeletons of Dachau resolved that they would now fight for their own land, that the Jews lost their newly-found friends. The world reluctantly came to accept our national existence but was prepared to mourn our imminent demise. For as it was said from the British Foreign Office to the halls of the American Department of State: "My God, man, you know Jews can't fight."

But fight and win they did. And for twenty years it appeared as though the world really did care about the fledgling Jewish state. Who can forget those days before the Six-Day War when every free-world capital saw massive rallies in support of Israel. From London to Warsaw the common man supported Israel in its fight to live. Even the leftists backed Israel, although one can only feel that the left would have rather avoided the subject entirely. But Israel's victory lost her any left-wing support she had. Israel suddenly became a "force of reaction," and a bastion of "antirevolutionary activity." If Israel had lost the war, she could truly have ingratiated herself with the leftists. They would have held their sympathy rallies and would wear the Star of David as the symbol of national liberation. She could have come to represent the fight for freedom; the universal struggle to exist. Her people, unfortunately "driven into the sea," would have been martyrs to the cause. It could have been beautiful; but Israel lost her one golden chance to be loved by the left. She survived. And for that she shall be punished. Many Jewish nationalists have remarked that our recent history has conclusively proven that the Jews are "damned if they do and damned if they don't." For hundreds of years they said we were too passive, couldn't fight, and finally that we allowed ourselves to be led "like sheep" to the slaughter. Today they say that we are a militaristic people with a fiercely bellicose streak. So we have been condemned both for a lack of action and for strong deterrent action. In the final analysis we must prefer the latter condemnation. It is better by far to be damned for action than for the lack of it. As the black nationalists have said, when the issue is survival, we must prevail "by any means necessary."

But Israel is not the central issue at this point. The issue is one of Jewish pride. The Jewish professor who makes a point of teaching on Yom Kippur with subtle mockery of those students who stay home, the Jewish kids who lower their heads when a Philip Roth story is up for discussion in their literature course, the Jewish radicals who are prepared to fight for the Czechs, the Greeks, and the Biafrans and yet reject Israel; these are our Uncle Toms and our shame. The Jew must accept his identity; and, like it or not, his Jewishness is his destiny. Hermann Goering was not far from the point when he said that, "I determine who is a Jew." Our only answer, as Jean-Paul Sartre has advised us, is to accept our Jewishness with pride. No anti-Semite, National Socialist, or Socialist Worker, will define my existence. The sad lesson of the past thirty years is that, in the final analysis, we shall stand or fall together. To speak figuratively, in the shower rooms it will little matter that one fellow was once Albert Shanker and the other was once Mark Rudd. Their destinies and fates are intertwined, for better or for worse. If we haven't learned that, we have learned nothing.

Black nationalism and Jewish nationalism will exist concurrently. To accept one, you must accept the other. The black is America's Jew and a common fight can be waged. But not at the expense of our own pride. Thus, when some black nationalist calls us "racist Zionists" or tells us that we are poisoning his children's minds, then we must see him for what he is: just another *goy*, using the Jew as the available and acceptable scapegoat. We must then fight him with all we have. That's the way it has to be; we must scrape for no one.

And thus from this point on, I will support no movement that does not accept my people's struggle. If I must choose between the Jewish cause and a "progressive" anti-Israel S.D.S., I shall always choose the Jewish cause. Not blindly, not arbitrarily, but always with full knowledge of who I am and where I must be. If the barricades are erected, I will fight as a Jew. It has been written that after "Auschwitz we retain but one supreme value—to exist." Masada will not fall again.

There is still time but the burden of proof is not on the Jewish nationalist; it is on you—you who reject your identity and attempt to evade the inescapable fact that it follows you wherever you go. You who mockingly reject every lesson of your people's history. You who are so trapped by your Long Island split-level childhood that you can't see straight. You who fight against everything you are—against the one element that gave you your goddamn social consciousness: your Jewish social idealism.

In the aftermath of the crematoriums, you are flippant. In the wake of Auschwitz, you are embarrassed. Thirty years after the Holocaust you have learned nothing and forgotten everything. Ghetto Jew, you'd better do some fast thinking.

Judaism and Revolution Today
Malkhut Zadon M'herah T'aker

Arthur I. Waskow

*V'lamalshinim al t'hi tikvah . . . umalkhut zadon m'herah
t'aker ut'shaber ut'mager v'takhneah bim'herah b'yamenu.*
"May You bring to nought the hopes of the slanderous in-
formers . . . May You speedily uproot the Empire of Arrogance and crush it, subduing it quickly, in our own day!"

So the nineteenth prayer of the *Sh'moneh Esrei,* the "Eigh-
teen Prayers" of the daily service. Nineteenth because it was
added, long after the others, at the direction of Rabban
Gamaliel II, head of the Sanhedrin at Yavneh, at the end of
the first century of the Common Era, when the Empire of
Arrogance was Rome. Added because, even at nonrevolu-
tionary Yavneh, even when the first wave of Jewish revolutionaries against Rome had been crushed and the Temple destroyed, even then the hope of revolution, of the crushing of the
Empire "in our day," was kept alive. Added because, above
all, there was to be no hope, even from Yavneh, for those
slanderers who informed upon the Jewish revolutionaries to
the Empire.

Copyright © 1971 by the Religious Community of Micah; reprinted from
Judaism, XX, No. 4, Fall, 1971. The argument of this piece is extended in
Waskow's book *The Bush is Burning,* Macmillan, New York, 1971, available
from Micah Press, 1808 Wyoming Ave., N.W., Washington, D.C. 20009,
for $2.25 prepaid.

What a clearly, vigorously "political" statement to be preserved alive in the liturgy even to our own day! Reading it,
who can help but know that Judaism is, indeed, intrinsically
"political," and that under some circumstances the most
honored upholders and developers of the tradition have called,
or hoped, for revolution? Almost by itself, even if there had
been no uprising against Pharaoh, no uprising against Antiochus, no Book of Jonah with its explicit command to preach
the imminent destruction of a "violent" city that was not
Jewish and was not oppressing Jews—almost by itself, the
deliberate insertion and preservation of the *malshinim* prayer
would annihilate the claim that Judaism absolutely prohibits a
radical stance against the reigning authorities.

The question that we must answer at this moment of crisis
in our history is, indeed, exactly the reverse: Does the Jewish
tradition impel us to believe that *at this moment* we must become committed *as Jews* to the radical transformation of
America and the world? And, closely connected with that question, a second one of overwhelming import: Does the Jewish
people stand utterly alone—or are there other peoples who
share our needs, face much the same disasters as do we, and
might, in concert with us, act to transform the world so that
we and they are free?

Many American Jews are puzzled and frightened by the
present crisis, and do not yet have answers to these questions.
But the answer of an increasing number of Jews—mostly, but
not all, young—is that the Jewish tradition does now call us to
a radical response, and that other peoples do share our dangers and could, therefore, join with us in seeking a radical
transformation.

What kind of "radical" response? The creation of a vital,
holistic Jewish people which pursues the basic principle of
halakhah—that life is a path, a Way, indivisible, in which
politics, religion, economics, culture, the family are fused. The
particular codification of *halakhah* in the *Shulkhan Arukh*
may not be the form taken by the new *halakhah* (or perhaps

halakhot). Such a newly-*halakhic* community would, necessarily, be a community of survival and resistance. Such a community, governing itself, feeding itself, teaching itself according to its own perception of its own path would, necessarily, be a threat to the American empire.

Why? First, because the modern superstates are preparing a new and much more thorough Holocaust: the destruction of the Jewish people and of the whole human race. Second, because such a reconstituted newly-*halakhic* Jewish people could not be the empires' accomplice or pawn in deforesting Vietnam, poisoning the air and water, occupying Czechoslovakia, letting people starve in the midst of plenty, locking Israelis, Egyptians, and Palestinians into a permanent arms race—to name only cases where it is not we alone who are the victims.

But there is another answer. It comes from a small but vocal band of older Jews who control some of the key established institutions of American Jewry—the Anti-Defamation League, the American Jewish Committee, *Commentary* magazine—and who have a political stance born of the 1940's and 1950's. Their answer is: the Jews stand alone, and radical change is disastrous. Any Jews who seek it and believe that other peoples can join with the Jewish people to do so are anti-Semitic and self-hating, should be proclaimed non-Jews, other Jews should enter into no dialogue with them and the authorities should be told that they are fair game. Not everybody in these institutions answers the crisis in this way, of course, but the institutions do, at least some of the time. For example:

Item: The Anti-Defamation League of B'nai B'rith circulated to it regional offices, and thence to hundreds of Jewish groups, a memo on Uri Avneri, an independent-left member of the Israeli Knesset who is committed both to the preservation of Israel and to the liberation of the Palestinian people, and who was beginning a speaking tour in the United States: "We advise that Jewish organizations not sponsor or cosponsor his appearances and not engage in public debate with him."

Item: The Anti-Defamation League issued a public state-

ment denouncing the Medical Committee for Human Rights
and the Health Policy Advisory Center as destructive of
good medicine, refused to make available to the organizations
attacked, or to the press, the "public report" on which its statement is based, and hinted that M.C.H.R.'s and Health-
P.A.C.'s support for community control of hospitals and the
health system smacks of anti-Semitism. Why? Because in some
big cities—notably New York—the great hospital empires are
at least nominally Jewish, though they are now closely tied to
Federal and business bureaucracies. Therefore, an attack on
their present structure as undemocratic and unhealthful might,
in fact, regardless of formal political ideology, be "anti-
Semitic." In any case, A.D.L. felt obligated to defend these
Jewish Establishment institutions. On the other hand, it had
no other interest in the many Jewish medical workers who
were involved with Health-P.A.C. or M.C.H.R.; perhaps
A.D.L. considers them "self-hating" Jews.

Item: Commentary magazine, in an editorial introducing a
major cluster of articles, recites an abject litany to the White
House—divorcing not only itself, but the whole Jewish people,
from the civil-rights, anti-war, and other insurgent movements
of the past decade: "David Dellinger is not Jewish; Tom Hayden is not Jewish; Staughton Lynd is not Jewish; Carl Oglesby
is not Jewish; Timothy Leary is not Jewish; Kate Millett is
not Jewish; and neither . . . is Stokely Carmichael Jewish, nor
Huey Newton, nor Angela Davis. . . . The Movement . . . had
a decidedly Protestant flavor, with its tone being set by divines
like A. J. Muste and Martin Luther King." And then, admit-
ting that there *were* some Jews in those movements, even some
rabbis, explains that there were not really Jewish. They were
self-hating Jews. They were anti-Semitic Jews.

How pitiful, how sorrowful! That the statement, so strongly
begging for the acceptance of Jews as trustworthy subjects of
the American king, itself betrays so deep a fear that the Jews
are suspect, are rejected, by those whom the statement most
dearly wants to honor.

Such a performance may fill us with pity, or with disgust;

with anger, shame, or dialogic zeal, or with them all. But it is important to understand the response. To do so, we must understand the crisis that we face—a crisis embodied in three simultaneous crises, enclosed like envelopes, each within the other.

To begin with, there is what might be called the eighty-year crisis of American Jewry. Since the mass migration began in the 1890's, we have felt more and more confident about our ability to "enter" America. But in the 1960's this confidence was shattered. When the blacks tried to enter the melting pot, the temperature inside got too high and the pot shattered. Simultaneously, the Vietnam war showed America, not as defender against a holocaust, but as perpetrator of one. From both events, many young Jews whose parents had proudly assimilated themselves to the American Promise, the quasi-Methodist synagogue, and the quasi-Rotarian B'nai B'rith, find they do not want to be "Americans" after all, and some older Jews begin to wonder. The eighty-year upward-mobile process was broken. It became, not simply impracticable, as during periodic economic slumps, but to some it became undesirable—a much more basic crisis in belief. Many of our youth began to celebrate, not mourn, the end of the melting pot, and to herald the creation of a real Jewish community. They began to criticize as assimilationists those Establishment elders who had triumphed in the triumphs of America. But most Jews have not quite understood this crisis, and most of the Establishment Jews of the 1940's and 1950's have responded to the disintegration of "America" not with celebration but with panic, and, to this criticism from the younger, not with change but with fury.

Secondly, the 1900-year crisis. For the first time since the destruction of the Temple, a large and self-governing community of Jews has settled in Eretz Yisroel. But that created several poignant conflicts, at least among the young. To begin with, in 1967, if not before, the Jewish community in Israel proved to be, in some sense, "ours." Then, by 1970, if not before, Israel turned out to be not truly "Zion," that is, not the Hill, the Center from which the Teaching was going forth. Israel, as well as the Diaspora, lived in *galut; galut* was, indeed, spiritual, not geographic. Until the Messianic transformation of the world, Israel would be a state much like other states, and that Messianic transformation required the Diaspora as much as it required Israel.

Psychologically most important of all, the very existence of Israel meant that the Diaspora was no longer, if it had ever been, a "necessary evil." It was no longer "necessary" to stay in the Diaspora and, therefore, if the Diaspora were to survive it could not be viewed as an evil. To those who were most serious about their own commitments, living Jewishly in the Diaspora could not even mean viewing Israel as "The Center" of Jewish existence. For, if Israel were truly The Center, one should go there; and if Israel were not "a focus" but *The Center,* then the Diaspora must be a shadow. But no shadow can create anything real. And so the psychological reality emerged that *Israel-centered* Jews must go there if they were to be real and there create reality, while those who intended to stay in the Diaspora must commit themselves to a belief in the Diaspora as a *positive good,* short of the Messiah, if they were to make themselves and their community real. Some young Jews, then, began to see the Diaspora and Israel as two sides of the coin of Jewishness. Without *either,* the Jewish people would not be whole or healthy (i.e., as whole and healthy as it is possible to be, short of Messiah). They began to celebrate, not mourn, the Diaspora. They criticized those Establishment elders who had left the American Diaspora so empty of content. And again the Establishment responded in panic: with virulent denunciations of anyone who celeberated the Diaspora or criticized Israel as not wholly "Zion."

And, third, the 3500-year crisis. From Sinai, to the Holocaust, to Hiroshima. For Hiroshima posed the same threat to all of humanity (including the Jewish people) that Auschwitz posed to the Jewish people specifically. To the Jews, World War II was a threat of their physical destruction; to the whole human race it threatened the universal holocaust. But these twin terrors were more than simultaneous in time; both stemmed from the same demonic organization of a potentially fruitful technology. Both, perversely enough, were indices of the new possibility of transforming the world into decency, rather than death, into freedom, rather than necessity.

But to some Jews the twin message got lost. Some focused on Auschwitz as if no other people were in danger, while others focused on Hiroshima as though all the differences between people had been annihilated in that blinding flash. The truth is that both Auschwitz and Hiroshima threatened the Jewish people and that both threatened all the peoples of the Earth. Auschwitz threatened all of us in our differences, Hiroshima threatened all of us in our samenesses.

But Hiroshima also threatens us *as Jews*, because *as Jews* we are commanded to build the Days of Peace and Justice, and not to permit the destruction of ourselves and of all the Earth. That is why some young Jews came to believe that *in this generation* of our history, Judaism itself requires us to be revolutionary. For they believe that we live today under kings like Pharaoh, Antiochus, and the Ninevan, and that the potentiality is clear of Hitlers even worse than Hitler. There are some who scornfully dismiss that belief. But ought we to trust that the thermonuclear arsenals commanded by the United States and the Soviet Union will not be used? Ought we to trust that deterrence works forever—not for a decade, not for a century, but *forever?* Are we supposed to forget that the magnificent 19th-century balance-of-power deterrent system in Europe ended, after many a success that "proved" its worth, in 1914?

Can the Jewish people survive a thermonuclear war? Can we survive the making of the Earth unlivable? Simply because all other peoples are threatened with us, are we the less threatened and are we, therefore, the less required to respond? Suppose we do respond—Jewishly, radically. Suppose we respond that the very structure of the modern superstate is what re-

quires it to threaten the world and that the inward structure of
Judaism provides an answer that requires the building of a new
society and the dismantling of the old, with loving care, so as
to prevent damage to people, but with thoroughness in the dismantling.

Suppose we rise to take the task upon us. Would we be
crushed? Not if the other peoples of the Earth are rising alongside us.

And that is a central question. For the final defense of the
Jewish Establishment for its own retrenchment, its own deliberate restriction of vitality, is fear. Fear that the Jewish people
is utterly alone, that if we decide that our own tradition in this
moment requires Prophetic radicalism, we will be destroyed
because we are alone. Fear of the White House, of the black
community, of the Czar and of the peasants. Fear that we live,
not at a crossroads, but on the brink of disaster. Fear that any
motion will plunge us into the chasm.

And so for Jews as Jews, quietism. Inwardness. Let us renounce our beacon to the nations, become a small people. The
politics this requires? An abject clinging to those rulers who
at the moment have the greatest power. And when the trembling paralysis of will becomes unbearable, an outburst of
hysteria—followed by a return to trembling paralysis. At some
moments, a fear so overwhelming that those who feel it try to
divert the attention of the rulers with a human sacrifice. "It is
those others who are standing firm against you. Not us. Not us
real Jews. Take *them*."

Some of the fear, the loneliness, comes, of course, from being Jews who have lived through the period of the Holocaust
and were formed by it. But some of those who respond this
way happen to have been formed by the 1940's and 1950's,
less as Jews than as social democrats, or as ex-communists or
ex-Trotskyists scarred by encounters with their parties into becoming social democrats. There is nothing wicked about this,
any more than it is wicked for a Jew to become a non-Jewishly
identified radical of the New Left. What is wicked is contempt
for another identity that is not intrinsically oppressive, whether

it be some Jews' contempt for those who chose a radical identity or some radicals' contempt for those who chose a Jewish one.

The puzzlement and disbelief of these more-social-democrat-than-Jewish Jews at seeing revolutionaries who define themeslves as Jews and feel their revolution as a Jewish one may stem from the fact that they see their own primary community and identity as that of social-democrats-without-regard-to-race-or-religion, not as a Jewish one. So perhaps they project their feelings onto us. Obviously, their tendency to do so is facilitated by the fact that some of us "started" radical and grew into Judaism. But that makes their mistake no less destructive.

They are social democrats for a reason. Facing the country that had conquered half the Earth between 1940 and 1945, they knew in their bones that no one could ever change it from the bottom. So they gave up agitation and insurgency for manipulation. Through the 1940's, 1950's, and 1960's, the social democrats saw themselves as a cadre leading A.D.A., A.D.A. as a cadre leading the Democratic Party, the Democrats governing America, America remaking the world. Under Lyndon Johnson the dream came true—and proved disaster. When Johnson tried to hand over power to Humphrey, the social democrats' favorite stalking horse, the disaster was confirmed in defeat. Will those days come again—the days that never quite came once?

Not likely. Something new, much more insurgent, is stirring in the land. The bright and energetic non-Jewishly-identified Jews who would have read *Commentary* in 1961, now read *The New York Review* and *Ramparts*. And the committedly Jewish young Jews read *Response,* sing Carlebach, and wear *talleisim* to march against the White House. Some even read both *Response* and *Ramparts*. Every success of this insurgent movement infuriates ex-radicals who gave up on insurgency, every failure delights them. So they feel alone. Indeed, as social democrats, they feel even more alone, without allies, even more dependent, than they would if they felt Jewish. And they write large for the Jewish people the role, writ small, which they play themselves: clerks for the king.

But this analysis is not enough. If there were not even a grain of truth in their perception of the world, they would not have listeners and followers. But there is a germ of truth. It is not easy for American Jews in 1971 to see the possibility of allies. Why?

Because the 1960's were a period in which the form that the American crisis took pitted others most directly against the organized Jewish community. Who moved into action? Blacks, Puerto Ricans, professionals, and students who were often Jewish, but, if so, were rarely members of specifically Jewish organizations. And against what bulwarks did they move? Against the structures nearest to them and, therefore, often "Jewish." For example, blacks moved against the marginal stores operating in the black communities—stores owned or operated by a higher than "random" number of Jews. Blacks moved against public school bureaucracies staffed by a higher than "random" number of Jews.

The syndrome was an old one. Once again, one of the key oppressions suffered by Jews at the hands of a Western society —this time, America—had been to be slotted into roles that seemed oppressive to the desperately poor. The Jewish grocer might charge blacks high prices because the non-Jewish bank was charging him high interest—but the blacks were likely to focus on the immediate oppressor. The Jewish teacher might jam Suburban English down black throats because a non-Jewish educational establishment had jammed it down his own, but the blacks were likely to focus on the immediate oppressor. Similarly for Jewish social workers, Jewish doctors . . . the poor began to move—even when that movement ignored or specifically discounted as unimportant the Jewishness of the grocer or the teacher—the targets of the movement saw it as directed against them for their Jewishness. Occasional outbursts of explicit anti-Semitism from some blacks merely confirmed the fear that the whole black movement was secretly anti-Semitic. So the response was a defensive, anti-black up-surge.

The alternative would have been for the Jewish grocers and teachers to ally themselves with the black energies against the social system that had oppressed them all. Some did—particularly among the young teachers and young physicians who had more flexibility of thought and life style, more leg room in status and, perhaps, in money, to shrug off a traditional career. But these were the least identified with organized Jewish life. Perhaps, indeed, the younger they were the more they had been deprived by a low-content Judaism of any opportunity to identify with it, and so were angriest at the emptiness which they had known in the *shuls* and *bar mitzvahs* of their youth. (Their parents had grown up in a Judaism more deeply rooted in the realities of Eastern Europe.) So those who felt most a part of organized Jewish life also felt more threatened by the blacks—and those Jews who felt most hostile to organized Jewry were also those who were most likely to welcome the blacks as allies.

When organized Jewry began to condemn the black de-mands as consciously or unconsciously anti-Semitic, the Jews who allied themselves with those demands had two ways to go: accept that they themselves were no longer Jewish, or indignantly assert that, although their lives had been deprived of Jewish content by the Jewish Establishment, their lives were more "Jewish" in form (and sometimes even in content) than were those of the Establishment that was denouncing them. So some of the uninvolved young Jews were thrust into Jewish life by the urging of the blacks to go home and organize their own community, and some were thrust into it by the de-nunciations of their own community's "leadership." Most often both. Then, when some blacks did, indeed, begin to capitalize on latent anti-Semitism among some of their own, some radical Jews found themselves grappling with *that*—and becoming more Jewish, but no less radical, in the process.

Thus, from several streams and eddies of the historic black-

Jew encounter, came three developments: a scornfully, non-Jewishly-identified wave of Jewish radicals; the radical Jewish movement, created chiefly by newly-committed Jews who welcomed blacks as allies; and a conventional Jewish leadership increasingly fearful of the blacks (and sometimes seeing as its reference group, not the Jewish communities in America, but the American Establishment or the Israeli government).

What kind of Judaism can assuage this fear and fury, bind together all the Jews who take Judaism seriously with all the Jews who take radicalism seriously? We—the celebrants of the New Diaspora, radical Jews, the Jewish "counterculture"—firmly believe that the only Judaism which can do this *in our generation* is one rooted in those strands of the tradition that command both resistance to idolatry and positive reaching out for the Messianic Age, those strands which look to the day when "Blessed be Egypt my people, and Assyria the work of my hands, and Israel my heritage"—the day of allies in liberation.

And in the 1970's many of us see the glimmerings of a present possibility, alongside the commandments of an ancient faith. Many of us believe there *are,* or *are about to be,* allies in the building of liberation—if the Jewish people will take the risk of seeking liberation.

Many of us believe that in the 1970's and 1980's the American crisis will deepen, not abate. The 1960's were just the first stage of the American crisis, the first peel of the onion. Those most affected were the outer skins of the onion, the marginal people: blacks, students, Chicanos. But now the crisis is starting to cut deeper into the onion.

Why? The substructure of America, what keeps people alive, has been allowed to rot away for a generation while money was being put into the super-war machine. Sewers are ready to fail, the health system is collapsing, houses have not been built. The substructure *has* to be replaced, fast, if there is to be internal peace; but it will *not* be replaced, because the money is not available unless it comes from the military budget, corporate profits, the middle class, or industrial expansion.

And there are strong political reasons why it cannot come from any of them.

As the substructure continues to falter and fail, most workers and suburbanites will see the collapse as clearly the fault of the Establishment, not of the blacks or the yippies. And now it will be the working class and middle class, the inner layers of the onion, who get hurt, who get furious, who get moving. There will be Jews among them—Jews solidly embedded in organized Jewry, not the "marginal" Jews of the movements of the 1960's. And they will be moving, not against the institutions where Jews have great stakes, as some of the movements of the 1960's did, but against the real power-centers of America—which are not Jewish. So the Jews, the Italians, the Appalachians, the Poles will find themselves moving as allies of the blacks and Chicanos against the Empire, rather than as minions of the Empire against the blacks.

How can they move? Partly as peoples, out of their own ethnic consciousness of similiar oppressions, but partly as workers, sharing the inflation/unemployment oppression, the health/pollution oppression, the bureaucracy/speed-up oppression that American workers are now rediscovering. As workers, sharing also the power which workers have: the power to stop working.

For there are the barest hints that the illegal postal strike, and the Teamster wildcat, and the campus post-Cambodia strike, and the first steps toward one-day "moratorium" events inside the Federal government reminded people of the power that inheres in refusal to work for the system, and that power can grow out of something other than the barrel of a gun. Not elections: they are too slow, a maze to calm and channel sudden floods of popular energy, or simply an elaborate way of collecting power from the people and handing it over to someone else.

What then? New lips begin to shape an old phrase in a new context: "general strike." Not planning, but remembering. Realizing that a "general strike" need not be really a work *stoppage,* but could be a *redirection* of work; that for such a general strike workers need to understand how to run their own factories and farmers how to get food directly to those in the cities. Realizing that it takes knowledge, comradeship, and hard work to build the alternative future in advance.

What does all this mean to radical Jews? That if we reach out to reconstruct our own lives, so as to break out of the "mini-oppressor" roles our real oppressors have slotted us into; if we reach out to join with other men and women who suffer in bureaucracies, who suffer from the two-hour tortured drive to and from work, who suffer isolated in their housewifery, who suffer from the speedup on the assembly line—we can build the kind of movement that liberates the Jewish people *and* the other peoples, not to abandon our differences but to build upon them in non-oppressive ways.

Specifically:

One area in which we are struggling to express our newly radical Judaism is through the traditional Jewish celebrations, not abandoning the tradition but clearly and consciously developing it. We must develop a Sukkoth celebration that makes clear in our own terms the danger of the destruction of a viable ecology on Earth, and takes seriously the liturgy's assertion that if the Torah be ignored, the rain will cease to fall. We must develop Tisha B'Av as a memorial not only of the Temple but of the Holocaust and Hiroshima—those modern warnings of the Destruction of the Temple of Mankind.

We must create, or recreate, a communal Shabbat that embodies in the present the vision of a free, unalienated society in the future as the tradition says the Shabbat, foretaste of the Messianic Age, ought to do. We need a Shabbat of dance and song. We need a Shabbat that can have dance and song because it is celebrated by thirty people sitting on the floor in a living room, instead of 300 sitting in rows in a synagogue. We need a Shabbat of study that helps all Jews to do what the midrashic commentators did—sit in a circle to read *Tanakh* and comment on it out of their own knowledge and concern. We need a Shabbat liturgy that treats Buber and Heschel and

Fromm as seriously as our forefathers' liturgy treated Maimonides in *Yigdal*.

The Freedom Seder, used by thousands of young and not-so-young, radical and not-so-radical Jews tried to develop the liturgy in ways that assert the liberation of the Jewish people *alongside* the liberation of the other peoples—not theirs as against ours, or ours as against theirs. Thus, it celebrates the Warsaw Ghetto Uprising of 1943 *alongside* the black uprisings of the 1960's; the liberation of the Jews *alongside* the liberation of the Vietnamese; Rabbi Tamaret on nonviolence *alongside* Gandhi and Berrigan.

Thus, *The Freedom Seder* is not simply universalist or particularist, but "multiparticularist," following the form and content of the Seder of Exodus, and then showing how that history has a universally particular meaning—how, indeed, it is appealed to explicitly by Muste and King in their own lives and work. Thus, *The Freedom Seder* is one experimental effort —there have been and will be others—toward what the tradition calls the Passover of the Messianic Age, the Passover of the liberation of all the nations. When all will still be different from each other—all still walking, as Micah says, each in the name of its god.

Specifically, again:

We must respond to the crisis of the American health system (to which the Anti-Defamation League responded with a defense of the great hospital empires) with an answer more rooted in the Jewish tradition: neighborhood-based, community-controlled health centers that treat the whole person, psychological and cultural as well as "physical"; centers in which health work and decision-making are shared, and artificial barriers between doctors, nurses, patients, and "nonprofessional workers" are lowered; centers that serve as focal points for political campaigns on issues of pollution, public health, garbage.

Specifically, again:

We must respond to the conscription of our bodies and our

money into a war of the American Empire, with the clear withdrawal of the Jewish people in the United States from that war, which is forbidden by our Torah, with the turning of our synagogues into sanctuaries (like the six cities in ancient Israel) for those who have refused their taxes and their bodies to the Idol Moloch.

Specifically, again:

We must build urban and rural kibbutzim in North America that embody in the present the dream of a future liberated Jewish people. Kibbutzim that work in the complete round of production that our people, and North America, need: food, industrial goods, child-rearing, sociology, prayer, and poetry, and that live, not on the oppression of others, but on our own work, our own love, our own play. Kibbutzim in which work itself is liberated, the Shabbat casts its light over all the week, and the kibbutz reaches out to other workplaces, other celebration-places, and other politics-places to transform and unify themselves.

A kibbutz does not grow overnight. We can see the bare beginnings in the Boston and New York *havurot,* in Jews for Urban Justice and the Fabrangen in Washington, in the Radical Jewish Community of Los Angeles, and The Brooklyn Bridge in New York. But all of these are fragile. Not one is a production cooperative, let alone the full cooperative of which Buber wrote. We must deepen them, federate them, break through to a better kibbutz. We must also recognize that not every Jew in America will see the kibbutz as the form of liberation most appropriate to him or her, and we must encourage the invention of other forms.

And finally:

We must begin to struggle toward a new *halakhah,* if the particular lines of the old one no longer engage our sense of justice and holiness. What we eat *does* have something to do with what we believe; what would a new *kashrut* be like? How men and women treat each other *does* have something to do with liberation, redemption; what would it mean for men and women to be equal, free, and holy? What kinds of property are forbidden? What relationship ought we to have with our work?

The last dread question of social democrats: Suppose the revolution wins, will it be better than the one which the Bundists touted in the Russian Empire? Will we be any better off?

To which some answers: Anti-Semitism survived in the Soviet Union because oppression survived there, too, and the revolution was not fulfilled. The Bund failed, perhaps partly because it was too state-socialist and did not build kibbutzim or in other ways build unshakeable power at the grass roots; perhaps, partly, because it rejected the religious celebration which is part of what makes the Jewish people and which is at its best an assertion of the human spirit against idolatry and tyranny. But, probably mostly, because it was almost impossible to succeed. It would have been very hard for Russia in 1917 to liberate her peasants to be full citizens: they might not have had the time to grow food if they had taken the time to grow human. But now we live in the era of abundance, when no one need be a slave in order that others can have the leisure to govern, when all *could* share in governing themselves, if the abundance were shared equally among them.

Now the conditions exist that make it possible—barely, but possible—for us to break through to the "era of freedom," the Messianic Age; and it would be as great a disaster to fail to try with all our strength to bring "Messiah" when the time is ripe, as ever it was to follow false Messiahs when Messiah was impossible. Never before could the human race be destroyed; never before could it be liberated. So also for the Jews.

Our tradition teaches us not only the goal but the method: to bring the Age of Shabbat, the whole Jewish people must celebrate two Shabbats in a row. Two meanings: First, it is *we* who are obligated to act—all of us. Secondly, it is exemplifying in the present what we foresee as the future society of Peace and Justice that will make the future real. The only means that we may use are those that partake of the ends themselves, and to reject illegitimate means is not to postpone the revolution but to bring it nearer.

Let our watchword be this: The Shabbat was the first general strike, a holy general strike; let us build an Age of Shabbat!

The Oppression of America's Jews

Aviva Cantor Zuckoff

The article below is an attempt at delineating the pattern of
oppression of Jews particularly as it relates to the American
galut (exile). Its underlying concept is that liberation begins
with the recognition of oppression and the understanding of
its exact nature.

"Jew Jew Jew Jew Jew Jew! It is coming out of my ears
already, the saga of the suffering Jews! Do me a favor, my
people, and stick your suffering heritage up your suffering ass
—I happen also to be a human being."

—Portnoy's Complaint

Are the Jews in the United States oppressed?
To begin to answer this question, we must first define
"oppression." As the term is used here, oppression in its various forms (economic, social, political, and psychological)
means the denial of the most basic human right: to be yourself.[1] It means being forced into a situation where your own

Aviva Cantor Zuckoff, founding member of the Jewish Liberation Project,
is editor of *The Jewish Liberation Journal*. She is active in the women's
movement and a former reporter for the American bureau of the *London
Jewish Chronicle*. Reprinted by permission of the author. This article
appeared in *The Jewish Liberation Journal*, November, 1970.

destiny is not in your own hands but in those of others, usually of your enemy. It is a condition of being powerless to act to gain control of your destiny, of being reacted upon by events without the capacity to affect, change, or prevent them. It means being exploited and used in the interests of the oppressor and against your own, and of being programmed for and forced into certain roles for his benefit. It is being forced to adapt to these conditions in such a way as to prevent retaliation on the part of the oppressor.

Thus, when we come to consider whether Jews in America are oppressed, we should not be side-tracked by the fact that they happen to be, by and large, economically well-off and not subject at the moment to the kind of physical oppression faced by blacks, Indians, and Chicanos. Oppression in America can be subtle and not easily recognized as such, as has long been the case with the oppression of women. It is necessary to look at what is going on beneath the surface.

For centuries Jews have been programmed into certain roles in society which they still play: the middleman, the "oppressor surrogate," and the scapegoat. In the Middle Ages, when the ban on Jews owning land began, Jews were allowed to function mainly as merchants and moneylenders, occupations closed to Christians for socioreligious reasons but necessary to the economy. Till today, Jews have not been and are not really involved in the production process but are predominant in the distribution end of the economy. The thin spreading of token Jews in such institutions as banks, utilities, large corporations, the diplomatic service and government only serves to illustrate the exclusion of the Jews from them.

Jews have always been allowed and even encouraged, however, to enter new areas of the economy that were too risky for anyone else. Jews were essential in the incipient stages of capitalism; the rising *goyish* bourgeoisie took it over when it became too profitable. When there are enough of what Khrushchev called "native cadres" to do certain work, the Jews are pushed out.

Nowhere is the Jew allowed to be in a position where he is

so essential, so central to the functioning and survival of the economy that it could rise and fall with him. This is, in essence, the meaning of the Jew's "marginality": if all the Jews went to the moon tomorrow, the economy would still function.[2]

Jews are also programmed to be the surrogates of the ruling elite in doing its dirty work of helping keep down other oppressed groups. Jews in 16th- and 17th-century Poland collected rent and taxes from the oppressed Cossacks for the hated Polish nobles; today they are welfare caseworkers, teachers, slumlords, and pawnbrokers in the black ghettos of America's cities. Thus the Jews are constantly forced into the dangerous position of being trapped between the nobles and the peasants, the ruling elite and other oppressed groups. In this role of oppressor surrogate, and that of scapegoat, the Jew functions as society's "lightning rod" for absorbing and deflecting the rage of oppressed groups that might otherwise be turned on the ruling elite. This was the case during the New York City school strike of 1968.

An oppressed group always poses a potential threat to the oppressing elite. Throughout the history of the Jews in *galut,* the ruling elite feared the Jews might become the focal or rallying point for a revolt of other oppressed groups in the society. The Jews, by their act of refusal to give up their religion and culture, denied the ruling elite complete domination; this rebellion was obvious to other oppressed groups. Also, because the Jews were perceived as being different in values and life style, the ruling elite feared it would be harder to keep them under control as successfully as other oppressed groups who did accept society's values and could be kept down by early and continuous brainwashing. The ruling elite, therefore, found it expedient to employ certain definite means to make sure the Jews would not initiate a revolt that might be joined by other oppressed groups.

The most successful method was the classic divide-and-rule. The Jews had to be kept apart—either physically or psychologically or both—from other oppressed groups. The invention and wide circulation of ugly stereotypes and myths such as the Christkiller, host desecration, and blood libels served to "inoculate" oppressed *goyim* against getting together with Jews. When the ruling elites became truly panicky about their loss of power they resorted to expelling or ghettoizing the Jews.

Another method of keeping the Jews down was to make the threat of retaliation so frightening that it served as an effective deterrent. Periodic pogroms served not only to keep the mind of other oppressed groups off the real source of their troubles, but to keep the Jews paralyzed with fear for their survival and unable to think beyond it.

The pogrom strategy operated along the lines of the classic urban protection racket. Either you pay off those (in this case the ruling elite) who are selling you "protection" from themselves, or they unleash against you the forces they control (the masses they have programmed to be anti-Semitic). The payoff the Jews were forced to make was their good behavior, i.e., performing the roles programmed by the ruling elite and passively submitting to its power. The pogrom strategy persists in America today, although it operates on a very subtle and sophisticated level not easily perceived.

The best way of keeping the Jews down involved conditioning from childhood to certain patterns of behavior which the ruling elite rewarded by letting the Jews survive. These patterns, still necessary to the ruling elite, persist to today. One obvious pattern is passivity and nonassertiveness in relation to individual *goyim* and society in general. Jews are taught not to "antagonize the *goyim*": do not provoke them by asserting your rights. Never give cause for criticism. "Nice" is a favorite word in the Jewish lexicon. A "nice Jewish boy" is nonaggressive and nonassertive with the *goyim*.

As part of passivity conditioning, Jewish antisocial behavior is always judged more harshly than similar behavior by *goyim* —a double standard Jews accept. Too many Jews believe that if all Jews behaved "properly" anti-Semitism would disappear; they are nervous wrecks if there's a Jewish *goniff* on the front page.

Whenever a Jew deviates from the prescribed nonassertiveness, i.e., asserts himself as much as a *goy* would, he is put down as "pushy" (the equivalent of "uppity" for blacks and "nonfeminine" for women) in order to intimidate him into returning to the previous passive posture.

Then there's the *"sha-shtil"* (keep quiet and lay low) pattern. On the theory that if you are not conspicuous they won't go after you with an ax, Jews try to fade into the woodwork and emerge in the pale, lifeless reincarnation of "good Americans." A good example of the Jewish fear of being conspicuous is the hue and cry by some Jewish organizations whenever there's a possibility that the census might record "religious affiliation"—a proposal they have succeeded in killing.

Jews are taught to feel guilty about seeking or using political power or taking political action solely in their own interests. Thus, whenever the Jewish vote is mentioned Jews rush to deny it exists. For years the so-called Jewish "defense" organizations "combatted" anti-Semitism under the cloak of fighting for civil rights for all; apparently it was not considered kosher for a Jewish organization to fight only for Jews.

Try to imagine, if you can, a group of Jews demanding reparations from the Church or some other oppressive institution, for 2000 years of oppression. Of course it's a complete wild fantasy. We wouldn't do it; we would tell ourselves we're above all that. The truth is, Jews are terrified of asserting their power in this manner. One of the main roots of so much Jewish antagonism to the black liberation movement is Jews' jealousy of blacks for not being afraid to do this.

Camouflaged as "respect for the law" is a great fear of authority and its retaliatory capacity. Two thousand years of oppression have taught Jews that those who survived were those who hid in the cellar or took to their feet in time—not those who fought. Jewish defenselessness is among the most dehumanizing aspects of Jewish oppression—and the most dangerous. For it is precisely this defenselessness that provokes and encourages attack. Jews will not riot and the *goyim* count on this. We do not know what would have happened had German Jews rioted against Hitler before or just when he came to power; but we do know the Nazis counted on the fact that they would not do so.

My favorite illustration is a quote by one Judge Christ Seraphim (*sic*). Contrasting the civil rights marchers whom Father Groppi was leading in Milwaukee to the Jews, His Honor said of the latter: "These people were baked in ovens. . . . They didn't do much marching. They are the most law-abiding people in the world."

This defenselessness is coupled with a pathetic dependence on others to fight our battles for us. Jews are constantly cultivating "allies" (read "protectors"). Jews were shocked when the Polish nobles turned them over to the Cossacks in 1648. Jews depended on Roosevelt, whose icon hung in so many Jewish homes, to rescue Jews from the Nazis. The shock of the recent, belated disclosure that F.D.R. would not move a finger, even to bomb the rail-tracks to Auschwitz (not to speak of changing the racist immigration laws) is just now beginning to be felt. Parenthetically, America refuses to this date to extradite hundreds of Nazi war criminals to stand trial for murdering Jews.

Jews are constantly falling in love with other peoples' countries, societies, and struggles. Like a woman oppressed by a long series of lovers, the Jew enters each new relationship with a society or group in the belief that, if he is useful to it and good, he will be protected ("this time it'll be different"). The Jews are the last believers in the American Dream.

In the quest for protection, Jews also play the "Jewish Mother Game." This involves submerging themselves in other peoples' work or struggles, or the sacrifices themselves—and then saying (as they did to the blacks), "look what we did for you." But the sight of a powerless group trying to use this kind of emotional blackmail in politics provokes only contempt.

Jews are constantly looking to the *goyim* for approval; the main question always is "what will the *goyim* say?" This is reflected in Jews' striving to prove how well they fit in to their view of society. Young Jews are conditioned to perform so well on the job and be so necessary that they can't be fired. This may be part of the reason they are pushed to achieve, achieve, achieve. (The obvious conflict, of course, between the compulsion to achieve and the conditioning to be nonassertive tears people apart.)

The Hoffman Syndrome (Judge and Abbie) is related. Jews bend over backwards to show the *goyim* that they can be harsher in judging their own people than would a *goy* in the particular circles (right or left) from which they crave acceptance. A non-Jewish judge would probably not have sentenced the Rosenbergs to death. Many young radical Jews go beyond their *goyish* comrades in denouncing Israel or parroting a particular group's line (even if it's anti-Semitic) to say, in effect, "Look Ma (or Mao), I'm a radical."

Worst of all is our eternal nauseating gratitude to those *goyim* who behave with the most elemental kind of decency expected by one human being of another. It is an obscenity that we should think it natural and proper to give medals to *goyim* who saved the lives of Jews in World War II. Has there ever been any other nation on earth which found it natural and right to give awards to people of other nations for treating them like human beings?

In the past two centuries ruling elites have invented a second method of keeping Jews down: the assimilationism game. Jews are conditioned to believe that the relinquishing of their cultural difference and distinctiveness will lead to an abatement—or even an end—to anti-Semitism, and to their total "acceptance into society."

This game, although Jews are blind to this, is based on a complete fraud. For it should be obvious that the complete assimilation of the Jews (or any other oppressed group) is not in the interests of the ruling elite. Oppression and power are too advantageous for the oppressor to give up or share; moreover, if the Jews would assimilate, who would fill the roles they are programmed for?

Assimilationism, however, achieves very desirable ends for the ruling elite. One, by getting Jews to accept its values, they become better and more pliable tools, more easily exploited and manipulated; and two, breaking down Jewish cohesiveness so that the ruling elite has to deal with Jewish individuals instead of with a Jewish people insures Jewish powerlessness. Peoplehood is powerful; keeping Jews apart means keeping Jews down.

Assimilation is the carrot held out in front of the Jew's nose (with a stick clearly visible in the background): give up your distinctiveness and be rewarded—OR ELSE, he is told. The Jew who gives up his distinctiveness is indeed "rewarded": he is allowed to rise on the socioeconomic ladder. He is not, of course, allowed to cross the boundary into the ruling elite, but is kept tantalized with this prospect. In this state of anticipation and frustration, he is scared to do anything that will jeopardize his chances and is thus even more susceptible to exploitation and less willing to acknowledge the existence of hostility.

In such a state, the Jewish assimilationist feels a great deal of rage against his oppressors (whom he does not define as such). Unable to turn this rage on them, he turns it on himself and on the Jews: if only he could eradicate the vestiges of his Jewishness made conspicuous by the all-too-visible existence of the Jewish group! If only the Jewish group would give up its distinctiveness! It is tragic that it is precisely these assimilationist Jews who rule the Jewish community. Denied the high status they crave in the *goyish* bourgeoisie, they accept substitute high status among the Jews. Because the Jews perceive them to be closer in values and life style to the ruling elite and thus have entree to them, they are chosen as "ambassadors"[3] to them, otherwise known as "court Jews." Because they see the conspicuous existence of the Jewish group as threatening their acceptance by the ruling elite, they push assimilation among the Jews and act as the transmission belt of its values and programming.

Assimilationism is, in essence, the conditioning and programming of the Jews to ethnic amnesia. The ruling elite with its Jewish collaborators, in order to get the Jews to give up their distinctiveness in return for a promised end to anti-Semitism, had to lead Jews to believe that 1) their distinctiveness was worthless to preserve, and 2) giving it up was paying off, i.e., anti-Semitism had disappeared. Since it has not really disappeared, Jews had to be conditioned into not perceiving its existence.

The perception and expectance of anti-Semitism had always been an important Jewish defense. Jews developed exquisitely sensitive antennae to anti-Semitism and learned that it was *real* and to be expected. This defense was and is necessary. Jews do have enemies; it is a bare 27 years since the end of the Holocaust. Should any Jew be surprised that anti-Semitism is alive and well? Women have come to realize how powerful a pattern sexism is; blacks know the same is true of racism. Why shouldn't Jews face the fact that anti-Semitism is a powerful, pervasive, useful social pattern conditioned and reinforced for over 2000 years, and not likely to disappear?

The ruling elite and the assimilationist Jews, however, have led us to believe that it is "paranoic" to recognize anti-Semitism as such in the U.S. ("America is different"), that the feeling of insecurity we experience is some sort of weird atavistic throwback (or perhaps a neurosis to enrich a shrink); in other words, an irrational response to a nonexistent danger. Jews are taught to feel guilty about harboring these feelings instead of recognizing them as real; this is one of the reasons Jews feel so uncomfortable about and unwilling to confront the implications of the Holocaust.

We are also conditioned to feel guilty about distrusting *goyim,* our leftists, especially, try to ignore the fact that while anti-Semitism was engineered by the ruling elite, most *goyim* have participated to some degree, actively or passively, in our 2000 years of oppression. We are taught to repress our rage when hostility is dumped on us, and even to feel guilty about using the word "*goyim.*" Most important, Jews are vulnerable because they are not conscious of their enemies.

It is, however, useful to the ruling elite to have Jews feeling guilty about distrusting or hating *goyim*. Let's consider a parallel with the oppression of women. Now it's a perfectly acceptable attitude for a man to be a misogynist. But calling a woman a "man-hater" is meant to be extremely insulting—and intimidating. Why? Because if women, who are oppressed, come to identify and hate the oppressor, he is threatened. For thousands of years anti-Semitism has been a perfectly acceptable attitude; even today it will not get you fired from personnel or censured by the Senate. But a Jew who recognizes *goyim* as his oppressors threatens them. So Jews are taught to repress this as "paranoia."

The American Jew who faces anti-Semitism today faces it alone and unprepared. What should he do when a *goy* makes an anti-Semitic remark? Smile and pretend he didn't hear or he's above all that? Walk out of what may be a very important meeting? Speak out and face the accusation that he's simply "too emotional" and that his "oversensitivity" and "insecurity" led him to "misunderstand"? Because Jews fail to expect anti-Semitism and discuss it, they experience it as a traumatic shock and have no way of coping with their rage.

The second defense the ruling elite and assimilationists broke down was the defense against the concept espoused by the *goyim* that Jewish difference and distinctiveness meant Jewish inferiority. In the Middle Ages, Jews were told they were inferior because they rejected Jesus. In modern times, they were told it was their "race" that caused their inferiority, or the "fact" that Jews were "economic parasites," incapable of doing constructive work, spineless cowards, money-mad maniacs, and so on.

Now it is natural for any oppressed group to come to believe this type of accusation, which has behind it the power of the ruling elite and is accepted by the majority. Blacks, colonized peoples, and women have accepted the myth of their inferiority for thousands of years. But the Jews, until about 150 years ago, did not follow this pattern of other oppressed people because they had built up strong inner defenses against the outside myths. The Jews offset the Christian myth of Jewish inferiority with the countermyth of Jewish intellectual and moral superiority. The "Chosen People" concept must be understood, therefore, in this context of a defensive countermyth, and Jews must stop being guilty and apologetic about it.

More important, each Jewish child was armed with the knowledge that the Jews were indeed different from the *goyim* and that the culture that made them distinctive was a positive, beautiful thing. Significantly, the Yiddish term for a "good Jew" is *"shayner Yid"*—a "beautiful Jew." Jewishness is beautiful.

The ruling elite and the Jewish assimilationists broke down these defenses by teaching that Jewish differences were negative, meaningless, and a barrier to equality with the *goyim*. The Jews who were (and are) into assimilationism did their utmost to give up or at least play down their differences. But while the inner defense was smashed, the outer hostility remained. With no barrier against the hostility, it quickly became internalized. And like most oppressed people, Jews came to accept the myths of the oppressor as valid.

The oppressor always advocates the concept that it is the difference of the oppressed that is causing the oppression. The oppressor knows that the difference was the excuse or rationalization for the oppression, but not the cause. But let the oppressed try to emulate the oppressor: it is impossible but it will keep them preoccupied, weak, apart, frustrated—and easy to manipulate and exploit.

American Jews have fallen right into the trap. Most of the efforts of the organized Jewish community, outside of fund raising, go into creating the image that the Jews are like the *goyim*. Yes, we say, American democracy is embodied in Judaism; yes, or religion is like yours, really—viva ecumenicism!; look how many Jewish boys died for the flag, just like *goyim!* In short, Jews behave as if involved in a life-long popularity contest, not realizing it was fixed a long, long time ago.

Jews are conditioned to feel guilty and act defensive and apologetic about being and wanting to remain different. They are taught that being Jewish is "petty," "narrow," and "confining," and somehow disqualifies one from being a human being. (A Haskala poet, Yehuda Leib Gordon, told Russian Jews to "be a Jew at home and a human being on the outside.")

So many American Jews have internalized the attitude that being different (Jewish) is bad (or parochial, reactionary, what you will) that they actually regard it as a compliment when someone says, "You don't look Jewish." Jewish women have their noses shortened and bleach their hair to conform to the Anglo-Saxon ideal of beauty, or at least, minimize their Jewish differences—for much the same reason that blacks used to "process" their hair. We spend years trying to eradicate what the high school and college speech *mavens* call a "Yiddish intonation" or a "Brooklyn accent." Some Jews go so far as to change their family names to something Anglo-Saxon sounding. Most choose Anglo-Saxon personal names for their children (remember the all-time favorites: Seymour, Irving, and Milton?).

Some Jews try to hide their Jewish identity completely. This involves at times the development of the "Laurence Harvey Syndrome." Yes, *kinderlach*, Harvey is a JEW (a Litvak, yet). But who would ever know? He comes off as the quintessential cool British cat. Assimilationist Jews try to overcompensate for their differences by being more British than the British, more American than the Americans, and so on. They hope that by doing this they will not only "pass," but that the outer personality will become, by force of habit, the inner personality. It sometimes does.

To these Jews, a conspicuous committed Jew or Jewish group is a threat. How many of us cringe when we see a Chassid in *shtreimel* and kaftan letting it all (*tzitzis*, that is) hang out, walking, say, in the East Village when we're in a mixed group? We're embarrassed and uncomfortable. The Chassid's garb is the external symbol of his refusal to assimilate; he is a living, breathing, walking reminder of Jewishness. His conspicuousness makes us conspicuous.

Similarly with Israel. Assimilationist Jews, of the right and the left, who seek to escape their Jewish identity are put uptight by Israel's highly conspicuous existence. Significantly, what they find objectionable about Israelis is always their "arrogance," i.e., their prideful Jewish identity and assertiveness, which contrast with the assimilationist's lack of these characteristics. Many left assimilationists reject Israel for this emotional reason, and other more complicated ones discussed below. Many right assimilationists, involved in Jewish communal affairs, use their power to try to make Israel become bourgeois American like them, i.e., less Jewish.

Too many of us have internalized Jewish stereotypes invented by *goyim*—the money-grubbing Jew, for instance. One young Jew even told me that the Jews' "special affinity" for money was a characteristic of the Jewish *race!* Another example: How many of us now believe that Jews are "too emotional" (the stereotype is "the loud Jew") and that it's not good to express or show emotion, particularly in political matters? It is a tragedy that Jewish emotionalism and expressiveness, one of the really healthy and positive characteristics of our tradition, has been so put down that we are intimidated into repressing them, particularly among *goyim*— and embarrassed when a Jew is emotional. How many meetings have I attended on Israel where I was told by Jews to stop being "emotional" about an issue which happens to involve my people's—and my own—survival? Why on earth should a Jew be unemotional about Israel? And if you really want to insult a young Jewish woman, even drive her to tears sometimes, just tell her she is "talking like a Jewish fish-wife" when she is expressing her feelings.

Jews are kept powerless by being taught to feel guilty about being together. Brainwashed into believing that the warm feeling of concern Jews feel for each other is "chauvinistic" and that the freeness Jews experience only in each others' company is "racist," Jews will always try to refute that most terrible of all terrible accusations: Jews are "clannish." Never do they stop to think, hey what's so bad about being clannish?

The technique of keeping people powerless by keeping them apart is used with other oppressed people. For example, women: when women get together to discuss their oppression, those opposing women's liberation try to intimidate them by saying "they're all a bunch of dykes." When Jews get together, those who are threatened by Jewish liberation will say, "this is chauvinism." The technique is the same.

Another example of our oppression is that others define us and, worse, we accept their definitions. The *goyim*—of the right and the left—sit around wracking their brains as to what is a Jew (something no Jew ever did until the assimilationist period), coming up with some pretty way-out definitions ("caste," "race," "class," and "religion" for example), and Jews do not find this infuriating. Jews don't even recognize that they should have the basic human right of defining themselves.

American Jews acquiesce in the definition of them by the ruling elite and the majority of *goyim* as a "religion." This is convenient because American society is tolerant about religious differences; nobody really cares about them anymore. But ethnic differences, the recognition and encouragement of which would lead to ethnic solidarity and power to the peoples, is a threat to the ruling elite. The "melting pot" is designed to break down ethnic groups and render them powerless. So Jews masquerade as a religion and have even come to believe this definition and try to function as a religion and not a people—in other words, to try desperately to fit themselves into a Sodomite (Procrustean) Bed, with results similar to those in the legends.

Jews accept with alacrity the nauseating term "Judeo-Christian civilization." The term is a fraud because it misleads people into thinking that it really includes the Jewish tradition of the past 5000 years, while in reality the only "Judeo" part is the "Old Testament." It successfully deceives Jews into believing that the two civilizations are really alike (when they are at opposite extremes), to minimize again our distinctiveness and the uniqueness of our tradition and culture, and to anesthetize us against recognizing and remembering that Christians oppressed us for many centuries in the name of their "civilization."

Jews also acquiesce in the definitions of others as to what constitutes oppression. For example, a persistent Old Left line has been that middle-class people (which includes most American Jews) are not oppressed. Many Jews have been intimidated into denying that the persecution of our people in the Soviet Union today, and even of our people in the past, constitutes oppression. While militant blacks do not hesitate to speak of their "300 years of oppression," Jews shrink from mentioning our twenty centuries of persecution. Many young Jews are even intimidated into sloughing over the Holocaust as an excess ("war is hell") whose significance as far as the survival of humanity is concerned is dwarfed by that of Hiroshima, and denying the particular Jewish tragedy of the Holocaust. They rush to point out how many Russians, Poles, gypsies, etc., were also murdered in World War II.

We arrive, finally at the attitude prevalent among many young Jews, particularly radicals, that "Jewishness is chauvinistic." What they seem to mean by "Jewishness" is the expression of one's Jewish identity culturally or in terms of commitment to and identification with the Jewish people and its destiny. In the past five years I have argued with hundreds of young Jews who told me this, and I in turn presented all manner of objective and rational refutations. Finally it hit me that most young Jews do not know enough about Jewishness to be able to say if it is chauvinistic or not. I realized then that it is useless to try to refute these irrational attitudes because what is involved here is simply another example of our oppression, and it must be treated only in this context. We must ask simply: What is the reason a Jew develops such an attitude? *Whose purpose does it serve?*

My conclusion is that this feeling is useful to the ruling elite in order to keep Jews apart and powerless. Young Jews arrive at this attitude because it is constantly being promoted by the ruling elite and its literary lackeys; any prideful Jewish identification or action is immediately put down as "chauvinistic" or "racist." Jews who are struggling with these feelings must see that they were programmed to feel them by the ruling elite for its own interests, not theirs.

This conditioning goes hand in hand with severe cultural deprivation—the absence of anything positively Jewish in the life experiences of young Jews. It is in the interests of the ruling elite to keep oppressed groups, including the Jews, culturally deprived, meaning, separated from the resources of their history and tradition. The Jewish tradition contains strong positive elements that develop pride and cohesiveness. A solid knowledge of Jewish history would give Jews the tools to analyze their oppression and rebel against it. Of course, this is against the interests of the ruling elite. Black history, women's history, Indian history, Chicano history—and Jewish history—have all been ignored by the textbooks and media. Cultural deprivation is a method of keeping oppressed people down.

The almost total absence of quality Jewish education is no accident: assimilationist Jews do not want their children to be raised as Jews. The arguments we hear against day schools are revealing of the motives of assimilationist parents: the day school will "separate the child from other children," make him "feel different"; he will not "fit into society."

The creation of a Jew takes place mostly in the home. It consists of the absorption, imitation, and internalization by the child of the parents' Jewish gut feelings, attitudes, and values. What has occurred in America is the partial or sometimes even total breakdown of the Jewish socialization process.

In families where some Jewish behavior patterns and gut feelings persist, they are not passed on to the child as part of a complete Jewish *Weltanschauung* but as isolated fragments of a jig-saw puzzle which no longer exists. Having internalized these fragmentary feelings, the Jewish youth will search desperately and in vain for the jig-saw puzzle to fit these odd pieces into. He will suffer from "Jewish schizophrenia," being torn apart between his Jewish gut feelings and his intellectual rejection of these feelings as purely negative and dysfunctional, having no relevance to anything else in his personality or life.

In other families, parents have so repressed their own Jewish gut feelings that none or very few are expressed. They are sicklied over with the pale cast of liberalism and "universalism." When a crisis arises, typically, an impending intermarriage, the liberal veneer is stripped off and the Jewish gut feelings push their way through. The young Jew, seeing the inconsistency between these gut feelings and everything else his parents have taught him (which he has internalized already), bitterly rejects his parents' "hypocrisy," which he identifies with their "Jewishness."

The essence of being Jewish lies in feeling love and concern for and identification with other Jews, the Jewish people, of the past, present, and future. The loss of this feeling becomes obvious when you compare writers of different generations: Sholem Aleichem and (lehavdeel) Philip Roth were both critical of many things in Jewish life. But Sholem Aleichem's work is permeated with love and compassion for *his* people. Roth's is infused only with bitterness and disgust for *those* people.

How many young Jewish radicals when criticizing American Jews always mention the mink coats? They do not see the spiritual nakedness underneath. For, regardless of its economic wealth, the Jewish community is suffering from a fantastic cultural and spiritual poverty which is as oppressive and dehumanizing in its way as is physical poverty. It is this gnawing spiritual hunger that drives young Jews to search for meaning in Zen, astrology, scientology, Hare Krishna, drugs, encounter groups—and sometimes, only sometimes, in Judaism.

Oppression is always destructive and dehumanizing for the oppressed. But oppression that is experienced as oppression at least frees the oppressed from his self-hatred and alienation. He stops internalizing the oppressors' hostility and begins to fight it with his sisters and brothers.

Oppression that is not experienced as oppression is, however, far more destructive to a human being. He internalizes the oppressors' hostility and mythology and turns it on himself, or more accurately in the case of Jews, the Jewish parts of himself. He tries to cut out these pieces in order to fit into and be accepted by those of his oppressors that he identifies with.

It is the Zionist thesis that all the various forms of the oppression of Jews discussed above derive from the inherently oppressive nature of *galut,* where Jews are always a tiny, "different," and powerless minority.

It is the ruling elite, of course, which engineers the oppression of the Jews. *But it is the* galut *condition which places Jews at the mercy of the ruling elite.*

The *galut* condition forces Jews, if they want to survive, to adapt to the values and roles set by the ruling elite. Now it is destructive enough to be forced to adapt to the values of one nation over a long period of time. But historical circumstances are constantly forcing Jews to leave one *galut* after another. Being forced again and again to adapt to totally different environments makes any kind of natural cultural and social development impossible. The vast proportion of energy (like in a neurosis) goes into adapting oneself in order to survive; not much is left over for any creative pursuits. If Jews will ever again produce a work of the creative stature of the Torah, it will have to evolve out of their unimpeded cultural development, and that means outside of *galut,* i.e., in Israel.

But even more horrifying and depressing has been the damage wrought by the *galut* on the Jewish psyche. Dr. Arthur Janov (in *The Primal Scream*) defines the neurotic personality as "unreal"—a description which, tragically, fits the collective Jewish people in the *galut.*

Janov's thesis, briefly, is that human beings are born with real needs, both biological and emotional; among the latter are the need to develop at one's own pace and to express oneself. When these needs are not met or not allowed by the parents—when the child cannot be himself—he tries to survive by becoming the person his parents want him to be. Turning off his real self, he begins to behave in the manner expected of him—he pursues "unreal" needs: those of this parents, not his own. He thus becomes increasingly not himself, i.e., "unreal."

Ahad Ha'am, father of "Spiritual Zionism," wrote in 1891 that every people has a "natural" aim: to create for itself "conditions suitable to its character, in which it could develop its latent powers and aptitudes, its own particular form of life . . . in obedience to the demands of its nature."[4]

The *galut* condition, however, denies the Jews the possibility of pursuing these real aims and needs, of being themselves. Living in constant fear and anxiety—conscious or unconscious—subject to hostility and abuse, surrounded by a majority programmed to be anti-Semitic—whose latent anti-Semitism can turn overt at any time—stifled in an atmosphere which denies the validity, uniqueness, and worth of Jewish difference, experience, and values, Jews survive by "turning off" their real Jewish feelings and needs and becoming only what the particular *galut* society's elite needs and allows them to become, approves of, and programs them for.

Each *galut* elite has its own rules of how long a leash to allow its Jews. It permits them to do or be what is consonant with its own needs. But in no *galut* has it been possible for Jews to develop solely according to their own needs, character, and aptitudes. There is always someone looking over your shoulder to make sure you are performing right, and his disapproval is dangerous; eventually, self-censorship replaces imposed censorship.

Galut life, increasingly unreal, creates Jews who are unreal themselves, for only unreal Jews can fit in and be part of such an unreal life. Young Jews leave the Jewish community in droves because it is so unreal, but they take their already-formed unreal selves with them.

The more unreal Jews become, the more dehumanized, the easier it is to regard them as nonpersons. As Richard Grunberger pointed out in *The 12-Year Reich: A Social His-*

tory of Nazi Germany, the Holocaust was unreal to most Germans "not because it occurred in wartime and in conditions of secrecy, but because Jews were astronomically remote *and not real people."*

It has been oft-repeated that power corrupts. But so does powerlessness. Being free means having responsibility for one's life—for the values and decisions that shape one's fate. Powerlessness is by its very nature a state of irresponsibility: someone else, the oppressor, has the ultimate control over your life and death. The longer the lack of responsibility continues, the more corroded and corrupted the mind and spirit become.

Irresponsibility, like a narcotic drug, produces a lethargic, almost trance-like state which can be comforting and comfortable and which can even block out the real stimuli from the environment. A people which becomes used to the drug of irresponsibility must, however, mutilate itself in the process, much as the human body does in order to adjust to the poison of heroin.

Withdrawal is painful.

The Jewish people in the *galut,* after two thousand years of being powerless and deprived of responsibility, finds itself in precisely such a state of mind and spirit. That is why, while the prison door of America is open, we sit in our cell, sit and argue about what the jailer is going to bring for lunch.

The neuroses caused by the *galut* and its oppressions affect all the Jews in the *galut*—no individual, class, or sex is exempt. In other words, the Jews in *galut* are oppressed *as a people.* As Memmi pointed out, each oppression is different and the revolutionary solution must be organic to the specific oppression. In the case of the Jewish people, our oppression is inseparable from our existence in *galut.* The specific liberation of the Jewish people, therefore, requires the specific revolutionary solution of liberation from the *galut,* and *aliyah* (immigration) to our own homeland, Israel.

The process of liberation begins with the consciousness of oppression. What Jews in America lack most is this consciousness. It is to raising, and even creating, Jewish consciousness among American Jewry—to breaking the state of ethnic amnesia—that our main efforts should be directed.

References

1. I am indebted to Albert Memmi, whose writings on the oppression of the Jews provided the basic analysis on which this essay was built. I have developed many of my ideas from Memmi's thesis, and a synthesis has evolved to the point where it would be hopeless to try to footnote. I feel it is a must for young Jews to read his three books, *Portrait of a Jew, The Liberation of the Jew,* and *The Colonizer and the Colonized* (Orion Press, New York, 1962, 1966, 1965, respectively).
2. Ber Borochov, *Nationalism and the Class Struggle* (Poalei Zion, New York, 1937).
3. Chapters 10–12 of Kurt Lewin, *Resolving Conflicts* (Harper and Row, New York, 1948).
4. Ahad Ha'am, "Slavery in Freedom" in the essay collection *Nationalism and the Jewish Ethic* (Herzl Press, New York, 1962). The concepts of Jacob Klatzkin also contributed to the development of this essay. Finally, I am indebted to all the *chaverim* in the movement with whom I have discussed so many of the ideas that have gone into the writing of this essay over the past five years.

Part Two
The New Left, the Jews, and Israel

The Jewish radical movement arose in part because of the growing concern over the New Left's increasingly anti-Israel posture. Coupled with militant black groups, particularly the Black Panther Party, the New Left's anti-Zionism made it uncomfortable for many young Jews to remain silent. Furthermore, they felt compelled to challenge their peers who apologize for or "explain away" these positions.

Amos Kenan's "A Letter to All Good People" has been widely circulated in Israel, Europe, and America. As one of Israel's prominent gadflies, Kenan commands respect of both the Jewish Left and its Establishment critics. His letter is both a defense of Zionism and a call for radical change.

J. J. Goldberg, who organized one of the first high school S.D.S. chapters, presents a concise historical overview of the relationship of Zionism to radicalism. His statement is a major document of the new radical Zionist movement which he helped to organize.

Itzhak Epstein also spent several years as an organizer for S.D.S His radical activities were the source of his being blacklisted in his chosen profession—city planning. An Israeli native who spent his high school and college years in this country, Epstein was a leading figure of the Jewish Left, as a founder of the Jewish Liberation Project and, before his return to Israel, as secretary-general of the North American section of the World Union of Jewish Students.

His open letter addresses Black Panther support of Arab guerrillas and his confusion over the Third World's rejection of Zionism. "Though you are my enemy, I am not yours," Epstein writes, in the hope of reconciliation.

A Letter To All Good People

Amos Kenan

"No true revolutionary ever talks of extinction."

—Fidel Castro

I am for Cuba. I love Cuba. I am opposed to the genocide perpetrated by the Americans in Vietnam. But I am an Israeli, therefore I am forbidden to take all these stands. Cuba does not want me to love her. Someone has decided that I am permitted to love only the Americans. I don't mind so much that someone, especially the good people everywhere, have decided to outlaw me. I shall be able to get along without their help. But I do mind that I am not permitted any longer to love and hate according to my feelings, and according to my political and moral inclinations, and that I am refused invitation or even admittance to parties held by the good people. I am not permitted any longer to toast justice with a glass of champagne. I am not permitted to eat caviar and denounce the Americans. I am not permitted to stroll in the sun-drenched streets of Havana, arm in arm with my erstwhile good friends from St. Germain, Via Veneto, and Chelsea, and celebrate

Amos Kenan is the controversial Israeli journalist. This article first appeared in *The Jewish Radical*, January, 1969, and is reprinted by permission of the Jewish Student Press Service in New York.

the memory of Che Guevara, casting a threatening look at imperialism. I am also finally and absolutely forbidden to sign petitions of all sorts for human rights.

This situation drives me slightly out of my mind. Therefore I wish to relate a few confused, disconnected stories. Perhaps some good man will find the connection. One day an Israeli submarine sank in the Mediterranean with its 69 crew members. Its S-O-S was answered, among others, by the British, Turkish, and Greek fleets. The Russian navy, which cruised very close to the location, did not join in the search. Moscow radio, in its Arab broadcasts, took the trouble to denounce the countries whose ships rushed to help the lost submarine. It is a sacred principle of seamen of all nations to hasten to the aid of distressed vessels. The Israeli submarine was not on a war mission, and Israel is not in a state of war with the Soviet Union.

I am not so naive as to believe that this is anti-Semitism, Soviet-style. I have never believed that the Russians are guided, in their calculations, by such powerful and sincere emotions as anti-Semitism, which is common to both progressive and reactionary camps. I know that the Russians conduct a cool and considered pragmatic policy, and are guided by clear political considerations. This was a political move, carried out as a part of a political game. The meaning of this move can only be: Israel must be isolated from the civilized human community. The rules that apply to the civilized community, rules of honor, consideration and mutual aid, do not apply to me. I am out. There is only one more step to the conclusion: the shedding of my blood is no crime.

Forgive my brutal way of putting things. I cannot conceive of it otherwise. If this was a move in a game, the game must have an object. The object is the penetration of the Middle East, and let us assume, for the sake of argument, that this is for the purpose of advancing world revolution and the overthrow of imperialism. The Middle East contains 100 million

Arabs and 2.5 million Israelis. But it is not so easy, in our enlightened world, to wipe out 2.5 million people. A reason, and a justification, are needed. You cannot wipe out just like that. First of all you must outlaw. Therefore you must not invite an Israeli communist party to a convention of communist parties. Therefore you must not invite a leftist Israeli author to a conference of leftist authors in Havana. There are no more class distinctions. There are only national distinctions. Even an Israeli leftist is an imperialist. And an oil sheikh is a socialist. Therefore it is permissible to compare me to the Nazis. It is permissible to call me a Gauleiter. It is permissible to mobilize all of the world's conscientious people against me—and without them you cannot do it—and all this because there is an object looming beyond the horizon, an object for the sake of which this tactic is justifiable and useful.

Until quite recently, I also belonged to the Good People. Meaning that not only did I sit in cafés and sign petitions for the release of political prisoners in countries not my own, not only did I join proclamations, after sipping my apéritif, for the release of the downtrodden from the yoke of imperialism in places I shall never reach; I also *did* something against what seemed to me to be oppression and injustice in my own country. During the twenty years of the existence of the State of Israel I helped with my pen, in my regular newspaper column, the fight against the injustices committed against the Arab minority. And not by the pen only, but also in demonstrations, and also when arraigned before a military tribunal. I am used to being called a traitor by local patriots. During the Six-Day War, in June, 1967, the battalion I served in was ordered to supervise the demolition of four Arab villages. I considered it my duty to desert from my unit, to write a report of this action, and to send copies to the General Staff of the Army, to members of the government, and to Knesset members. This report has been translated and circulated in the world as proof of Israel's crimes.

Return to the Army

But permit me to conclude the story. The action I undertook was in flagrant violation of any military law. I have no idea what would have happened to a Red Army soldier were he to violate national and military discipline in such a manner. After returning to my unit, I was ordered to present myself—I, in rank a private—before the general commanding all the divisions on that front. He told me that he had read my report, and considered it his duty to inform me that what had occurred was a regrettable error, which did not recur. Deep in my heart I disbelieved his statement that this was only a mistake. I was convinced that whoever ordered such an action did not expect such resistance from within—the men of my battalion refused to carry out the order—and was alarmed at the impression such an action might create abroad. But I was glad that he found it necessary to announce that this was only an error. I asked him how he intended to ensure that the "error" will never recur. On the spot he signed an order permitting me free movement in all occupied territories, so that I could see with my own eyes that such an action had not recurred.

But since then, in all the peace papers in the world, my report about the destruction of villages has been reprinted over and over again, as if it happened only yesterday, as if it is happening all the time. And this is a lie. It is like writing that witches have been burnt at the stake in England—omitting the date. I hereby request all those who believed me when I reported a criminal act, to believe me now, too. And those who don't believe me now, I hereby request to disbelieve my former report, too, and not to believe me selectively, according to their convenience. I should also add that the town of Kalkiliya, which began to be demolished during the writing of my report, is now in the process of being rebuilt, after the expelled inhabitants have been brought back. This does not mean that other injustices are not perpetrated now. The less you fight me, the more you would help me fight them.

David and Goliath

Even the most leftist of men will not consent to be slaughtered when a sword is pointed at his throat. Even when the sword is a progressive one, it does not make it any the pleasanter. The trouble is that not a single serious person in the world believes today that Israel was really in danger of being annihilated. This is the optical illusion of 1968. The gigantic Goliath is threatening little David. The fact that Goliath is a giant, and that David is small, is only an optical illusion. If Goliath triumphs and tramples David under his feet, it is a sign that he really is a giant. But if little David beats the giant, people say: the giant David has trampled poor little Goliath in the dust. I claim that Israel played the role of David. And I claim that even now, after the stunning victory, it still is little David who has indeed beaten the stunned Goliath, but Goliath still is a menacing giant. Today, no less than in June, 1967, Israel is in danger of annihilation. Unless the enlightened world mobilizes now, immediately, perhaps it will be too late. But I am afraid that there are not many people in the world today who will be sorry if victorious David is destroyed. A bitter suspicion rises in me that even the most enlightened among the most progressive people still adhere to the Christian tradition that they imbibed with their mothers' milk: Jew, stay on the cross. Never get off it. The day you get off the cross and hurl it at the heads of your crucifiers, we shall cease to love you.

Al Fatah not Viet Cong

Today the Arabs boast of waging revolutionary guerrilla warfare. They claim to have copied the Viet Cong method of warfare and to apply it in the Middle East. They march with Che Guevara's picture. This makes me laugh. Just as Che Guevara's picture hanging in the luxurious salons of Montparnasse made me laugh. I have always wondered whether

Che Guevara had a picture of Che Guevara hanging in his salon. What is the Viet Cong? The Viet Cong is not white flags on buildings. The Viet Cong means fighting to the last man. The Viet Cong of the Middle East, whether those who demonstrate with Che Guevara's picture like it or not, are we. We are prepared, at any moment, to wage the battle to the death. After the death camps, we are left with only one supreme value: existence.

Our existence today is inconvenient for those who work at the global balance of power. It is more convenient that there should be two camps, one white, the other black. We number, as I said before, only 2.5 million people. On the global map, what is the value of a few hundred thousand leftists, opposing the Eshkol government policy and striving for a genuine peace with the Arabs, who strive to liberate themselves from the one-way dependence on American power? Somebody has already decided to sacrifice us. The history of revolutions is full of such sacrifices since the days of the Spanish Civil War. At one time, world revolution had been sacrificed on the altar of the revolution in one country. Today the calculation is somewhat subtler. Today they try to explain to us that there is an Arab socialism. That there is an Egyptian socialism, and an Algerian socialism. There is a socialism of slave-traders, and a socialism of oil magnates. There are all kinds of socialisms, all aiming really at one and the same thing—the overthrow of imperialism, which happens to be one and indivisible. Once there was only a single kind of socialism, which fed on principles, some of them moral. On the day the morality died there was born the particular, conventional socialism, changing from place to place and from time to time, for which I have no other name but National Socialism.

Who am I?

I want to live. What can I do if Russia, China, Vietnam, India, Yugoslavia, Sartre, Russell, Castro, have all decided that I am made all of a piece? It is inconvenient for them to admit that there is an opposition in Israel, too. Why should there be an opposition in Israel if in the Popular Democracies, in Cuba or Algeria, there is only one party? And perhaps they do have pangs of conscience, but they have made their calculation, and found out that I am only one, only 10, only 100,000; and on the other side there are tens of millions, all led like a single man, in a single party, towards the light, towards the sun. And if so, who am I? I will tell you who I am: I am the man who will confuse and confound your progressive calculations. I have too much love for this vain world, a world of caviar, television, sunny beaches, sex, and good wine. You go ahead and toast the revolution with champagne. I shall toast myself, my own life, bottle in one hand, rifle in the other.

"I Refuse to Play this Game"

You send Soviet arms to Egypt. You isolate me. And in order to make it easier to isolate me, you change my name. My flesh, which you eat, you call fish. You don't want to protect me—neither against the Arabs, nor against the Russians, nor against Dayan or Johnson. Moreover, when I try to call on you and tell you that I am against Dayan, against Eshkol, against Ben-Gurion, and ask for your help, you laugh at me and demand that I should return to the June 4th borders, unconditionally. Hold it! I refuse to play this game. If you give me back the pistol with which I tried to kill you, I won't kill you. Because I am a nice fellow. But if you don't give it back to me, I shall kill you, because you are a bad fellow. Why were the June 4th borders not peace borders on June 4th but will become peace borders now? Why were not the U.N. partition plans borders of 1947 peace borders then but will become so now? Why should I return the bandit his gun as a reward for having failed to kill me? I want peace peace peace peace peace peace peace. I am ready to give everything back in exchange for peace. And I shall give nothing back without peace. I am ready to solve the refugee problem. I am ready to accept an independent Palestinian state. I am ready to sit and talk. About everything, all at the same time. Direct talks, indirect talks, all this is immaterial. But peace. Until you agree to have peace, I shall give back nothing. And if you force me to become a conqueror, I shall become a conqueror. And if you force me to become an oppressor, I shall become an oppressor. And if you force me into the same camp with all the forces of darkness in the world, there I shall be.

Alliance: With Whom?

There is no lack in Israel of rabid militarists. Their number is steadily increasing, the more our isolation becomes apparent. Nasser helps Dayan, Kosygin helps Eshkol. Fidel Castro helps the Jewish chauvinists. Who of the world's giants cares how many more Jews, how many more Arabs, bleed to death in the Sinai sands? There is no lack here of mad hysterical militarists. All those quiet citizens who went out to war with K.L.M. handgrips and in laundry trucks, who scribbled on their tanks: "We Want Home." All those who fought without anger, without hatred, only for their lives, are becoming militaristic, convinced that only Israeli power, and nothing else in the world, will ever help us.

The only ones who are prepared to defend me, for reasons I don't like at all, are the Americans. It is convenient for them, for the time being. You are flinging me towards America, the bastion of democracy and the murderer of Vietnam, who tramples the downtrodden peoples and spares my life, who oppresses the blacks and supplies me with arms to save myself. You leave me no other alternative. You don't even offer me humiliating terms, to be admitted through the rear door into the progressive orgy. You don't even want me to overthrow my government. You only want me to surrender, unconditionally, and to believe the spokesmen of the revolution that henceforth no Jewish doctors will be murdered, and that they will limit themselves to the declaration that Zionism is responsible for the riots in Warsaw.

And in the End of Days?

Very funny. The truth is that I and Sartre, two people with the same vision, more or less, with the same ideal, more or less, and if I may be permitted the impertinence, with the same moral level, more or less, are now at the two sides of the barricade. We have been pushed to both sides by the cold calculations of the people who sent us, or abandoned us. But the fact remains—these are not Americans shooting Russians, or capitalists shooting socialists, or freedom-fighters shooting the oppressors. It is I shooting Sartre. I see him in my gun sights; he sees me in his gun sights. I still don't know which of us is faster, more skilled, or more determined to kill or be killed. Neither do I know who shall be luckier—the one who has no other alternative, or the one who acts out of choice. One thing is clear to me: if I survive, I shall mourn Sartre's death more than he would mourn mine. And if that happens, I shall never be consoled until I wipe from under the heavens both the capitalists and the communists. Or they me. Or each the other. Or all destroy all. And if I survive even that, without a God and without prophets either, my life will have no sense whatsoever. I shall have nothing else to do but walk on the banks of streams, or on the top of the rocks, watch the wonders of nature, and console myself with the words of Ecclesiastes, the wisest of men: *For the light is sweet, and it is good for the eyes to see the sun.*

Open Letter to the Black Panther Party

Itzhak Epstein

I don't believe the bourgeois press any more. As a matter of fact, I hardly believe anybody. But I still read *The New York Times* because I've developed the habit of deciphering their coverage of events to add a few more pieces to the jig-saw puzzle of the world in which we live. On July 23, 1969, I read *The Times* dispatch from Algiers reporting that Eldridge Cleaver backed Al Fatah and opposed Zionism. I may have been skeptical at *The Times* but I saw similar comments by David Hilliard in *The Guardian* a short while later. At this point I felt certain things must be said and I chose this rather awkward format of an open letter, though I hardly know any of you. I must, however, go back a bit to put things in some perspective.

Some months ago, radical Zionist teenagers in New York published a tabloid called *Thorn*. The first issue discussed the reactionary nature of Al Fatah, the quality of kibbutz educa-

Itzhak Epstein has been a member of various Zionist youth movements, an S.D.S. organizer in the Great Plains area, co-founder of the Jewish Liberation Project, and secretary-general of the North American Jewish Student Network. He presently lives in Israel. This article originally appeared in *The Jewish Liberation Journal*, September, 1969, and is reprinted by permission of the author and editorial board.

tion, and Eldridge Cleaver. The poster, with Cleaver's picture and the caption "Eldridge Cleaver Welcome Here," accompanied this last article, which quoted from his essay on the land question and expressed fraternal solidarity with your struggle.

Later, I was present at a conference where some "progressive" Jews of the older generation came upon this tabloid and expressed disapproval of the irresponsible way in which the younger generation selects its heroes. They were obviously influenced by some of the nasty things they had read about the Panthers in the bourgeois press. In the ensuing argument, I backed the kids' identification of their movement with yours because I felt that we were all struggling for similar goals against the same enemy. I did not do so because I lack folk heroes of my own.

Anyway, despite my feelings of solidarity, I did not get around to establishing the necessary contacts with the Panthers. I was busy participating in the building of the Jewish Liberation Project and figured that when the proper time arrived we would find each other. I do not know how many Panthers there are or how much support you enjoy in the black community, but the Jewish Liberation Project has only a few dozen members, not very much power, and no weapons at all. We are attempting to create an insurgency in the Jewish community, to radicalize and Zionize it in order to be able to control our own destiny.

In July, the J.L.P. got this flyer in the mail—"People! Organizations! Groups! Yippies! Political Parties! Workers! Students! Peasant-Farmers! You the *Lumpen*! Poor people! Black People, Mexican-Americans, Puerto Ricans, Chinese, etc. [etc. very often stands for Jews]. We must develop a UNITED FRONT AGAINST FASCISM."

So we got together and talked about how the Panthers were being repressed by the power structure, about C.P. tactics in the 1930's and Georgi Dimitrov, about the difference between fascism and plain old-fashioned piggish police behavior, about how the Jews might get it if fascism became rampant in these United States of America. We decided to send three brothers and a sister to Oakland to express solidarity, present our politics, and see what the Panthers and we could do for each other.

So the four of us went to Oakland ready to consider joining a united front against fascism, assuming that such a movement would be good for the Jews. Figuring that resolutions might be introduced, we prepared two in advance. The first stated that Jews and blacks have been singled out as special targets of fascism and should therefore unite with all other progressives against fascism and racism and against anti-Semitism, which is used by the ruling class to divide us. The second resolution, entitled "For Peace With Justice in the Middle East," was prepared for the contingency that an anti-Israel resolution were presented by pro-Arab elements. As it happened, the conference turned out to be a two-and-a-half-day pep rally and no resolutions were adopted at all.

I was impressed by the seriousness, dedication, and discipline of the Panthers. The conference staff was most courteous and cooperative in providing us with suitable facilities to set up a literature table with other Jewish radical groups. Jews were mentioned either as victims of German fascism (by the theoreticians) or as the children of Israel liberating themselves from the Egyptians (by the clergymen). But though we related quite well to most individual Panthers, there was little opportunity to relate politically to the party.

The whole affair was a one-way top-down tag-team presentation reminding me more of a high-school assembly than of any radical conference I can remember. After just one year's absence from the movement at large, I found out where it was at and I do not like it. I do not like the smug self-righteous manner of most of the new sects that have emerged in the last few months. I do not like the gap which is emerging between the inflated rhetoric and the serious tasks ahead. I find the rehabilitation of Stalin and the resurrection of the Stalinist cult reprehensible. I find little-red-book waving juvenile, and mass clenched-fist heiling quite out of place at a conference against fascism. I am not afraid to be tagged with some hollow epithet by a self-appointed vanguard, for I derive my radicalism from my understanding of this world and my accumulated experiences, and not from the pronouncements of central committees and the oratory of stage affairs.

Though I was quite turned off by the conference's style, I considered it my responsibility as a Jewish radical to relate to the content of the program which its leadership asked (rather, instructed) us to undertake. We were told to form committees against fascism in our own communities with the main task being to push city charter amendments to decentralize police departments and place them under community control.

At the time I thought it was a good idea, though, to be quite honest, not very politically practical. You just could not unite enough people to push it, let alone vote for it. It was quite obvious at the conference, before the ensuing fratricidal accusations and counteraccusations, that it had not succeeded in molding a united front. The kind of nice kids who in the past participated in electoral politics were turned off by the Stalinist tone and top-down format of the affair. The other kind of nice kids present would rather erect barricades in the streets of America or seize the factories; but with all their professed revolutionary Marxist-Leninist discipline, they just do not have the inclination to explain charter amendments to John Q. Public from door to door. By the time this was being written you had managed to offend everybody on the organized left with the possible exception of Y.A.W.F. and the C.P. These cats are the least capable of communicating outside their particular sects without causing giggles. Whatever the accuracy of the charges of C.P. influence at the conference, it seems that they managed to kill it by the adoption of their political program and style. And as we all know, the C.P.–U.S.A. is the sorriest bunch of losers on the left.

But despite the political bungling, I still thought that the police decentralization campaign could hinge on the participation of national minorities, and this is where the Jews come in. To be quite honest, the first question which I had to consider was whether police decentralization is good, bad, or indifferent for urban Jews. If it is bad for the Jews (which it is not), we might have to oppose it; if it is good for us (which it might be), it probably would have to be assigned a rather low priority; and if it is indifferent for us, but important for the Panthers, we would have to justify dropping or slowing the rest of our work and enlisting in a popular front with the Panthers, the C.P., and other thus-far unmobilized minorities because it is good for the blacks.

(Parenthetically, it would seem strange to fellow-travel in a popular front inspired by the C.P., which acts as the Soviet Union's senior apologist in this country. You see, there are three million Jews over there and that pig structure [to use a Panther phrase] is committing cultural genocide and practicing physical oppression against my people. By the way, how do you people stand on the Jews in the U.S.S.R.?)

I returned to New York more confused about the Panthers than I had been before. From what I had heard and read about you up to that time, you were the most relevant, most together radical organization in this country. You talked about a radical nationalist struggle and behaved as responsible revolutionaries. It is this correct practice (I am picking up the lingo) which made you the primary target of the power structure on the one hand, and the revolutionary vanguard for the whole movement on the other. But from some of your statements I got the idea that you confuse this vanguard role with some inherent right to dictate the rest of the movement's politics. Your leadership will be accepted only when it makes sense to the rest of the movement. When your practice is incorrect, and you refuse to critically recognize your errors, you are not the vanguard any more but just another black radical group.

On July 23rd, *The Times* reported on Cleaver's appearance

in Algiers with Al Fatah dignitaries, declaring his fraternal
solidarity with their cause and mouthing their bullshit about
Israel being an American "puppet and pawn" and a usurper
of the land. I have read before about Third World politicos
making anti-Israel statements in Arab capitals. I was urged
by a J.L.P. comrade to expose Al Fatah, defend Israel's right
to exist, and appeal to Cleaver's sense of fairness. Since the
facts are amply available elsewhere, I will not burden you
with them on this occasion.

Let it suffice to say that the Panthers have declared themselves to be the enemies of my people's national aspirations,
and supporters of those who want to commit genocide against
us. Whatever justice there is in the Panthers' own struggle,
I must view them from now on as my enemies.

I do not know whether to attribute the Panthers' position
on Jewish self-determination to stupidity and lack of political
sophistication or to sheer opportunism. But what puzzled me
even more was another part of *The Times* dispatch which described a Panther cartoon displayed in a window of the new
Afro-American Information Center in Algiers saying "racist
ethnic groups battle for pig power" in the United States. The
dispatch continues, "These groups were identified as the
Italians, Irish, Anglo-Saxons and Jews." Is this the way you
want to build a united front? But hell, we all know—don't
we?—that *The Times* and the rest of the bourgeois press lie.
I still wait to hear from you that it was all a figment of Eric
Pace's imagination.

But *The Times* article seemed to fit into the pattern. The
August 16th issue of *The Guardian* reprints a statement by
David Hilliard, the Panther Party Chief of Staff, denouncing
practically everybody on the left with the possible exception
of the Young Patriots. Towards the end of the statement,
while rebutting the Y.S.A. and I.S.C.'s anti-Stalinist criticism
of the conference (not convincingly at all), Hilliard says,
"perhaps they will call the Black Panther Party anti-Semitic
for supporting Al Fatah's liberation struggle against Zionism."
After the poor Y.S.A. opportunists had gone out of their

way to embrace the Al Fatah line they (and the I.S.C. which has a more principled though erroneous position on the issue) are being labeled Zionists, which is the in-phrase among Stalinists (such as Moczar and Co.) for radicals who oppose their dogma and heavy-handed tactics. The reason behind these outfits' "Zionism," Hilliard implies, is that they are run by Jews, and since Jews are counterrevolutionary by nature, they would have to criticize the Panther line. This is the other side of the coin of the ruling class' myth of the Jew as a revolutionary and troublemaker by nature. The Jew is thus singled out for condemnation whenever dictatorships of the right or the left clamp down on dissent.

The Black Panther Party is not anti-Semitic in its ideology —though the Algiers cartoon and the Hilliard remark still have to be explained. However, by your actions you shall be known, and you have lined up with our enemies and the name for any enemy of the Jews is an anti-Semite.

There seems to be some kind of preposterous fratricide on the left. Short of describing it all as the work of an *agent provocateur* among the Panthers, one finds it difficult to explain the destruction of the left as we have known it within a few months. Perhaps it is the work of the American ruling class, perhaps it serves the interests of the Soviet ruling class. The constituencies of the American left, with the Panthers in the vanguard, are fratricidally going for each others' jugular veins.

We all know that the Panthers are not the first on the American left to embrace the Arab cause. It is just that we all had more respect for your maturity and radicalism. We still hope that the present madness will be recognized and overcome, and that the Panthers will again behave as principled radicals rather than caricatures of mindless Stalinists.

Though you are my enemy, I am not yours. But I would have to be plumb out of my mind to go out of my way to save your ass from the cops. Even if I were a superaltruistic liberal and campaigned among the Jews to support the Panthers' program, I would justifiably be tarred and feathered for giving aid and comfort to enemies of the Jews. I would rather it were not this way, but it was you who disowned us, not we who betrayed you.

POWER TO THE PEOPLE! ! ! and I mean the people.

Is Zionism Compatible
with Radicalism?

J. J. Goldberg

The question always seems strange to the Zionist—silly at best, obnoxious at worst. But as it is asked often enough, it may merit an answer: Zionism *is* a radical movement. The most concise definition of Zionism is the national liberation of the Jewish people. Liberation? The idea of Jewish liberation usually sounds odd to a North American, rather like saying women's liberation in the White House. So perhaps a brief outline of Jewish history is necessary to clarify the issue.

Roots of Zionism

Political Zionism finds its origins in the unrecorded history of the second millenium B.C. At that time a small nation grew up in the area now called Palestine, travelling under the name Israel. Some 1500 years later that nation, by then called Judea (and its inhabitants Jews), was subjugated by the forces of Roman imperial colonialism. After a protracted

J. J. (Jonathan) Goldberg, a native of Washington, D.C., is a student in Jewish studies at McGill University and a writer for *Otherstand*. He is a member of Habonim and the Radical Zionist Alliance. This article appeared originally in *The Activist,* Spring, 1970, and is reprinted by permission of the author.

people's war, lasting roughly from 67 to 165 A.D., the nation was totally crushed. The Roman occupation forces decided to ban all national cultural and political life, expelling a major proportion of the population for good measure.

The national leadership was by this time, however, in the process of devising a code of law, now called Talmud, which laid out a transportable life style to preserve the communal life of the nation until such time as territorial polity would be restored. As is well known, these pockets of Judea ("Jewish communities") abroad flourished under varying degrees of economic, religious, and physical persecution for about 2000 years. They were held together by their code of law, and by a common faith; belief in the unity of God, in the unity of the Jewish people, and the inevitability of territorial restoration, all of which were repeated three times daily in prayers.

Around the year 1800 two important movements grew up in European Jewry. In Western Europe and America, then under the influence of the liberal Enlightenment, the Jews were emancipated. This was a sort of deal between the leaders of the Jewish communities whereby the Jews would be allowed to disband their organic, internally self-governing communities and enter society as individuals—Frenchmen, Americans, or Germans. Jewishness might be retained as a "religion," i.e., those aspects of Jewish culture which in form resembled Christianity: theology, personal ethics, and sexual practices. Thus Jewish civilization and Jewish people were no more; the Jewish religion had been invented. The motto of western Judaism was (and is) "be a Jew in the house and a man on the street." The Jew had finally accepted the distinction between Jew and man.

Unfortunately for the majority of the Jews, liberalism never hit Eastern Europe. The largest segment of the Jewish people (about five million before Hitler) were denied the opportunity of departmentalizing themselves. In the Russian Empire the traditional approach to Jews remained in force—continued economic pressure, starvation, and periodic massacres.

Eastern European Jewry, not offered the option of becoming Russians or Poles, developed Jewish novels, Jewish poetry, Jewish theater, Jewish journalism, and Jewish politics. By the end of the century a combination of the unbearable oppression (the year 1881 in particular saw a sudden outbreak of pogroms and new restrictive laws) and the growing nationalism, resulted in a major movement demanding political self-determination for the Jews.

Jewish Liberation

This movement took two forms. One of them, the Bund, fought for Jewish national autonomy within the framework of a socialist Russia. To this end they called, in 1898, a congress of Russian socialists which formed the Russian Federated Social Democratic Party— later the Bolsheviks. The Russian communists at this time numbered close to a thousand. The Bund numbered a little over 5000. It grew until it numbered 500,000 at the time of its forced disbanding (along with all other Jewish communal life) in 1917.

The other approach was that of Zionism. The Zionists reasoned that real national self-determination was possible only upon the base of a territorial national economy. Historically the Jew in Europe, always an outsider and barred by Christian canon from most occupations, had been forced into the economic position of middleman—petty merchant, small moneylender, tax collector for the nobility, and occasionally (in the West) international commerce and finance, making him an enemy to the working class and usurper of the rising middle class. This would and did inevitably lead to anti-Semitism, fostered by the ruling class, massacres, and occasionally (1648, 1939) to holocaust and genocide. The only answer, for the Zionist, was to seize the time and bring about the abovementioned restoration of the territorial polity, the return to Zion, hence Zionism.

Again, Zionism carried on the struggle at two levels. One was the practical level: in 1881 a small wave of immigration (the First *Aliyah*) made its way to Palestine and began to settle on the land. In 1906, with the failure of the Revolution in Russia and the resulting pogroms, a large wave of young workers and university students, the Second *Aliyah,* fled for Palestine and began the intensive settlement of the Yishuv, the Jewish community in Palestine. Not true colonists, but rather refugees, this wave was the founding generation of modern Israel. It consisted of membership of the various socialist Zionist parties, and accordingly they demanded and made innovations in the existing community, and indeed in the Jewish people of their time. They established a Jewish national economy of Jewish workers and Jewish capital, hoping in accord with the teachings of Ber Borochov to establish the conditions for a healthy class struggle. Borochov pointed out that the constant pressures of anti-Semitism forced the Jews into an abnormal inter-class solidarity which could be eliminated once the nation's existence was normalized territorially. Others hoped to bypass class struggle and establish a socialist Israel from scratch, and they started the kibbutzim, the workers' cooperatives, the Histadrut labor union with its worker-owned economy. In addition, they attempted, though in a regrettably small way, to organize Jewish-Arab friendship leagues and to agitate among the Arab masses for labor organization and the overthrow of Turkish imperialism. This did little to endear them to the Arab bourgeoisie and ruling class.

On the international level, Zionism began to organize for the legal establishment of a Jewish national home in Palestine. A World Zionist Congress was called in 1897 by a Viennese journalist named Theodor Herzl, and the World Zionist Organization was formed. A Jewish National Fund was set up to purchase land in Palestine, for settlement by poor, young, Russian socialists (somewhat to the chagrin of the liberal intellectuals who were the leadership of W.Z.O. and J.N.F.). Diplomatic representations were made to various world powers to obtain recognition for the Jewish polity. Approaches were made to Arab leaders to achieve some measure of understanding and cooperation in the development of the region.

Conflict in the Mideast

Things did not all go well for the Zionist diplomats. The Turkish Empire, which remained firmly opposed to Zionism, was dismembered in 1918 and southern Syria (Palestine to us) went to England. England owed the Zionists a favor because an English chemist named Chaim Weizmann, who was also president of the Zionist Organization, invented a product called acetone, a major component of dynamite. Britain also owed a favor, as it turns out, to Emir Feisal, Sherif of Mecca, for his cooperation with T. E. Lawrence, and as Feisal's clan was in the process of being driven out of Arabia by the Saudi clan, he was promised the Kingdom of Syria (including the provinces of Lebanon and Palestine). The Zionists, meanwhile, were offered in the 1917 Balfour Declaration a Jewish national home in Palestine. At the Versailles Peace Conference, Weizmann and Feisal met and agreed to cooperate in joint Jewish and Arab development of the region.

During this same period (1900–1930) another force was developing, this time in the Arab world. Arab nationalism was fundamentally a response by the new Arab bourgeoisie and intelligentsia to centuries of foreign domination (Mongol, Turkish, and later English and French). A conception developed of the Arab homeland—*Wantan al-Arab*—which had been raped for centuries and had to be redeemed. The demand grew for Arab hegemony over the entire traditional territory, including non-Arab Kurdistan, black Sudan, Lebanon (one-half Maronite Christian), and Palestine (some 500,000 Arabs, 85,000 Jews). In this respect the movement came to resemble the politically insignificant but much publicized right-wing faction of Zionism which aspired to Jewish hegemony over the entire territory of Palestine. This latter hope was dashed when the British, having deferred most of Syria to the French, gave

Eastern Palestine to Feisal in 1924 under the name Transjordan.

The resulting situation was tailor-made for British imperial designs: divide and rule. By encouraging Zionist hopes for some form of autonomy, they enraged the Arab leadership which sought absolute hegemony over the entire Middle East. By continually backing the Arabs—periodically shutting off immigration, arming Arabs for occasional pogroms against the Jews, outlawing Jewish defense units—they infuriated the Zionists. As a result, they were able to direct Arabs and Jews in Palestine into fighting against each other over a piece of land which had plenty of room for both, instead of joining together to drive out the British colonial occupation.

By 1939 relations between Jews and Arabs had deteriorated to a point where the British had no choice but to shut off almost all Jewish immigration and land purchase and to declare their intention of staying indefinitely. The Jews were now in active resistance against the British occupation, the Arabs were in frequent uprisings against the Jews, and there was a war going on in Europe. To complicate England's problems, the leadership of the Arab world was openly cooperating with Germany. The chairman of the Palestine Arab Higher Committee, Haj Amin al-Huesseini, Mufti of Jerusalem and Moslem spiritual leader of Palestine, spent the war years in Berlin.

The State

By 1941 the situation of the Jews inside Europe was becoming obvious to the outside world, and heavy pressure was put on England by the Zionists to open immigration to Palestine. But to no avail—boatloads of Jews smuggled out of Germany by the Yishuv were placed in internment camps, sunk, or sent back to the crematoria. By 1946 there was open rebellion in Palestine by the Jews against the British and by the Arabs against the Jews. Britain, unable any longer to "control" the situation, turned it over to the United Nations, which in 1947 recommended the partition of the country into two independent states for the two peoples living there. The Zionists had achieved their dream, political independence, and they were dancing in the streets of Jerusalem, Tel Aviv, and Times Square.

The Arabs, however, were in no mood for compromise and rejected the Partition Plan, demanding complete autonomy in Palestine. They went to war, and Jerusalem was placed under siege. On May 15, 1948, the date set by the U.N. for the establishment of the two states, the Provisional Assembly of the Yishuv declared the Jewish State of Israel in the territory allotted them by the U.N.; and the British withdrew leaving their fortresses around the country securely in Arab hands. Five Arab states—Egypt, Transjordan, Syria, Iraq, and Saudi Arabia—declared war. They called (by radio, sound truck, and leaflet) upon the Arabs of Palestine to flee, promising that they could return in a few weeks to find the Jews gone. They called for a sea of blood and marched in to create one. The Palestinian Arabs took them up on it, encouraged in their exodus by the right-wing splinter Zionist army, Zvai, despite pleas by the Yishuv's provisional government to remain and live in peace.

The Zionists' state was recognized immediately by the Soviet Union, and soon after by the United States. Supplied with arms by Czechoslovakia, they managed, when the cease-fire was arranged in 1949, to stand on lines outside the borders allotted them by the U.N. The Arab states refused to recognize Israel or sign peace treaties (Iraq never even signed a cease-fire) and the cease-fire lines stood as *de facto* borders until 1967. The territory allotted for the Palestinian States was annexed by Egypt and Transjordan, thus aborting the Arab state of Palestine. Five hundred thousand refugees who fled during the war were by and large denied entry into Egyptian and Jordanian society, and were kept interned in camps for 20 years, fed on U.N. rations and promises of seas of blood. The history of 1948–1967 has been the history of Arab determination to make good on their promises, and Israeli determination to exist, to have self-determination for the people of Judah after 2000 years of exile and colonial oppression.

Israel and Imperialism

During those first nineteen years, Israel was very much accepted as a member of the community of nations. She had successfully absorbed half a million penniless refugees—North African and Asian Jews—from the Arab states starting in 1949. She was building an egalitarian, social democratic state with lots of cute kibbutzim. The right wing (defined in Israel as any party supporting free enterprise) was politically powerless. The world was as ready as the Jews were to believe the bloodcurdling threats of the Arabs, who were, besides, a convenient place to hang the guilt which the West shared, but refused to accept, for the death of six million Jews. And the Jews were playing their traditional role of underdoggish losers who refused to give up. Supporting Israel was very progressive.

Then in 1967 this tidy little arrangement fell apart. Israel won a shockingly successful victory, and all by herself, against $1 billion worth of Soviet arms. Jews aren't supposed to do that. France, suddenly an enemy of imperialism, realized the moral implications of her position: she had been Israel's closest ally and main source of armaments, and this was losing her support among the progressive Arab states of the Third World. With all their oil. So Israel was forced to turn to the United States for arms sales. The State Department (read oil lobby) and the Foreign Relations lobby (check upon Fulbright's race relations record) tried to block it, but the Democratic Party has traditionally been very conscious of the Jewish vote. The U.S. suddenly became Israel's traditional ally.

But disregarding the maneuvers of the imperialist powers, the question remains one of the rights of Israel and Palestine to exist, and this issue is becoming clearer. Now that the Arab governments—particularly Egypt—have been shown to be morally and physically bankrupt, the Palestinians have begun to reassert themselves. Their leadership still totes the classical Arab nationalist line of total hegemony, and the traditional gentile line of denying the right of the Jews to exist as an independent group. Their major organization, Al Fatah, is still not a leftist organization—"revolutionary" yes, but strictly apolitical. Yet there are strong indications that Palestinian forces are beginning to recognize the necessity of dealing with the needs of the people of Palestine, rather than the land of Palestine: not hegemony, but independence. Israel is now getting used to the idea of disregarding, at least politically, the neighboring Arab states and recognizing the Palestinian nation, as demanded by the radical left in Israel (which ranges from the Israeli Communist Party to the secretary-general of the ruling Labor Party). There may be, then, a good chance for peace on the basis of mutual recognition of the rights of the two nations of Palestine, as Israel so futilely called for twenty years ago. Since 1967, however, Israel has not called for negotiations with the Palestinians; but to be a Zionist does not mean to support the Israeli government.

What of the idea of a democratic, united Palestine with equality for people of all faiths? Well, first of all, we're not a "faith." Nor are we a class of colonies, or an army of occupation. We are a people, a nation with workers, students, writers, garbagemen, exploiters, exploited, movies, dope. Jews from Europe (although not "white"), Jews from the Middle East (although not Arabs), Jews from Ethiopia, Liberia, and Bedford-Stuyvesant. They are all Israelis, with an economy, class conflicts, revolutionary movements, and a shared determination to be allowed to exist as a nation.

But the idea of giving up separateness is an attractive one— a cosmopolitan one-world brotherhood and unity. Many Zionists are willing to work toward that goal. When the United States, or Russia, or England (or maybe Vietnam?) voluntarily gives up its right to exist, we volunteer to go second. We're tired of being told to go first. And those Jews who have begun to disband in our name—the rulers of the American Jewish community who speak of the "Jewish faith," the Uncle Jakes —are being fought. Fought at the fund-raising drives, fought in the Hebrew schools, fought on all levels where they try to make us what we are not. Jewish kids who are tired of tomming to the *goyim* are learning from Israel, from the blacks, from the Vietnamese that it's better to extend the hand in solidarity than in charity. The radical Zionist movement is getting its shit together again, and we won't be denied.

Part Three

Socialist-Zionist Ideology

During the past half decade, two prominent Socialist-Zionist theoreticians, Ber Borochov and Nachman Syrkin, have been resurrected to provide the radical Zionists with their own prophets, their own equivalents of Marx and Engels.

Socialist-Zionism was the creed of the early Jewish settlers in Palestine, especially those of the 1900 to 1914 wave of immigration from Eastern Europe. They called themselves *chalutzim* (pioneers) and organized agricultural kibbutzim and trade unions. These Founding Fathers are today the "power elite" of Israeli society. Most of them are in their late sixties and seventies and have lost the revolutionary zeal of their youth.

Likewise in America, the Zionist movement changed drastically following World War II and the founding of the State of Israel. The Socialist-Zionists were overshadowed by the big Jewish fund raisers whose commitment to *aliyah* (living in Israel) and to a socialist Israel were negligible at best.

The revival of radical Zionism is a response to these two trends. Jews in both America and Israel have become complacent with affluence. Young Jews are offered a historical picture of Israel—a plastic Utopia, a land of milk and honey— which exists only in postcards and films from the Israeli Ministry of Tourism.

The private sector of Israel's economy has grown considerably. Israel now has the slums, poverty, and organized crime which urbanization and industrialization breeds. At the same time, it spends more of its gross national product (27 percent) on defense than any other country in the world. The authors in this section are all Zionists, committed to making *aliyah*. But they are also radicals, and their love for Israel does not blind them to the inequities within Israel and the misplaced priorities of its leaders. While accepting the reality of hostile neighbors, they believe that Israel cannot and must not use this as an excuse to ignore the internal problems which exist. Nor can the Jewish Establishment in America adopt an "Israel right or wrong" position, thus challenging the loyalty of radical Zionists.

These pieces analyze the present posture of American Zionism, America's relationship to Israel and the Arab nations, and Israel's relationship to its neighbors and its own political and cultural minorities.

A Radical-Zionist
Strategy for the 1970's

Tsvi Bisk

The Radical-Zionist faces a dilemma: Ethically he belongs on the left but emotionally he belongs with all Jews (reactionary or radical) because he knows that if in the end he is attacked as a Jew, *only* the Jews will fight and die side by side with him (all the liberal, heart-rending *goyishe* protestations notwithstanding). So who can the Radical-Zionist align with? The self-righteous ass-kissing assimilationist Jewish leftists or the overweening assimilationist schmucks of the Jewish Establishment?

The answer is—neither. We must define our own course— outline our aims and hopes, state a strategy and develop tactical and contingency plans for each phase of operations.

First, I would like to define a Radical-Zionist. A Radical-Zionist is not radical out of wholesale endorsement of the radical style nor does his Zionism mean that he must necessarily be oriented towards *aliyah* to Israel—although he must agree that Israel is central to Jewish existence in the 20th century and must be devoted to its survival. This does not preclude a radical analysis of Israel or Israeli society. The Radical-Zionist does not equate being radical with being accepted

Tsvi Bisk presently lives in Israel. This article orginally appeared in *The Jewish Liberation Journal,* November–December, 1969, reprinted by permission of its editorial board.

by the radical establishment—S.D.S., the Panthers, or *Ramparts*. He does not hang up black power posters at his Freedom Seder nor does he submit the script to *Ramparts* for approval. For him being radical is not a matter of being invited to the right radical conventions. Being a Radical-Zionist means fighting Jewish causes in a radical way, first in defining the enemies of both the Jewish people and the Jewish ethical tradition and second, in combating both with whatever tactics are deemed necessary (i.e., without the self-imposed restrictions of liberal nice guys). In the context of the Jewish liberation struggle, the Radical-Zionist has the right and responsibility to combat all enemies of the Jewish people and of the Jewish ethical tradition whether they be left or right, white or black, gentile or Jew.

Who are the enemies of the Jewish people?

1. *The power structure elements that instigate falsehoods such as the recent one by F.B.I. men that Al Fatah is behind the campus disturbances.* Such statements drive a wedge into the heart of the Jewish community, inhibiting proper analysis and action. Whenever such statements are made they should be answered promptly and sharply by Radical-Zionists in statements that clearly analyze the true situation and delineate the ulterior motives of those making them.

This particular lie is a classic example of mixing issues in order to confuse, compromise, and neutralize the Jewish community in a period when revolutionary activity is reaching its peak. By presenting this "analysis" to a community already frightened by the specter of the rising anti-Semitism of the left, the reactionaries hope to represent themselves as the true friends of the Jews. By doing this, the hand of the court Jews (who owe everything that they have to a lifetime of serving the establishment and, indeed, help to propagate such tripe) is strengthened, and those radical and liberal Jews who still function within a Jewish consciousness are emasculated. Equating participation in the revolutionary struggle with pro-Arab activity leaves the role of spokesman for the Jewish community in the private preserve of the most conservative elements of that community—a community that has the cultural potential of being one of the strongest moral forces in that revolution. This tactic is similar to the fanning of black anti-Semitism by the establishment and must be seen as the forerunner of imminent repression—first demoralize the left and then hit it hard before it is able to make a proper analysis and regroup its forces.

This pretended concern is a classic tactic of establishment anti-Semitism. In Europe the royalty fanned peasant anti-Semitism whenever the peasants' poor conditions threatened to erupt into revolution. They would then pretend to give succor to the Jew and would, in fact, give the Jew certain privileged positions (such as tax collector, holder of whisky licenses, and court Jew). This enraged the peasants even more against the Jews who were driven ever further into the arms of the king.

This time the Jew must not make the same mistake of thinking of the king (in this case the white corporate structure) as his ally, because in times of stress he throws out a few soothing words to the tortured Jewish soul. However, we must at the same time not make the mistake of the Russian Jewish radicals who viewed the pogroms of 1903 as just and good revolutionary practice for the Russian peasant with no long-term ill effects for the Jew. Black anti-Semitism and the anti-Semitism of the left are a reality and they are an issue. Although because neither of these groups has, at present, any real power the ill-effect is predominantly moral and not physical, by divorcing the moral force of the left from the mainstream of the community's consideration, the community is driven into taking positions that run counter to its interests and its moral heritage.

2. *The white anti-Semites hidden in the bosom of the Minutemen, the John Birch Society, and the Nazis.* Because these groups have access to the hearts and minds of middle-class America and ultimately to the power structure, they constitute the most frightening long-term danger to the Jewish people.

Being fringe groups in periods of *relative* calm will not prevent them from growing tremendously in times of political upheaval. In the 1970's the political upheaval in America will reach its peak; we are therefore constrained to keep a watchful eye on these groups and to engage in pre-emptive strikes if we deem it necessary.

3. *LeRoi Jones, Stokely Carmichael, and other black militants who find it necessary or expedient to operate in an anti-Semitic ideological context.* We have no obligation to super-objectivity or to the "tolerance" of those ass-kissing Jews who say, "We must understand the sociological conditions that make these statements possible." Fuck sociological conditions! While we must use them for a comprehensive understanding of any problem, we should not be so infatuated with them as to be unable to draw proper conclusions for action when the end result of these conditions is to be our own destruction. Statements turn into action if repeated often enough. Should one tolerate the K.K.K. because a particular set of sociological conditions has produced their hatred?

At Cornell a cross was burned in front of the Afro-American house and the blacks responded quickly and ruthlessly to dramatize the event. To a black, a burning cross means that someone out there has a rope and a tree, and the cats at Cornell didn't stop to make any sociological analysis—they struck. To a Jew swastikas and anti-Semitic rhetoric means that someone out there has an oven, and fuck me where I breathe if I am going to allow a sociological analysis to inhibit my ability to defend myself when confronted with these symbols.

4. *Russia is the enemy of the Jewish people—the Russians are different from the Nazis only in that they are more patient.* The cultural genocide of the Jews of Russia must be seen as less evil than the Nazis' final solution only in degree. It has as its aim the same result: the end of the Jewish people. Russia's Machiavellian attitude in the Middle East compounds her crime against the Jewish people—by supplying the Arab states with the means to destroy the Jewish state and then instigating them to try to do so.

5. *The Arab states—for whatever reason, they want to destroy the Jewish state.* Also their treatment of the remnant of Jews in these countries is indefensible.

6. *The situation of the Arab refugees.* The emotionalism of the Middle East situation is exacerbated by the truly horrible conditions of the refugees (especially in Gaza; the situation on the West Bank is better although one may assume that the situation on the East Bank is just as bad, if not worse, than in Gaza). These camps produce the terrorists, the instrument of the refugees' hate and frustration. If war is seen as the enemy of the Jewish people and peace as her ally, then the application of thought to the solving of the refugee problem as the first step to peace must take priority in the consideration of the Radical-Zionist.

7. *The current trends in Israeli society.* Ignored by the Soviets and rejected by the international left, Israel has been forced to depend for her economic development and political alliances on the western Jewish bourgeoisie. To say that this fact has undermined the position of Israeli leftists would be a gross understatement. Jewish philanthropists are seen as the saviors of Israel (and make no mistake, they are) and therefore the habits, values, and materialism of the West are making rapid inroads into the life style of Israel. This Americanization must be seen as the ultimate spiritual danger of the Jewish people if Israel is seen as the focal point of the Jewish messianic urge.

8. *Jewish millionaires and court Jews.* As disgusting as the phenomenon of people who buy their immortality with plaques on buildings is, we should not be quick on the draw in condemning but should, rather, view the problem in terms of the historic predicament of the Jew. As we have indicated above, it was the Jew's marginal survival quotient that drove him into the hands of the king. To a large extent this marginal survival quotient exists today. The Zionist revolution in Israel is not complete as long as Israel still depends on the "king" (the developed world) for jet planes and the right of export of Jewish capital to the Jewish state. As long as this situation

exists, the hand of the Jewish philanthropists applying pressure at the court of the king is an absolute necessity to the survival of the Jewish people. These are our brothers too, and their condition is another sorry element in the dreary history of the Jew. These people very often use their power for objective good and for the good of the Jewish people and considering the traditional avenues of power open to the Jew this class must be seen as historically *necessary and justifiable* for the Jewish people. However, it must be recognized that as the Zionist revolution progresses this class will increasingly lose its relevance in existing as a class and, indeed, will soon be obsolete in terms of *any* benefits to the Jewish people.

It must also be recognized that these people very often use the power of being rich or the prestige gained by being influential in a *goyish* framework, to dominate Jewish communal activities and make them the private preserve of their own lust for power and social eminence to the exclusion of the meaningful participation of the rest of the community. They are rich people who, in the wake of the demoralizing effects of the Enlightenment on the ghetto culture and the great economic needs of the Jewish people after the Holocaust, created philanthropic institutions and installed themselves as the leaders of these institutions and, thus, as the leaders of the Jewish community, since these institutions have become central to Jewish life since World War II. They have never held elections open to the community at large but rather have constantly reappointed themselves as leaders of the Jewish people, thus becoming inbred groups that pat each other on the back and give each other trophies. They keep the masses of the Jews out of the decision-making process but periodically dun them for money. Jewish prominence in the twentieth century is not, therefore, based on piety, learning, or a cultural ideal but rather on money alone. This is the most dangerous phenomenon happening to the Jews and must be confronted.

9. *Immorality and ostentation within the Jewish community —racketeers, blockbusters, and profit mongers of essential services such as funerals and old-age homes, and the disgust-*

ing ostentation of Jewish bar mitzvahs *and weddings.* The edifice complex of the American Jewish community is a good example of this ostentation: magnificent Frank Lloyd Wright-type synagogues to show the *goyim* that we can do it too, but absolutely lacking in Jewish content. The centrality of money in *every* aspect of Jewish life with its subsequent glorification of moneymen as "paragons of Jewish life." These are all the enemies of the Jewish people precisely because in combination with ignorance of true Jewish values they repel every sensitive Jew and drive him from the fold. From here on in, the criterion of a good Jew must be if he is righteous, learned, and ethical and not if he has bought a forest in Israel.

10. *Jews like Albert Shanker.* Whatever the justification of his stand (and I will not comment one way or another as I am not familiar with the particulars of the situation), it is clear that Shanker himself fanned the flames of anti-Semitism into a roaring fire. Like the reactionaries, he mixed issues to confuse the Jewish community. There is decentralization and there is black anti-Semitism and while many blacks endorse both, they are clearly separate issues which Shanker deliberately merged in order to widen his political base by a coalition with a hysterical and paranoic Jewish community. This was done out of consideration for his own political gain and should be condemned because it probably caused more anti-Semitism than there was before and also because a hysterical Jewish community is an unthinking Jewish community at a time when clear thinking is clearly a survival factor. As with the corporate white establishment, this kind of hypocritical and paranoic issue-making should be promptly and clearly exposed and condemned.

11. *Jewish paranoia—the thing that makes the above tactic possible.* The Jewish response to decentralization must be seen as the right response to the wrong provocation. After the "sheep going to the slaughter" attitude under the Nazis there is inherent in every Jew the desire to prevent a repeat performance. The Jews are quick on the trigger, and decentralization elicits a ferocious response—a whale is created to devour a

minnow (and the reactionary and racist Jewish Defense League
to the right). The Radical-Zionist must assume the responsibility for the defense of the Jewish community both to combat
the attraction of the right and because the minnow is potentially
dangerous and growing.

12. *Jewish cowardice.* As exemplified by the historically re-
petitive scene of the Jew's chronic disregard of an analysis of
his place in society so as to forestall catastrophe—we are the
ostriches of history. When catastrophe does come we are unable to formulate a strategy and act on it.

What should Radical-Zionist strategy be at this stage?

1. *To make it clear that politically, ethically, and culturally
the place of the American Jewish community in the American
political spectrum is on the left.* By "left" I mean that part of
the spectrum which rejects American values and resists its
corporate structure. I do not refer to any particular group or
ideology calling itself at the moment "left." Given past American history and present American conditions, the militant
(often Marxist) splinter groups are completely irrelevant to
real social change in America; traditionally ethnic groupings
have been responsible for more social change in America;
traditionally ethnic groupings have been responsible for more
social change than such splinter groups or the nonexistent
class struggle in America. The white radical groups (especially
S.D.S.) are going through a splintering phase and will soon
become totally impotent. The black revolution (with its real
visceral needs as opposed to the "spiritual revolution" of the
suburban radicals) is the true vanguard of the present American social struggle.

The American Jewish community is spiritually dispossessed
and economically marginal (i.e. dispensable) in relation to
American society. It is increasingly paranoic in terms of this
situation. It is this situation which gives rise to a real visceral
need which in turn qualifies the Jews to be a partner with the
blacks in a revolutionary struggle.

A black-Jewish partnership does not mean the sentimental

brotherhood horseshit of the past nor does it mean the present
ass-kissing relationship of some Jewish intellectuals to blacks,
but, rather, an alliance based on enlightened self-interest. It
should be made clear from the beginning that we are making
a *Jewish* revolution and not a black one; that when we can
cooperate on particular issues we will and when we can't we
won't; that the alliance is issue-oriented and that on any given
issue we may have to go against the interest of the blacks.

2. *To democratize the Jewish community.* We should strive
to form a Jewish Citizens' Union in which all Jews (whether
they belong to a synagogue or not, or to any other organization
for that matter) will have a right to speak and to vote. The
Union would bypass the existing organizations and thus
emasculate the political power of the Jewish Establishment.
The Union would be involved in all phases of Jewish life in
America and in the distribution of funds raised in the community. The existing organizations (B'nai B'rith, American
Jewish Congress, and the American Jewish Committee) would
have to be accountable to the Union.

We should strive to redirect community funds from glory-
seeking prestige projects (such as hospitals) to the more immediate needs of Jewish education. Educational reforms
should consist of the teaching of modern Hebrew in all afternoon Hebrew schools with parallel English-language instruction in the Bible and the Talmud. The *bar mitzvah* boy should
be able to at least translate his *haftorah* and comment on it
intelligently before he is to be *bar mitzvahed.*

Pressure should be applied on local school boards to intro-
duce Hebrew as a modern language in public elementary,
junior high, and high schools in cities with a large Jewish
population. A reversal of policy should occur in that we should
align ourselves with the Catholics for federal aid to parochial
schools. This would give Jewish day schools a shot in the arm.

3. *To identify Israel with the Third World.* This must be
done both in the eyes of the Third World and in the eyes of
Israel's own citizens (who, as noted before, have become
slavish imitators of the West). There has not been a people in

the world that has suffered as much from Europe as the Jew
and while this does not mean that he should automatically
identify as part of the Third World, he should not reject such
a tendency either. While it is true that Israel is presently dependent on the West for survival it also is true that peace in
the Mideast will only come if the Third World takes a neutral
stand and applies its moral force and influence in the Arab
world to bring it about.

If given recognition by the Third World as a Third World
entity, Israeli leftists will be redeemed in the eyes of their
countrymen and will be able to steer Israel to such a course.
Given such an opportunity Israel will do more than her share
for the Third World struggle, but denied such an opportunity
she will refuse to offer herself as a sacrifice on the altar of that
struggle. After Auschwitz we have one duty: to survive—even
if it means taking arms from the Devil himself.

We should make it clear that the Middle East conflict is
basically one between two Third World combatants and that
this is exploited by the imperialist powers to weaken the
revolutionary potential of the Third World. The role of Third
World members such as the blacks should not be to take
sides but to act as referees in this situation so as to direct the
energies of the Third World to its proper forcus—the combating of imperialism, and their own self-liberation.

4. *For those of us who see Israel as the center of our future
and wish to settle there, we must devote our energies towards
creating a social revolution in a New Left context—i.e.
against capitalism and against bureaucracy.* We must strive to
formulate a pragmatic ideology that takes into account the
unique features of Israel—a flexible nondogmatic analysis that
can accommodate the realities of each stage of development.
We must also act as an instrument of defense of the rights of
the minorities in Israel and also as a vanguard group in pres-
suring against undemocratic and unethical practices in its
public bodies.

5. *To strive to relieve the plight of the remnant of Jews in*

*the Arab countries and to facilitate the emigration of Jews
from Russia.*

What should be our tactics in realizing these aims?

First, *research:* An intensive study should be made of the
American Jewish community to determine how the power is
distributed and manipulated, what the sources of funds are,
how many people in the community participate in Jewish
affairs, and Israel's dependence on the fund raisers and
philanthropists and how this affects her policy in an adverse
way. A historically documented analysis should be made of
how, traditionally, the Jews have been in the middle and have
been used by the establishment to repress popular movements;
an investigation of the relations of the various U.S. minority
groups to each other is also necessary.

Confrontation tactics of an educative and influential nature
within a Jewish framework should begin immediately. For example *halakhic* law allows one to challenge the congregation at
a certain point in the service to demand justice, and the service
cannot continue unless the complainant is heard. The Beth Din
offers innumerable opportunities to confront elements in the
community, such as Jewish slumlords. A Talmudic Research
Committee should be established to determine other traditional
methods of Jewish protest. Teach-ins of Hebrew to Jewish kids
in public places (such as parks) by long-haired radicals should
prove an embarrassment to the Jewish Establishment and would
dramatize the lack of interest in Jewish education in the Jewish
community.

The organization of the Jewish Citizens Union should utilize
grass-roots political organizing techniques, doorbell ringing,
storefronts, local meetings, etc., and should be directed especially to those who are dissatisfied with the present structure of
Jewish communal affairs. I suspect that we will find a surprisingly large number of dissatisfied Jews in the middle and lower
middle classes.

Second, *the blacks and Israel:* the blacks have no real political interest (other than possibly a temporary tactical one) in supporting the Arabs. We might present to them the following proposition: "The Mideast struggle is not central to your liberation struggle but it is central to ours, thus your stand on the situation is more a tactic than a result of objective inquiry and analysis. Because of this you are not willing to die for your stand on the Mideast, (or even fight for it) but we are. If you persist in your stand you will find yourself wasting more revolutionary energy on this side tactical issue than on the main issue of your liberation in America because if you insist on acting as our enemy we will be forced to fight you as our enemy. We are working now for a reformed and restructured American Jewish community and if you let us we will succeed and you will have a potential powerful ally. But if you fight us we will also waste our energy and will not succeed, and we will both be the losers." Faced with this analysis, perhaps the blacks may opt for neutrality on the Middle East.

This would be one prong in combating the Arabs; the other prong would be to *educate the Afro-Asians in the universities to the true nature of the Mideast conflict,* and the neo-imperialist nature of Pan-Arabism (using the issue of black slavery in Arab history and Arab suppression of Africans). We should picket all Afro-Asian houses who don't condemn Arab anti-Semitism (in terms of propaganda and the treatment of Jews in the Arab countries).

In terms of *Russian Jewry* it is clear that our role is limited and that, in fact, the Jews best in a position to help on this issue are the Jews who act as a pressure group in the government. However, we should try as much as possible to link South African racism with Russian anti-Semitism by offering ourselves as an ally on the American scene to African students. Large demonstrations in cooperation with Africans against Chase Manhattan Bank and the Stock Exchange in New York would help their cause greatly and, of course, the identification of the Africans with our cause against Russian anti-Semitism will embarrass Russia greatly. We might also align ourselves with Greek students in demonstrations in front of the Stock

Exchange—to be associated with the junta is just as bad for Russia; and we would be giving the Greeks a real vehicle that they up to now haven't had.

The work outlined above that faces Radical-Zionists is a tremendous undertaking in terms of effort and devotion to the cause of Jewish liberation. One thing is clear: time is of the essence. While not neglecting logical analysis, we must also act. The battle for Jewish dignity and survival must be carried from the salons and caucuses of the intellectuals to the streets and the campuses. There is much to be done and no time to lose.

Borochovism

Moshe Zedek

When Nachman Syrkin offered his eulogy at the grave of Ber Borochov, he said, "Borochov has passed away, but the fruits of his labor for Socialist-Zionism will survive forever."

Little did Syrkin anticipate that not long after Borochov's death on December 17, 1917, at the age of 36, the contributions of the founder of Socialist-Zionism would become as marginal to the Zionist movement as the Jews were marginal to the socioeconomic structure of modern capitalist society.

The fate of Borochov and the Jewish proletariat were inextricably intertwined. Borochov's views, which helped to forge, nourish, and revolutionize the Zionist movement declined and almost disappeared in proportion as the Jewish working class diminished and Jewish Socialist-Zionist consciousness waned and became submerged in the class collaborationist view of establishment Zionism.

But today, Borochovism is emerging from the long historical winter of ideological hibernation and lives again in the thoughts and actions of growing numbers of young radical Jews for whom the ideas of Borochov serve as the basis of Zionism as

"Moshe Zedek" is the pseudonym for a New York-based writer and lecturer. He is also a founding member of the Jewish Liberation Project. This article originally appeared in *The Jewish Liberation Journal*, February, 1971, and is reprinted by permission of the author.

the national and international liberation movement of the Jewish people. The revival of Borochovism is proportional as radical Jewish youths become increasingly aware of their Jewish identity and increasingly dedicated to the struggle for the termination of *galut* (exile) which Socialist-Zionism must bring about.

During the past two years, Jewish national liberation consciousness in the United States and abroad has deepened into a greater concern for Jewishness, *aliya,* and Israel. There are signs that this year will witness an even greater recognition of and rededication to the two basic principles of Borochovism: there can be no normal socioeconomic Jewish life in the *galut,* and the liberation of the Jewish people from the exploitation of the ruling class of each nation and the oppression of the Jewish establishment must be the tasks of the Jews themselves on a grass-roots level. Organizations in many countries in the West and even in Israel have been formed which adhere to Borochovism. What was, over the years since his death, carried on almost exclusively by groups such as Hashomer Hatzair, is now being put into practice by numerous organizations.

But Borochovism lives not only in the hearts and minds of growing numbers of radical Jewish youths. The theoretical and practical contributions of Borochov are being vindicated daily in the most diverse ways throughout the world. What is the substance of Borochov's views? What are their essential elements? Are they relevant to the Jewish condition in the U.S. and elsewhere?

Borochov was the first to apply the ideology of scientific socialism-Marxism to Zionism, and was the first Zionist to apply Marx's method of dialectical and historical materialism to the national problems of the Jewish people. In so doing, Borochov showed that the economic situation of the Jews was a recurring and insoluble condition under capitalism and that the Jewish people could not develop a normal nation and a normal socioeconomic structure of the *galut.* The struggle, therefore, has to occur in each country in a permanent fashion until the Jews extricate themselves from the *galut* and build their own nation on their own territory. With that, a normal class struggle can develop which will lead to the establishment of socialism.

The essential elements of Borochovism can be summarized in eight points:

• The Jewish socioeconomic structure in the *galut* takes the form of an inverted pyramid: Whereas the base of the pyramid of other peoples is comprised of industrial workers, and its apex of capitalists and landowners, with the center comprised of small shopkeepers, intellectuals, technicians, white-collar workers, and professionals, the base of the Jewish pyramid is comprised of ruling-class elements; and the apex of industrial workers.

• This abnormal and peculiar structure is the consequence of an absence of territory upon which to build a normal nation and which, therefore, forces Jews to adapt themselves to the economic mode of production and ruling-class life style and isolates them for the basic process of productive activity. Under these conditions the Jewish people cannot develop a viable working class and must exist in the crevices of the economy. They become, therefore, a marginal people.

• The main enemy of the Jewish people is the ruling class of the nation which exploits and oppresses them just as it does the working class as a whole and all other national minorities. In addition, however, there is another enemy: the Jewish Establishment within the Jewish community. This Jewish Establishment acts as a transmission belt for the ideas, values, and mores of the nation's ruling class into the Jewish community. The Jewish people, therefore, must conduct a simultaneous class struggle against both ruling elements.

• Unlike other minority groups which are national minorities—the blacks in the U.S., the French in Quebec, the Catholics in Northern Ireland, the Basques in Spain—the dispersal of the Jews throughout the world makes them an international minority—the victims of ruling classes and elites in all nations.

This, consequently, provides the Jews with an internationalist outlook.

• The most that Jews can obtain in the *galut* is national autonomy, but this, in Borochov's words, "is not a radical solution of the Jewish problem and, therefore, cannot remove the anomalies of the Jewish strategic economic base. However, it provides the Jewish proletariat with the necessary political forms" to conduct a struggle for immediate rights.

• There is no contradiction between genuine national consciousness and class struggle. In fact, the nation provides the base for developing the conditions of production and, hence, class consciousness. A movement or person with genuine national consciousness, while recognizing the existence of a common national character created in the environment of common conditions of production, realizes that "within every nationality the separate characteristics of each class appear more acutely and can be more readily discerned."

• There is no dichotomy between work in the *galut* and work for a Jewish homeland. "*Poale* Zionism (literally, proletarian Zionism or Socialist-Zionism) has to integrate the *galut* and Zion," Borochov wrote. This requires a development from trade-union consciousness to class consciousness to socialist consciousness to Socialist-Zionist consciousness.

• The condition of marginality—the phenomenal form of what is generally referred to as the "Jewish condition"—can only be solved in the Jewish homeland where a "normal pyramid" and a "normal" class struggle can be developed. There is, therefore, a permanent revolution in the development and fusion of the struggle against marginality and the establishment of a homeland.

These elements, which constitute the essential contributions of Borochov, were distilled by him in "Our Platform," written in 1906. In it, he wrote: "Our [Socialist-Zionist] ultimate aim, our maximum program, is socialism—the socialization of the means of production. The only way to achieve socialism is through the class struggle of the Jews within the world-wide social democracy . . . Our immediate, our minimum program, is Zionism. The necessity for a territory in the case of the Jew results from the unsatisfactory economic base of the Jewish proletariat."

The validity of Borochovism is borne out currently by world events: the growing anti-Semitic policies of the Soviet Union's ruling elite, reflected in the population, is intensified by the fact that Jews are dispersed and lack an autonomous, self-determined territory (Biro-Bidjan was not self-determined but created), and by the fact that relatively few Jews are members of the industrial working class.

In countries such as Chile and Cuba, and in other nations advancing toward socialized economies, Jews are obsolete to the process of production because their former economic status and activities have no place in the new social structures.

Ironically, even Israel vindicates Borochovism, but in ways unforeseen by him. The entity which is Israel—its modern economy, Jewish culture, and institutions, its highly politicalized development with multiple parties, and its class struggle —is marginal to the region as a whole compared to the socioeconomic backwardness of the Arab world. It is Israel's development—its unilateral marginality—that makes it vulnerable and an object of scorn and hatred. In fact, Israel, which personifies the Jewish people, emphasizes the historical fact that marginality is the basic functional element that generates scorn and hatred of the Jewish people everywhere and makes them the object of vilification and attack by other oppressed peoples.

How does the form and content of the Jewish condition manifest itself in the United States—the citadel of world imperialism? What is the perspective for Jews in this country?

The Jews in the U.S. are oppressed on three levels: they are economically marginal, politically disunited, and dependent on the ruling class' political structure and parties, and psychologically schizophrenic in that they lack identity.

The Jews in this country comprise three percent of the population, compared to the Catholics and Protestants who comprise 25 percent and 67 percent of the population respectively. Yet, 67 percent of America's Jews are professionals, white-collar workers, and businessmen, while only 36 percent of the Catholics and 31 percent of the Protestants are in those economic categories. At the same time, 68 percent of the Catholics and Protestants combined are manual workers, while only 14 percent of the Jews are in the industrial labor force.

The income of the Jews is also out of proportion. Sixty-six percent of the Jewish population has an annual income of $7,000 and more, while 47 percent of the Catholics and 88 percent of the Protestants earn $7,000 and more. At the other end of the income spectrum, only 15 percent of all Jews earn $5,000 a year or less, while 28 percent of the Catholics and 39 percent of the Protestants earn less than $5,000 annually.

From an economic point of view, the workers generally and the majority of Jews in particular are faced with the beginning of generalized unemployment affecting both the industrial and white-collar workers. Prosperity, based on a continuing war economy, is coming to an end. The vast majority of American Jews, white-collar workers, technicians and professionals, like their non-Jewish counterparts, rode on the crest of an economic wave between the Korean War and now. But a new era is emerging that will be marked by social unrest in which competition for jobs that are vanishing daily with increased automation and cutbacks in military expenditures will make the Jews the prime target of popular resentment.

The fact is that the growing national rate of unemployment, currently six percent or close to five million jobless (it is close to 75 percent jobless in the ghettos) despite the war economy, is hitting those technical and professional job sectors in which there is a greater proportion of Jews to non-Jews. But because of their marginality, which will increase even further when their skills are no longer required in the emerging era, the Jewish scientists, technicians, and professionals could all disappear tomorrow and it would not essentially change the system of production. This was evidenced tragically in Nazi Germany when Jewish scientists, technicians, and professionals were first ousted from the economic sphere and then thrown in concentration camps and murdered or forced to emigate; the economy continued to function without their skills.

By contrast, the blacks, Puerto Ricans, and Chicanos who are oppressed, exploited, and discriminated against today are vital to the capitalist mode of production. Capitalism needs their labor force—unskilled or skilled—to keep the economic gears meshing on the level of primary production. These minority groups can be either engaged as required as producers or as a reserve labor force. The Jews offer no such economic advantage to the capitalist class. In short, the Jews in their marginality are necessary to no one.

However, the nature of the Jews' marginality is such that those Jews who are being and will be fired from white-collar jobs will not be conspicuous to the majority of the unemployed. Jews (and others) in such jobs are eased out individually or in small groups, not, as in the case of industrial workers, in huge percentages and, sometimes, by whole factories. Since such Jews generally have some savings to fall back on, they will not be conspicuous on the unemployment lines or the welfare rolls, at least not for a certain length of time.

However, those Jews who are in favored economic positions are, by the very nature of these positions, conspicuous in contrast to exploited or unemployed workers. Such Jews create the impression that their economic situation is true for all Jews. This situation will provide the ruling class with the opportunity to make use of the Jews as a handy scapegoat to divert the attention of the jobless and oppressed groups away from the social system responsible for their plight. The identification of the Jewish Establishment with the ruling class and the opposition of both to revolutionary social change will stigmatize all Jews as oppressors.

Hostility will be directed by workers against Jews seen rising to the top of the economic ladder while they remain on the bottom, and from the professionals and corporate elite which view all Jewish advances in these areas as threats to their own economic security.

Because a large segment of the Jews are involved in reshaping the techniques of production which makes it possible to increase productivity with less workers, the ruling class will hold Jews responsible for intensifying the contradictions of capitalism and the workers will hold the Jews responsible for their joblessness. While revolutions in the techniques of production (automation) are welcomed by the capitalist class in their quest for greater profits and required in the struggle for world markets, and while workers generally can be absorbed in other industries during periods of relative prosperity, the emerging era of depression will be ruinous to both workers and a portion of the capitalist class.

In this situation, the Jews in the U.S. will be subjected to pressures from three directions: from below—the working class; from above—the capitalist class; and from within— the Jewish middle class itself.

Borochov, in an article published in 1911 entitled "The Anti-Zionist Concentration," observed that one of the contradictions in Jewish *galut* life is "the extraordinary strength of the individual and the unparalleled weakness of the group." This situation, he continued, "gives rise to the conflicting, antithetical 'material' interests within Jewish life."

This is reflected in the very nature of the inverted pyramid Borochov described. This pyramid has four tiers:

1. The capitalists—the owners of large factories, realty, investment brokers, stock exchange and banking magnates, and oil men—whom Borochov described as "aristocrats (who) . . . turn philanthropists," find their best interests served by assimilation. Were it not for the poor Jews (here and abroad), this Jewish capitalist class "would not be disturbed by the Jewish problem." The Jewish capitalist, Borochov wrote further in "Our Platform," "is engaged in the search for a Jewish solution and a means of being delivered

from the Jewish masses." He would like nothing better than "to lose (his) individuality and be assimilated completely by the native bourgeoisie."

2. The Jewish middle class—small shopkeepers, professionals, technicians, scientists, intellectuals, doctors, lawyers —is bound more closely to the Jewish masses because its economic interests "depend on the market which the mass of people affords" since a major portion of its capital is invested in consumer goods and services. As long as this middle class retains its economic position it is "relatively unconcerned with the Jewish problem." This primarily white-collar class faces competition for jobs with the non-Jewish segment of the labor force which compels them to face the Jewish problem. "Jewish misery is closer to them than to the upper bourgeoisie" and they are, therefore, "the chief supporters of all types of 'cultural nationalism.' "

3. The Jewish working class—a steadily diminishing number in the needle trades, fur, millinery, jewelry, and some manual workers, sales clerks, social workers, teachers, journalists, and government employees. Many are not the classical industrial proletariat but are part of the "new working class." The condition of these workers in the marginal industries makes them least susceptible to assimilation although the upper-income strata of workers seek a *shidach* with their non-Jewish neighbors. The older generation retains a semblance of a vague and faltering Jewish socialism or Bundism while many in the younger generation (including those still in high school and college) develop varying degrees of Zionist consciousness. In this tier of the pyramid are also the declassed, aged, and impoverished who reside primarily in the urban centers that long ago lost their Eastern European *shtetl* character.

4. The Jewish "community leaders"—the officials of the communal organizations "elected" by their own closed organizations but which lack a mass base and constituency in the Jewish grass-roots communities—are a unique segment not found in this form within any other ethnic group. These

"leaders," who function without any democratic participation of the Jewish masses, are recruited from the upper and middle Jewish bourgeoisie and control and expend vast incomes and employ thousands of "staff personnel" for domestic and overseas philanthropic activities.

Borochov reserved the greatest scorn for the establishment Jews. In the 1911 article he excoriated "these new rulers" whose activities had one aim—"to obtain the recognition of the neighboring peoples, and to achieve personal integration in the *galut* through the medium of the Jewish people."

He scorned them because the services the establishment Jewish leaders and organizations rendered "satisfied only the most temporary needs. . . . Since these activities brought some amelioration, the *galut*istic intelligentsia boasted to the outside world of the partial confidence in them displayed by the Jewish people. . . . Their chief concern was to be the 'only representative' of Jewry to the mighty, enticing, outside world. Therefore they maintained that 'within the Jewish people, under our care, peace must reign.' " Borochov concluded that to unify the Jews to face new dangers and to retrieve all that has been usurped by these Jewish lackeys, this "anti-Zionist concentration," the Jewish people must establish "a national front against the anti-Zionist front."

This, then, is the nub of the Jewish situation in the U.S.: too liberal for the WASP community and too conservative for the oppressed minorities. The Jew is marginal even when deeply involved, an outsider even when thoroughly committed, a stranger even when he is in undisputed leadership.

The most important question still facing the Jewish people in the *galut* at this time is: How can we be ensured against the recurrence of the horrible persecutions and tragic events which so often befell us in various countries and epochs?

When other peoples suffer from oppression and persecution they all struggle for their own national causes; should they lose in the struggle their defeat is not permanent because they remain on their own soil and can always wait for the opportunity to rise again and regain their rights.

But the Jewish struggle in the *galut* is altogether different. In the August 6, 1915 issue of the *Yiddisher Congress,* Borochov wrote: "The *galut* condition of the Jewish nation is not only tragic, but also hopeless. Our *galut* tragedy is not temporary but permanent. We do not fight for a Jewish cause— we suffer for foreign interests." Cutting through the Gordian knot of "solutions" offered to Jews by various ideologists and ideologies which avoided dealing with the "Jewish condition," Borochov declared:

"We Socialist-Zionists are convinced that our freedom depends primarily upon the national self-help of the Jewish masses." The emancipation of the Jewish people, he asserted, "can be gained only by our own efforts . . . Organized national self-help [must be the national political slogan of the Jewish masses]. We must unite ourselves in the struggle for our own future."

Radical Political *Irbutz**
in Israel

David Mandel

The concept of urban collectives has floated around Zionist circles for a long time, and history records a few failures. Discussion has resurfaced recently, with the development of an independent radical Zionist movement, whose members are dedicated to their own self-realization through communal life in Israel and to serious socioeconomic changes in the Israeli structure. Also, the Sha'al group in Israel has received wide publicity since its establishment three years ago as a "kibbutz" of professionals who chose an urban setting. In all due respect to the Sha'al group, which has seriously pioneered a life style that looks as though it may succeed, we should differentiate between them and what we shall call the "political *irbutz*." This concept has been proposed as not only a life style, though certainly the stability of such communes as permanent homes is crucial. The "political *irbutz*" is seen primarily as a means to effect political, economic, and social change in Israeli society.

* *"Irbutz"* is a contraction of the Hebrew words for city and kibbutz, connoting an urban collective settlement.

David Mandel has been a long-time activist in the New Left. After returning from a year in Israel, in Fall 1969, he organized the Hebrew House at Oberlin College and became active in the Radical Zionist Alliance in Ohio, and was elected National Chairman of the R.Z.A. in February, 1971. This article is reprinted by permission of the author.

The Kibbutz

Let us begin with a look at the history of the kibbutzim. Recent research has shown that the communal institutions of the early kibbutzim were not, as had been widely assumed, arrived at haphazardly. They were, to a large extent, calculated attempts at solving what was seen by the founding Socialist-Zionists as the crucial problem that needed to be solved in order to create any sound Jewish national existence —a base for the national economy. This meant that there had to be an organized Jewish working class, a widespread Jewish presence on the land itself, and, if the economy was to be a socialist one, ownership of these newly-created means of production by the Jewish workers themselves. The subsequent creation of the collectivist movements of different shades, and of the large Histadrut union, were the fruition of these intentions. But also on the cultural level, the work ethic that permeated the kibbutz society, its valuing of group spirit, and its nationalism, became the models for the whole society. These group-oriented values created the national conditions of production that are still the foundation of the state, and its values and goals.

The kibbutz was certainly a revolutionary vanguard movement of its time, aimed at solving the problems necessary to achieve Jewish national existence with a socialist bent. It achieved a great deal, but fell far short of bringing complete socialism to Israel, and seems unable to effectively continue the struggle today, at least on its own. In fact, socialism as a value and a goal seems lately to be less and less important and even less popular to all of Israeli society. Why?

First, there was created out of the early kibbutzim and labor movement an incredibly powerful Socialist-Zionist elite, still holding a great deal of power. For many of them, political and social reality is the same as it was fifty years ago, and a natural resentment has built up among aspiring younger leaders, and an "anti-ideological" spirit among the young public. Private ownership has increased, but the largest private owner by far remains this gigantic labor union complex, and the fact is that it has become, to large portions of the population, oppressive.

The Urban Problem

Take, for instance, a scenario from one of the proper development towns, created around 1960 for the masses of immigrant Jews from backward Asian and African countries. The population is, say, 95 percent Moroccan and Tunisian, totaling maybe 5,000 people. The poor educational and cultural facilities and overcrowded housing are given factors, as is the cultural gap between these citizens and many Europeans of the large cities and kibbutzim. In addition, the town's residents are trapped in poverty: Professional services are usually provided by outsiders who often do not live in the town. Except for the minority who own or work in small businesses or trades, the vast majority of the labor force are relatively unskilled workers in one of two large basic industries in the town. And here's the catch: These industries are almost always owned by the Histadrut, the union supposedly representing the workers it hires. There is an obvious contradiction. Furthermore, the Histadrut bureaucracy is controlled totally by outsiders, and relatively little has been tried in these unskilled factories in the way of worker participation in management. Needless to say, there are few strikes in these industries. Another obvious result: There is a good deal of resentment—when elections come around the only anti-Histadrut opposition is the chauvinist right-wing and religious parties; and they receive large support in these towns in the absence of any effective left opposition. This only hurts the chances of these towns receiving new investments from bureaucratic Histadrut decision-makers.

Kibbutz-Town Interaction

And the kibbutzim? Often a development town like the typical one described above is literally surrounded by kibbutzim. And usually the social contact is zilch. If anything, the kibbutzim hire some workers from the town, not the best example of socialism at work. The standard of living on the kibbutz is way above that of the town. And the kibbutz movement is the backbone of the labor bureaucracy that ostensibly prevents the development of these "development towns." In terms of the modern social and economic problems of Israel, the kibbutz is removed from the struggle for socialism, no longer in the vanguard, in fact, and is a social and economic elite. The younger kibbutz members, if they stay on the kibbutz, are less concerned about the general struggle for socialism, taking even the life style more or less for granted. The kibbutz succeeded in its revolutionary purpose of creating an organized Jewish working class, and, in fact, the present state and its institutions, but is not geared to solving the problems of today, found in the development towns and in sections of the large cities. The kibbutz is still valuable as an example of communal life style, and even as an economic institution; and there *is* a potential for the kibbutzim assuming once more an active role in the large struggle. But something will have to stimulate this from the outside.

A more active struggle towards true socialism will come about with the development of a movement of lower-class workers in the cities and towns; a movement of organized leftist labor against the Histadrut bureaucracy, either from within or without the existing organizations. Progressives of the old left parties and intellectuals may support such a movement, but it will somehow have to generate a momentum of its own. The recent Israeli Black Panther incidents were certainly a hopeful sign, even though only a small faction of the movement talks in terms of class conflict as well as struggle for ethnic equality.

Problems of Urban Collectives

Here enters the idea of the radical *irbutz,* aimed at agitating for such a socialist movement by actually involving itself in the urban setting with its problems. They are obvious immediate problems in creating an urban commune that will succeed merely to exist, let alone build a revolution. The Sha'al group has always been in danger of falling apart communally. Let us analyze why this difficulty exists: The isolation of the kibbutz, with its obvious political disadvantages, does, however, create a ready-made setting for a successful community—owning its own means of production, working and consuming together, and apart from others. *Any* urban group is many times less isolated, making it very difficult to just stick together. Furthermore, a group like Sha'al, which neither owns its own means of production nor works together, has only the social bonds holding it together. From the outset this has been recognized as the major problem to the group, and for three years the *chaverim/ot* have claimed to be looking for a project which could involve the work of a large proportion of the members. This may be impossible, since most of the members joined specifically for their own personal occupational reasons; many even work outside the town in, which they live. It remains to be seen whether such a group, held together only by strong social bonds, will succeed.

Two Possible Solutions

Two possible solutions to this problem of lack of an important binding force in an urban collective had been proposed. Both are aimed directly at affecting politically the surrounding community and the country. (Some Sha'al members are somewhat politically involved in the town, but the group as a whole has chosen not to involve itself).

One idea has been to have a group enter a town or city

and, from the very start, own and work at its own means of production, a factory of sorts. One such proposal now in the planning stages is for a print shop that could serve as the nucleus for information and education for a national radical movement and serve the community at the same time. Of course the group would actively involve itself in the politics of the surrounding community. Problems and advantages of this approach include the following: Owning such separate means of production as a group would somewhat isolate the group from the surrounding workers but would serve very well to keep the group itself together and dedicated to its goals. Establishing such a project would be difficult, however, requiring capital at the very beginning, and if successful, immediate expansion. Help would have to come from somewhere on the outside, and the question is where? Probably *not* the Jewish Agency-Histadrut establishment that usually helps immigrants' enterprises.

A second idea is for a group whose primary motivation is the political one to live in a town, and all find jobs in the town, with many, if not all, as laborers in the factories. This would involve little initial capital and has the advantage of providing close and real proximity with the workers, the most advantageous situation for agitation. There is no common economic enterprise to hold the group together other than consumption, but common political action could play such a role to some extent. If a basic requirement in the establishment of the group is primacy of political motivations over personal and professional ones, then there is something concrete on which to build the community. This plan could also bring in new members very easily, even from the town itself. It has been a question of considerable debate whether such a commune should include professionals or only laborers. Most, however, are willing to include professionals to a certain extent: A majority of the members should be non-professional, and those who are should work within the town itself, and as radicals in their profession, thus serving the town in an important way. The crucial requirement would be that *all* members consider the political purpose of the community more important than professional and personal aspirations (high priority to a successful and happy community is assumed).

The Need for Garinim*

Experiments along these lines will have to be planned carefully, pioneering the development of communal institutions adaptable to urban life—strong enough to hold the groups together but flexible enough to allow the necessary interaction with the surrounding community. The biggest drawback, however, is that neither idea has yet been attempted. More and more radical Zionists are arriving in Israel all the time, and more are becoming active in movements outside of Israel. No *garinim* oriented strongly toward these or other possible plans have been formed, though many people are discussing the ideas. Disillusionment often sets in once a radical arrives in Israel and sees that little has been done, that many like him are also floating around.

Serious groundwork would be laid by those in Israel already, and contacts should be made with Israelis ready to participate in such projects. And in America and other countries, more serious efforts need be made to form groups dedicated to these ideals—groups that will arrive together in Israel to set up their communities. These groups have not come into being, often because there were not enough committed people in one place to form a real group. In spite of the disadvantages of lack of personal contact, perhaps we should form mail-order *garinim;* gatherings can be held, summers spent together, and perhaps a year either in America

---

* Literally, the Hebrew word for "seeds"—groups of people who collectively leave for Israel to settle there.

or Israel before the foundation of the community. We are spread out, and in spite of some growth, are not becoming a mass movement. No one will know if these nice ideas can work until we try, and that means serious commitment and organization of *garinim*.

Part Four
The Jewish Counterculture

Since Biblical times, the Jewish people, in the course of their wandering, have come in contact with many other cultures—some hostile, some friendly. In each case, the Jews and their hosts engaged in a cultural give-and-take. Jewish culture, then, is as varied as the number of stops along the way. In fact, it is unwise to speak of a monolithic "Jewish culture." The American Jew visiting Jewish communities in South America, India, or even Israel is likely to experience a form of "culture shock," so different are these styles of Jewish life.

If we cannot speak of a "Jewish culture," then how do we talk of a "Jewish counterculture"? The restless young Jews of today make no claims on *the* counterculture. In fact, it is just the flexibility of Jewish tradition which allows these young Jews to find the Jewish experience so relevant to their own.

Sifting through Jewish history, these young Jews—American born and bred—hope to develop an alternative to the sterility of American-Jewish existence. Perhaps five years ago, a young American Jew involved in poetry, or theater, or filmmaking, would not look to Judaism for inspiration. What, after all, did his Jewish education and experience offer? A cultural tradition gone sour, perhaps, but certainly no valuable insights into the human experience. The chaos of the immigrant generation and the marginality of their children provided America with a new genre: Abraham Cahan's *The Rise of David Levinsky*, Bernard Malamud's *The Assistant*, Meyer Levin's *The Old Bunch*, Michael Gold's *Jews Without Money*, Henry Roth's *Call it Sleep*, and later, Herman Wouk's *Marjorie Morningstar*, Philip Roth's *Goodbye, Columbus*, and Saul Bellow's *Adventures of Augie March* describe in fiction the torment of two generations of Jews learning to deal with America. In poetry and drama, too, Emma Lazarus, Morris Rosenfeld, Abraham Goldfaden, George S. Kaufman, Paddy Chayefsky, Clifford Odets, Karl Shapiro, and others expressed themselves through Jewish themes, not simply as artists "of Jewish origin."

The tensions and torments of the Jewish immigrant and his offspring were fertile ground for artistic expression. But what of the third and later generations? We have heard very little of their Jewish experience. The generation that reached maturity in the 1960's and 1970's, while energetic and perceptive in teaching the world the lessons of fall-out shelters, war, the campus revolt, civil rights, drugs, and of an awesome rootlessness, alienation, and predisposition for change, has been curiously silent about things Jewish.

The pieces in this chapter offer a brief taste of the cultural renaissance of this third generation of American Jews. By reaching back into Jewish tradition, by exploring the experiences of their own generation, and by creating for themselves a Jewish life style—these young Jews are writing an exciting new page in Jewish and American cultural history.

Listening to J.,
What J. said, or may have

David Nachum Yaakov Twersky

Listen to this story:

When Rav Kutler came to America,
he drove
a strange suburban route.

teaching, as he was, to open inside,
he pulled away the curtains in new jersey,
raise blinds. which reminds me,

in Vienna, Reegner says,
they threw him out
university windows.
some said they weren't
until fallen
silently cursing the perfect gardens,
while only dormitory away,

David Nachum Yaakov Twersky is a founder of the Jewish Student Press
Service and an undergraduate majoring in English literature at the City
College of New York. This poem is reprinted from *Response*, Spring, 1971,
by permission of the author and editor. Copyright © 1971 by *Response*
magazine.

the orchestra plays Bach
in a straight line
through stained glass.

teaching to open up a soul,
as he was,

driving, j. says, from lakewood
to brooklyn,
he wanted to shift lanes

in his mind he glanced quickly
from Hanasi to Ravinah.

as they were closer to toll
than to messiah, a disciple
warned (*oi,* he may know Talmud,
no traffic)
Rav, we'll back the cars up
from here to Philadelphia.

Never mind, he decided,
and it was law.

Later on,
as was their habit,
they pressed him for a story.

Later he explained
I saw that in our line
one hands the change
to a machine.
While in the one we rode through
a man's rough hand
outstretched over this diaspora.

It was better,
was it not?

that the man should not feel
a machine can do his work.

They say we learn from this
the traffic of a *tzaddik*.

Some say, (but very few believe),
the hudson parted when Rav Kutler died.

new year

___

d. a. levy

When i was
          six years old
we dipped
apple slices
& bread
in honey
touched small glasses
of wine
& sed 'to life'
          'to life'
that was the only time
my father ever hit me
his eyes were very sad
& he sort of walked away
knowing he was wrong
or that he couldnt reach me

___

d. a. levy shot himself to death in Cleveland on November 24, 1968. This poem was sent to *Jewish Currents* six weeks before the author's death. It had appeared earlier in *Connections,* an underground paper in Wisconsin. Among his other poems is one saying he had "decided to commit suicide at the age of 17." The poem appeared in *Jewish Currents,* September, 1969, and is reprinted by permission of *Jewish Currents* and its editor, Morris U. Schappes.

i dont think he knew who i was
perhaps even asking if i was really his son
that was 1948—it is now 1968 and i know
he is watching a football game on television
in another city—his grey hair
                    his sad eyes
and he is probably still wondering if i
am really his son
what father wants to admit that his
son really is a 'poet'

i think i was ten when i asked the difference
between christians & jews
and his reply was
'the jews think jesus was a bastard'
he was wrong again
the jews believe in living, the christians
believe in jesus and have formed a death cult
around his image
a cult dedicated to suffering & love
as a means of liberation
the jews know, that one becomes liberated
thru living, not *only* thru programmed acts
of masochism or blindness

it was sometime afterward
my father and i
went to a temple to hear
the services
                    sat down in time
                    to hear that haunting
                    language for just a moment
when someone told us we had to stand in the
back—we had chosen 'reserved seats'
seats that had been paid for
we left & it was thus i completed
my external jewish education

my father was right
we never visited another temple
& now i wonder how many jews are
destroyed in this country each year
my father with his lonely eyes
trying to return home
only to have the american god of money
slapped in his face
when we left it was as if
he passed the message on to me
'there are no jews left in this place'

and i spent years
trying to fill in that

hungry space denied me
on holidays i did not
know about i found myself
thinking of the old man
and later trying to remember
what i dreamt when i was
a child
i kept discovering his quietness
   when did the first images
   appear in my head?
'a place with sand where it was warm
the blue sky—strange trees'
      my fathers eye
had never turned from israel
i don't even know if he knew
what was inside his own head

once visiting hillel house
i was told about keeping
traditions alive
                  lighting candles

the secrets i learned from my father?
how does one pass them on?
            my fathers terrible eyes
            the loneliness

            flésh phrases like
            'genetic memory?'

this poem?
that i remember once
being free to walk
through all secret doors
to walk with a free people

where did i learn that

when i think of my father
i wonder if he can hear me

this poem?
for my father
who will someday be reborn in israel
& this poem
for my father
that i may once again be his son
& the name we carry
was once a name to be proud of

now it is new years 1968
in a barbarian country
that has always *felt*
alien to me

while blind men struggle
to keep traditions alive
my father watches football
games on television

to pass time
& i dream of his sad eyes
and i wonder about those blind men
do they ever wonder who wrote
their fucking traditions for them?

what songs will be sung
in israel for the young jews
beaten or murdered in the south
trying to keep alive
the internal spirit

what songs will be sung
in israel to remember
the young jews
who took drugs into eternity
trying to find the Spirit
they couldnt find in america

what songs will be sung
in israel to commemorate
the subtle murders
while rabbis danced the hora
ate dates & figs
& looked the other way

to keep traditions alive?

my father watched football
on television
his eye did not lose sight
of israel for even a moment—

and once a year
i break bread with him
quietly in my mind

Maybe

Danny Siegel

"Jew-Ostriches of the world unite!"

—Straight A. Marx

Maybe they don't know what they is doin
  even though they think they do
  or think they might
Maybe they is wrong
                all
                or partly so
                or just a little bit
    and they don't know
      or care to know
      or care to know that they don't know
Maybe.
Maybe they is just a little scared to face the fact
      that they ain't sure just what to do or think
      but then again factfacing ain't quite as easy as
                        factknowing or peoplefacing

Danny Siegel, born in Arlington, Virginia, has a B.S. from Columbia University, and a B.H.L. and M.H.L. from the Jewish Theological Seminary. This poem is reprinted from *Soulstoned* by permission of the author. Copyright © 1969 by Danny Siegel and Allan Sugarman.

We're the Ostrichjews
       (post June six-days
       chicken we're not no more)
     down Miamiway there's lots of sand where we put our
                              heads to hide into
     so we don't have to look to see what they don't
                             want to care to see
     even though they haven't bothered hiding hungup
                            heads down
          deep down deep in Southern Sand
       (ever notice how our heads don't get Miami
                        Sun-of-God Tan?
         cause we got our heads in sand
                     up to our necks
                     upside down
                     down to our necks)

They're just blind . . . them
     those birds will never see again
                 unless they get some
                 eyes from us
     we disenchanted Jewish anti-Jewestablishmentarian
                      kiddiefolks
     who so kindly forgot that one can't see
             or give his eyes to others
             or that worldmess ugliness
             looks awful blurrydark
             with heads deep two feet
             in Southern Sand

That makes sense
       we'll all rebel
       revolution über Alles
       we'll show them that
             that we ain't blind
             oh no we see
                 a lot of sand

we'll show the blind old bats how
                we don't like
                blindbattiness
we'll show them how to see
                since we're so
                good at seeing
JEW-OSTRICHES OF THE WORLD UNITE!

Jeweyes are hard to find around
        even harder than the fivecent see-gar that our
                        daddies wanted years ago
        rebbe's eyes that used to see the soul of all the world
                                and every little Jew
        bloodshot and all kinds of holy
            from hours and hours of Jewbook lookin
            dawndays latenites years of years
            lookin up to see where they were needed
                to straighten crooked lines in wobbly worlds
                to put a lotta little white where too much
                        black (sometimes bibleblack)
                                war paint
                    made things a little dorkydark
            to help a gropin blindman sit down in the
                                sunlight
                so's that he could feel the light
                even if he couldn't see it
Yes Charley Jeweyes are hard to find
        unless you got a lot of time to do some runnin
                        round the beach
        to see the sandlumps where the Jeweyes lie
                                buried
                                probably
        and that don't seem like too much
                        PesachKosherPepsigeneration fun
        in fact it's pretty stupid
        hey kid where you goin to
        Oh just down to beachville lookin for

some Jeweyes
(My son the beachcomber!)
It wouldn't even be so bad if we got blinded by the light of
God
and truth
and right
but we're just lousy *shmutzig** rebels
there's some things that we don't like
so we choose some other things we like and say
they're better
or at best the only way
today
to do it
or cause its different
Being different means being better
and being very different means being very better
and being as different as little-old-teenager can
be means
being little-old-teenager better
Man, there ain't nothin more different (better) than walkin
round on Collins†
on your hands (stark naked helps) singin
Lookie here
we're better (different)
bringin you the news of
different (better) things
to come
in this
young world
of ours
(now ain't the world just so much better?)
We're just lousy rebels, ain't we kiddies?
cause we don't see too well from two feet sand

---

* Messed up.
† Main Street in Miami Beach, Florida

                                        down under
                    our eyes is burnin and our brain don't work
                                           so well
                                 I can't imagine why
              (I thought that our *tsedrayte* heads work better
                                  always upside-down)
With so much water
            and blue Jewsky all around
                          this town
            I don't see why you choose
                        you Jews
                          to keep your heads in sandsville
You want to make some noise
            so call them Jew-ostrich people all together for
                                    the great big plop
            as everybody all together now on the upbeat
            has an uploose pullout
            a thousands-headed plop as everybody pulls out
                                    his Ostrichjeweyed head
                                    from Southern Sand
            then the greater bigger whoosh as thousands
              (thas right, man, thousands—it's gonna be a
                                      sublime moment)
                    thousands lay their birdybodies down
                                    on Southern Sand
            to let their eyeballs rest *a bisl** on the big blue
                                                      Jewsky
            that's been there all the time
                                  though hard to see
                                  through Southern Sand
            and since no grass don't grow nohow
                                    on Southern Sand
              but natural sunshine lights you up instead
              well then lightup under Southern Sun

---

* a little bit

and let your upside-down cerebral hangups do
a semi-modified flip-trip
(no flop included)
and relax
There's somethin nice about this sittin on the sand
and lookin up at a Jew
bluesky
its quality clarity goes on forever
wayway out and
wayway in
and nice and warm
and sorta quiet
kinda gets you somewhere down inside the *kishkas*
(Middle Malay for the Latin *kishka-kishkae*)
gets you kinda thinkin bout the world
gets you kinda clearly thinkin
gets you askin all them questions you done clean
forgot to ask
cause your mind was sorta gettin eaten by the crabs
when you used to live headdown downside uptight
Sorta nice jus lookin up not down at your own Jewblue
Jewsky
compliments of our friend
*HaShem**
the Good Old Man
who went to all that
trouble givin us a sky
to look at
(Gee, that's awfly nice
and He didn't even ask to have His ~~Tetrachloride~~
~~Tetrahedron~~
~~Tetragrammaton~~ John Hancock
put on a plaque on the wall)
"This sky contributed by the Lord (or is it

---

* The Name, God's Name

Endowed by the Lord)
to the Jews of all the world."
Bet you never thought the sky belonged to us alone
it don't belong to no birdmen-astronauts
(That there is the stratosphere, son, N.A.S.A. Route
Eleventy-Four to Lunacy)
and others call it heaven
(where they think they think they gonna go
when the last freighttrain
blows the last whistle)
and the starry general LeMay, Curtiss E. thinks its
how high we oughtta blow
them Vietcong baby chilluns

But it's *our* sky
and it goes all the way round this world, Baby
and it did
in the days that used to wuz it
and it will
in the days that gonna be
and that no-plaque Lord done put it there for us to look at
whenever we decide to see what
we oughtta see
or oughtta wanta see
Now let's use them nonblue Jeweyes to look
at Jewblue skies
for just a little while
and forget the little broad who's with you on the beach
just forget the little broad
and leave yourself to see
if you can see
what you can see
Just lie like
quiet like
and listen to the waves
and all that Godblessed silence
and ask yourself,

"Self, why is the bluesky Jewish?"
that's bein different
    cause no one ask that kind of question
    cause they're double dangerous
    cause then the other questions just come pourin in
    like
        "Self, what are we doin here?"
    and
        "Self, why are we askin all these
                  Jewquestions?"
And so you'll want to take a break
           from askin
           cause it jiggles up your mind
        and cause you don't quite know the answers
    (not like the answers on the school examinations
        true-false
        right-wrong
        triple-choice
        blot out the blank
        guess wrong-don't leave blank
        blankety blank blank
    which, because *the* answer is there
    you hence and therefore subsequently
                consequently find it maybe
    easy, likeable, warm as a pistolhandle,
             and very very stupid)

So take a break
    and watch the peoples passin by
    just drop those nonblue Jeweyes
            and watch the kinda people
                walkin by
    the ones who wonder why
        you ain't havin fun
        and movin with the crowd
            (Old Celtic for *chevra*)
        making that big move

                                and makin it mighty fast
                        just keep movin
                        don't just lie there on the sand
Those is your blueeyed
        trueblue buddies
        the ones you sorta love
                        kinda
        but you shouldn't hate em
        and then again you shouldn't kinda sorta love em
        you really oughtta love em
                        whatever that means
And now the fun begins
        cause you don't love em very much
        sometimes you don't even like em
        and so you look back up to
                        bluejew Skysville
        (not to be confused with Jewskylakesville) *
        and that don't even help
        cause it's gettin mighty hot
        and you're roastin just a little
                        burnin up
        what's He doin to me BlueJewSkyGod
        what's He want

(Logically, if you stop to think, there are really only two you
                                know rational choices:
        Number 1—I may alter my reclining bod position by
                        turning over (it's called Revolutionizing the
                        Bod) and cookin the other side to a medium
                        brown while lookin at the sand.
    Or Number 2—I may get off my fat Jew*tuchiss*† and
                                move out of the sun

---

* Sky Lake is a section of Miami Beach where the more well-to-do Jews
are making the scene.
† rearbutt bottom

and if I move, whereto shall I move to
I can always go with them
                    cause they're movin
or maybe go somewhere else
                    that's somethin else
wherever Somewhereelseville may be)

November 17, 1968
Miami Beach, Florida

April 18, 1971
Nisan 23, 5731

Mark Hurvitz

The week of Pesach, the festival of our liberation is over.
Today is the ninth day of the counting of the Omer which we
will continue another forty days until
Shabuoth: the celebration of our receiving the Torah.
During the period between these two ancient holidays we
commemorate the occurrence of two recent events
Yom ha' Shoah—the day of the Holocaust
Yom ha'Atzmaut—the independence of the State of Israel
In this context

Shalom

Our liberation from slavery is symbolically complete;
wandering now in that chaotic period immediately following
the winning of our freedom,
we are faced with the devastation of one of our largest and
most creative communities.

Mark Hurvitz is student ombudsman for the Jewish Federation of Los
Angeles, a member of the Jewish Radical Community, and editor of *Davka*,
where the poem first appeared in the Summer, 1971, issue. He also studies
music at California State College, Los Angeles. The poem is reprinted by
permission of the author.

We have returned to our oasis and have begun digging wells
      resolving never to be set adrift in the sands again.
The winds around us are turbulent and the risen dust clouds
      our way.
We have not yet received our Law and although we are
      liberated, we are not at peace.
This week (Shavuah ha'Shoah) the scar that remains from our
      experience with Europe,
glows bright as we heighten our awareness of the Nazi horrors,
      Christian complicity and our own cowering silence.

"I only followed orders" was the answer:
      as they drove their chariots after us into the mud,
      as they aimed their artillery at our decimated bastions in
      Warsaw:
and as the waters of the sea flood over them we do not rejoice.
And today we cry out as our host nation strays deeper into the
      jungle getting sucked in by the mud:
Obeying orders.
      To resist!
the struggle against all odds
that defiance
in the midst of the passivity
      of not "causing trouble"

      Today one quarter of our people
      brothers and sisters
are in turmoil and doubt as their host becomes more
      repressive.
A handful of them, aware of our interwoven future have
      resolved to cause trouble.
Our host and theirs strain to reach an accord.
That oasis we share and dream of is the fulcrum of their
      antagonism
And we, aware of our impotence, scream and shout
      if for no other reason than to say to our children:
we were not silent.

We have been guests all over the world and have learned that
    a host does as it pleases.
In our oasis the wells are dug and irrigation has begun.
Only when we are planted in its fertile soil will we blossom,
    bring forth fruit and flourish.
Our contemporary resistance is not limited to firing small arms
    smuggled in through sewers,
but offers us opportunities for harvesting fruits and reaping
    fields.
This struggle shapes our Way through the wilderness
till that time when the pine and cypress trees we plant
will shade their own seedlings growing wild in the replanted
    forests:
We will be secure in our Law and sustained in peace.

Evolution of the Jew as Poet

Joel Rosenberg

. . . the world is laden with so many obvious needs. This we
know. They hang like stones or clumsy ancient coins on the
silver chains of dreams, dropping to our heads, bobbing to our
unready touch. One need not be a Jew or Sufi, poet or mad-
man, to know what the world needs. That we are torn apart by
barbed wire, poison gas, usury, abstraction, and loneliness does
not surprise. That we are prisoners even of our hopes and acts
of generosity may be harder to understand. I say it is the poet
who must catch the Way. The Jew as poet who is most a Jew.
But that's not all. I say, as well, we have only the shadow of
understanding about what is poetry. The real name of what I
mean is in disguise. A Moslem scholar says with embarrassment that Muhammad was a poet (and that the *aswak* of
Mecca and the tents of Hijaz were brought with a song). Say,
as well, Jesus and Isaiah, and Moshe de Leon—that they were
poets. Spinoza shows that even abstract language can become
a poem, depending on one's *kavanah*. I say, there are rabbis

Joel Rosenberg, a former member of Havurat Shalom in the Boston area,
is currently pursuing a Ph.D. program in the history of consciousness at the
University of California at Santa Cruz, where he is teaching a course on
aspects of Jewish mysticism and social history. This article is reprinted
from *Response* (#11), Fall, 1971, by permission of the author and editor.
Copyright © 1971 by *Response* magazine.

all around us, in disguise. There are men who are pillars of the world unknown to us. There are beggars and despised ones who will put us to the test. Every sunset that is ignored will ring like a cash register at the gates of death. Every child rotting in Bengali streets will become an earthquake. I say, with Blake, that we will have to jump through our eyeballs and grab the world vigorously, that the rising sun is no flat, abstract orange disk but a band of angels crying "Holy, holy, holy is the Lord of Hosts!" With imagination we redeem the world. Pictures, not "symbols." Animals that live and deeds raised to the stage of poetry. Alphabet letters that prance and Heraclitean fire that evaporates the sleepy bureaucratic fog. But I don't mean your tender, pansy, effete poets. I don't mean your closet Jews and court painters. I say that works of imagination are not "occasional pieces," are not the trivialities of a lazy, royal diversion. But I mean cities with drinkable air. I mean countries with open borders. I mean children raised to love their play, and who see their work as play. I mean cities of students, whole countries that are schools. I mean great-grandfathers at their tents telling ancient tales. I mean mosques with Jews, churches with Muslims, synagogues with Christians. I mean men and women alive as partners, sharing work and sharing birth. I mean the cherishing of silence.

Three Cartoons by Jerry Kirschen

Jerry Kirschen was born in 1938 and settled in Israel in 1971. The cartoon strips are reprinted by permission of the author and the Jewish Student Press Service.

joke time

As activists take to the streets to rail at the RUSSIAN PIGS who oppress our people the "leaders" of "major" jewish organizations speak out against extremism... they express the fear that the activists will only make the situation worse... this joke is dedicated to these concerned leaders...

the scene is a small town in europe... the time - a few short years ago... the nazis have just killed every jew in town... when suddenly the nazis discover two jews they missed... the two are marched to the edge of town, stood against a brick wall... and, as the nazi firing squad aims its rifles, one jew says to the other...

Say! when they kill you with a firing squad you're entitled to one last request...I'm going to ask for a cigarette

Keep quiet!..you'll get us in trouble!

jerry Kirschen.

The *Havurot:* An Experiment in Jewish Communal Living

Stephen C. Lerner

Two views of 1970: Somerville, Massachusetts. In a yellow frame house on College Avenue, seven young people sit around a bare table with books before them. Their clothes, the hair, are very much in the style of this college and graduate generation. But the six men wear *kipot;* the books are copies of a Chassidic text. On the wall a sign announces: "*Shavat vayinafash*—slow down and live."

Cambridge, Massachusetts. In crowded Harvard Square, a few miles away from Somerville, six girls pass, beating tambourines and chanting "*hare krishna.*" Two young women sell incense sticks and one fellow stands with a sign: "Philosopher available."

Stephen C. Lerner is rabbi of Tifereth Israel-Town and Village Synagogue in New York. A contributor to English and Hebrew journals on Jewish affairs, he is a member of the Editorial Board of *Conservative Judaism* and chairman of the Publications Committee, Central Youth Commission, of the United Synagogue of America. This essay first appeared in *Conservative Judaism*, 24, 3, Spring, 1970, copyright © by the Rabbinical Assembly of America, and reprinted by permission of the publishers and author.

We have come to expect the Cambridge scene. We have come to lament—and accept—that young people, a disproportionate number of them Jews, go questing after every offbeat movement. For many, however, the Somerville scene is a surprise. The modest house on College Avenue is the home of Havurat Shalom, an experiment which marks a new direction in American Jewry and which, for many in America's Jewish leadership, is as threatening as the action in Harvard Square. In much the same way that the firebrands of Orthodoxy castigate Conservative Judaism more than Reform, because Conservatism is close enough to the real thing to confuse and mislead, there are many who worry more about Havurat Shalom and its younger counterpart in New York than about the more prevalent manifestations of young Jewish activity across America.

Havurat Shalom does not afford a foretaste of the messianic age, but neither does it presage the fires of Gehenna. It is a serious attempt to provide a new alternative to the traditional modes of Jewish study carried out in seminaries, Hebrew colleges, and universities. Dissatisfied with the model of Jewish *Wissenschaft*, it values the religious quest above the dispassionate search for knowledge. Turned off by the formal and often cold relations between faculty and students in the established institutions, its members seek to develop an atmosphere of fellowship in which serious study is pursued without fixed lines separating teacher from pupil.

The Havurat Shalom Community Seminary opened in the autumn of 1968. After a year and a half of operation, it has its own building, approximately thirty-eight members, and an *élan* that few institutions possess. By virtually any yardstick, it has made more than modest progress toward its goals and it has stimulated the establishment of a similar, if less ambitious, group in New York as well as rudimentary organizations elsewhere. The basically anti-institutional nature of the *havurah* may endanger its long-term survival, but at this writing it constitutes as vibrant a center of Jewish life as may be found in these United States.

Origins

The idea of a *havurah* did not begin with the Boston group. The notion had been in the air for some years among young Jewish intellectuals. More than six years ago Rabbi Jacob Neusner spoke about *havurot* or fellowships which existed in Talmudic times, and commended their application to our day. The Reconstructionist movement had also talked of building *havurot*. It remained for Rabbi Arthur Green, a brilliant if erratic Seminary graduate, to give shape to the amorphous concepts. Rabbi Green traces the genesis of his active interest in the project to a discussion, while still a Seminary student, with Father Dan Berrigan, a radical priest, about the underground church and the inner-city Protestant parishes. Rabbi Green began to speculate about the establishment of an experimental synagogue where intensive study would be carried on and where a more total sense of community would prevail. He explored the subject with Alan Mintz, a Columbia student and former National President of United Synagogue Youth (U.S.Y.), who was also deeply interested in such a venture.

Returning to graduate study at Brandeis after his Seminary ordination in 1967, Rabbi Green pursued his ideas in discussions with Rabbi Albert Axelrad, the dynamic director of the Brandeis Hillel Foundation. Green was especially troubled by the fact that many young religious seekers found nothing of value in Judaism, while Axelrad's particular concern was the alienation of politically active youth from Jewish life. They hoped a new kind of institution might meet both needs. "When we realized we weren't out of our minds," as Green phrased it, they began to look in earnest for students, teachers, and an advisory committee. All three searches proved successful. The Havurat Shalom Community Seminary opened its doors in the fall of 1968, with twelve students and a faculty including Rabbi Zalman Schachter and some of the brightest recent Seminary graduates. Its impressive advisory committee included leaders from all walks of Jewish religious and intellectual life: Brandeis Professor Nahum Glatzer, *Commentary* writer Milton Himmelfarb, Hillel directors Max Ticktin and Richard Israel, and Conservative Rabbis Jack Riemer and Herschel Matt. (In most cases, however, the men on the advisory committee lent nothing more than their names to the enterprise.)

The students who found their way to the *havurah* had impressive academic credentials, and most had good Jewish backgrounds. One chose the *havurah* and the Harvard Graduate School of Education over the Jewish Theological Seminary; one came after having been rejected by the Seminary; another came from Shlomo Carlebach's West Coast House of Love and Prayer after being somewhat unhappy there. Personal association with Green and Axelrad brought some members; others were recommended by sympathetic Hillel directors. Not all found the *havurah* to their liking. Three dropped out during the first year, variously finding the center too Jewish, too "straight," or too communal. Axelrad dropped out as well, citing the demands of family and Hillel. But most of the students continued and during its second year of operation the enrollment has grown significantly. In New York, meanwhile, Alan Mintz and a group of graduate students formed the New York Havurah in the fall of 1969.

Though it is at odds with the shape of America's educational institutions, the *havurah* necessarily maintains some of their trappings. It is chartered by the Commonwealth of Masachusetts as an educational, nonprofit corporation. Its full-time students (those taking a four-course program) may receive 4-D draft classifications, since Havurat Shalom is recognized by the authorities as a rabbinical seminary. (Green is quick to point out that only half the students have availed themselves of the 4-D's.) It projects a four-year curriculum leading to the title of *haver* (fellow). There has been some discussion about the future ordination of rabbis. According to Green, those students desiring ordination would be given a bibliography of Hebrew texts and secondary sources which they would be required to master. Then a board of examiners, consisting of the ordained rabbis on the faculty with the possible addition of outside rabbis, would pass on the candidates' qualifications.

Communal Framework

The absence of sophisticated administrative procedures makes it difficult to gauge enrollment accurately, but there are apparently 38 members this year, of whom 18 are full-time students, 6 are part-time students, 7 are teachers, and 7 are wives who belong to the *havurah* but neither study nor teach. There are also wives who are student-members. Admission to the *havurah* is not easily gained. The members feel that the size of the group must be limited in order to maintain a communal experience. Some may be admitted next year to replace those who drop out or go to Israel. The institution, according to Rabbi Green, is interested in Jewish religious seekers rather than in those with either an "Orthodox mentality" or a Jewish secularist orientation.

All members are expected to participate in the religious and communal life of the fellowship, in addition to its study program. There are financial obligations as well. Each member, whether teacher or student, is expected to contribute $500 toward the upkeep of the house on College Avenue. A $10,-000 grant from the Danforth Foundation enabled the group to make an $8,000 down payment on the building. The group employs a part-time secretary; two of the younger teachers receive small salaries; the other members of the faculty receive no pay.

Rabbi Green hopes that the *havurah* will eliminate the category of part-time student (except for wives) in the future, and permit only such outside graduate study as dovetails with the learning at the *havurah*. At the present time the group is far from this ideal; nor is it true that all members share equally in the life of the *havurah*. Rabbi Joseph Lukinsky participates at best tangentially in the group's activities, but the *havurah* appears content to retain him as a member. (Lukinsky is a rare person who manages to have entree to and to feel at home in a multitude of Jewish spheres. He is a member of the *havurah*, a faithful *davener* at Brookline's Congregation Kehillath Israel, and a faculty member of both Brandeis University and the Jewish Theological Seminary's Teachers Institute.)

While the institution has no true hierarchy, and lines of authority are fluid (all are equal members), there is nevertheless a leader—Rabbi Arthur Green. The force of Green's personality, his primary role in the founding of *havurah*, his devotion to its goals, have made him clearly a sort of *moreh d'atra*, although the term *"rebbe"* might more properly describe his position. Green has always been a seeker, fascinated by *agadah*, cabala, and Chassidism. He was once described by a fellow student as an *epikoros* who *davens* like a Chassid. Green is more interested in experimenting with the full range of religious tradition than in maintaining the *halakhah*, and the *havurah* generally shares these emphases. As Havurat Shalom's most constant shaping force, Green's charismatic personality has led the institution along a certain line of development. Its spirit, as Green defines it, is the "ethic of becoming a religious human being through the sources of Judaism rather than through the ordinary concepts of Jewish commitment." To this end, there is a great stress on developing meaningful prayer styles, and an openness to fellow members and to the tradition. Saturday morning services, informal *Kabbalat Shabbat* gatherings, a group *seudah shelishit*, communal weekly meals, and a general willingness to work together and share chores all contribute to the growth of a total religious and interpersonal relationship. The spirit of Buber's writing reigns supreme.

A Day of Spirituality

The one *havurah* activity open to the public at large has been the worship service on Shabbat mornings. Many outsiders come to *daven* with the group regularly, and onlookers and observers come from near and far. Services are held in the main room of the building on College Avenue. Many sit on cushions scattered on the floor. A different *hazzan* each week has leeway in leading the service. The traditional liturgy is followed for *Shacharit,* and when English is used it is chanted to traditional *niggunim.* The weekly Torah portion is not read in its entirety but is studied intensively, utilizing various approaches. Sometimes the atmosphere is that of a Quaker meeting; people read silently until someone wishes to comment. At other times there is simultaneous Hebrew and English reading (Hebrew in an undertone and English aloud). There is no *Musaf,* but services conclude with singing and dancing.

What the *havurah* has created, it may be said, is a contemporary *shtiebel,* where intensity of feeling and unembarrassed exuberance are combined with study in a modern vein. Even those for whom prayer is not a central quest find that participation in a service conducted in an atmosphere of fellowship has heightened their religious perceptions.

The moderately traditional style of worship evolved by the *havurah* is typical of what has transpired there in other areas of Jewish practice. Green admits that he has been surprised by the marked growth or reemergence of respect for the Jewish tradition on the part of most members. The Shabbat in particular is a meaningful experience. Green estimates that approximately ninety percent observe the Sabbath (not necessarily according to *halakhic* guidelines). Seventy-five percent of the members maintain kosher homes while only a third observe *kashrut* outside the home. One quarter have gone beyond traditional Jewish law and are now vegetarians. These figures indicate where the *havurah* differs from a more typical sampling of committed American Jews. Within the American community, more Jews observe *kashrut* as a symbol of family loyalty, of national identity, than observe Shabbat as a day of spirituality, of relationship between man and man and between man and his God. In the *havurah,* however, it is not the claim of group loyalty which draws the members' allegiance, but rather the potential for religious growth.

Emphasis on Study

Study is at the center of the *havurah* program as it is at the center of the Jewish tradition. Last year, courses offered included a study of Buber's *I and Thou;* a survey of the biblical, legal, and *agadic* sources relating to Sukkoth; Zalman Schachter's varieties of spiritual quest which included a lab in *davening* techniques; an introduction to Talmud; an introduction to Jewish mysticism; and courses in *Siddur* and *Chumash.* In addition, students arranged individual readings with the members of the faculty. Besides Rabbis Lukinsky, Schachter, and Green, last year's faculty also included Rabbis Edward Feld, David Goodblatt, Burton Jacobson, and Mr. Michael Fishbane, an instructor in Bible at Brandeis University. By September, 1969, Zalman Schachter had returned to his academic post in Canada, David Goodblatt had left to study with Jacob Neusner at Brown, and Edward Feld had become the Hillel Director at the University of Illinois. They were replaced by equally able and interesting figures: Rabbis Everett Gendler (see page 209), Hillel Levine (see page 183), and Michael Swirsky, plus nonrabbinic faculty.

The current courses in large measure are following last year's pattern, although there is no apparent sequential arrangement to them. Among other offerings, Rabbi Green is teaching two courses in Chassidism, Rabbi Jacobson a course in Amos, and Rabbi Lukinsky a course in Talmud. Rabbi Gendler offers a course in male and female symbolism in the Jewish tradition and, with Rabbi Levine, leads a seminar in Judaism and contemporary social problems.

The choice of courses seems to derive from the interests and competence of the teachers. Given the general tendency of the *havurah,* it is not surprising to note that formal courses have as yet not been offered in such classical fields as medieval

Hebrew poetry, medieval Jewish philosophy, modern Hebrew literature, or Jewish history, and that, by traditional standards, a disproportionate amount of time has been devoted to mystical, mythical, and Chassidic thought.

Perhaps the most old-fashioned program of the *havurah* is the *bet midrash* organized this year. This is designed for the small number of members with weak or nonexistent backgrounds in Jewish learning. These students study Hebrew, *Chumash* with Rashi, *Siddur,* and other traditional texts five days a week, four hours a day.

Although it is extremely difficult to judge the academic standards of the *havurah* faculty and students on the basis of a few cursory visits, it is this writer's feeling that they are an unusually able group. Except for Albert Axelrad and Zalman Schachter, the rabbis have been graduates of the Jewish Theological Seminary, generally among the Seminary's outstanding students of recent years. Whatever their deficiencies as accomplished scholars, they are a knowledgeable, imaginative, and committed group although they are not *baale halakhah* in the *yeshivah* sense.

A session with Rabbi Gendler, for example, leaves one more impressed with the moral and visionary concerns of the man than with the rigorousness of his knowledge. At a class the writer attended, Gendler read and discussed a Sephardic-cabalistic compilation for Tu b'Shvat, *Sefer Pri Etz Hadar.* Interspersed among his grapplings with the Hebrew names of the various fruits and his remarks about the significance of each kind, were asides about the importance of developing contemporary rituals for the holiday, and of creating a mood which would enhance appreciation of the world of nature. After class, Gendler told the writer that he wanted to reintegrate Judaism with the vegetation cycle. He sought to "provide the *Kudsha B'rich Hu* with His consort," to "lead Him out of solitude," and to develop a Jewish style in which "rabbinic asceticism and *mitnagdic* defensiveness" were not the norm.

Classes were held in an atmosphere of informality. Interchange between student and teacher was easy and pleasant and there seemed to be a genuine interest in learning. Green's intermediate-level class in Chassidic texts, for example, was marked by interesting comments about Catholic quietism and Agnon, and references to the *Zohar*, as well as close scrutiny of the class text, *Sefer Ba'al Shem Tov*. Each of the seven students participated, and the discussion was intelligent if not illuminating.

The Haverim: Attitudes and Activities

To this writer, the most remarkable revelation is that the students are clearly contented. Whereas students all over the country express widespread dissatisfaction with institutions of higher learning, both Jewish and secular, the members of the *havurah* actually like their courses. According to Joseph Riemer, a graduate of Queens College and a product of New York *yeshivot*, the teachers are "very competent and very inspiring." He praised the atmosphere of "fellowship with people of my generation" in which study was carried on. For Riemer as well as for others, study in the *havurah's* religious environment contrasted favorably with the nonreligious, depersonalized approach which they believe is common to universities and seminaries alike. For some, the *havurah* represents the essence of *Torah lishmah*. Other mystically oriented young people seek exposure to the Jewish tradition as a source of nourishment. Richard Siegel, Brandeis 1969, was excited by a college course in Eastern religion; at the same time, he realized that "there were Jewish parallels to Eastern concepts." He became steadily more interested in religious attitudes and discovered that an intended career in law was not for him. Wishing to continue his religious search, he came to Havurat Shalom. He has found his choice a good one: "I'm engaging in the most serious study I've ever done in my educational life, in the most positively creative atmosphere I've ever been in." This is not the sort of comment we expect to hear from a student in an American Jewish academy.

While the mood of the *havurah* is introspective, the image of an urban commune or latter-day Essenic settlement is not entirely accurate. Most of the members are involved in outside activities. Rabbi Green had been a graduate student at Brandeis until January and currently lectures to Jewish organizations on the theme "A Critique of the Jewish Community." Rabbi Gendler is a member of Packard Manse, an ecumenical retreat in Stoughton. Rabbi Jacobson is principal of the Temple Emunah religious school in Lexington. Joseph Riemer is principal of the Kehillath Israel Hebrew high school in Brookline. Others are graduate students, Hebrew teachers, or Jewish youth leaders. Furthermore, while political activism is not the major thrust of *havurah* life, members of the seminary were active in the Washington protest against the war in Vietnam, and in the Boston campaign to pressure the Council of Jewish Federations and Welfare Funds to allocate more money for Jewish education and Jewish culture.

Though many members work in the community, a definite current of antagonism to existing Jewish institutions and a clear sense of apartness and superiority do exist. The members see themselves as nonconforming young Jews. Some do, however, wish to become new-style Jewish leaders who would attempt to revitalize the Jewish community. For this group, Jewish education, Jewish community work, or Hillel positions are all viable options. The one field excluded by virtually every member is the congregational rabbinate. For other members, communal matters are of no great concern. Indeed, as Green noted, there has never been a resolution of the basic tension between those who see Havurat Shalom as a center for the creation of new types of religious leadership and those who see the fellowship only as a place in which the members may experiment with new forms of religious and community life.

While the *havurah* judges the Jewish community and finds

it grossly wanting, the "Establishment" is somewhat equivocal in its views of the fellowship. A leading Conservative rabbi in the Boston area welcomed the contribution of *havurah* members to Jewish education and youth work. He felt that they were fine teachers and had good rapport with adolescents. As for the *havurah* itself, "It's a kind of *shtiebel*. . . . But I don't mean that as a criticism. I was raised in a *shtiebel* and I like them." Rabbi Herbert Rosenblum of Temple Emunah (Lexington), where the school principal and members of the teaching staff are drawn from Havurat Shalom, agrees that the presence of the fellowship has enriched Jewish education in the Boston area. Nevertheless, he laments the isolationist stance of the *havurah:*

> To the extent that they may verbalize the psychotic gulf between themselves and the synagogue, they have made an absolute type statement which is just a misconception. People change and mature, synagogues change, and perhaps a meeting can take place in a more relative way, if not completely. . . . These kids are still fighting to retain the umbilical cords of Camp Ramah and their college experience. They are postponing the acceptance of mature responsibility.

Professor Jacob Neusner, too, has expressed reservations about contemporary *havurot*. In a recent column in the *Boston Jewish Advocate* he wrote:

> One of their problems is the selfishness of the quest; another is the episodic quality of their fellowships, which have no place for married, mature people already embarked on the adventure of raising children and making a living.
> The *havurot* depend on a great purpose to unite the *haverim* and give their social life worthwhile tasks. Otherwise, they are destined to continue their present irrelevant and solipsistic life, to concentrate on their spiritual belly-buttons, so to speak, and to exclude from their concern the large part of the Jewish people.

At the Jewish Theological Seminary (J.T.S.), the *havurah* receives both support and criticism. Stories of the real and imagined doings of *havurah* members at Camp Ramah in Palmer, Massachusetts, and vague reports of excessive permissiveness in Somerville are factors in the critical assessments. In turn, some of the *haverim* feel that Ramah leaves much to be desired religiously.

Rumors of drug-taking at the *havurah* seem greatly exaggerated. In fact, one of the few rules existing in the *havurah* is that there may be no use of drugs on communal property. (Another rule is that only kosher dairy cuisine may be served at communal meals.) Of course some *havurah* members may experiment with drugs privately. Nonetheless, Rabbi Green calls the atmosphere "post-drug"; he feels that the challenge now is not drugs. Anyone who wants to can get high, but "the question is how to integrate the highs into daily living."

Challenge to the Seminaries

The impact, actual and potential, of the *havurot* on student recruitment is one that Jewish seminaries will have to treat seriously. The Jewish Theological Seminary has already lost one applicant to Havurat Shalom, as has the Jewish Institute of Religion (J.I.R.). The challenge becomes clearer if one looks at the roster of the New York Havurah, the Boston group's younger relation. Virtually all its members have strong backgrounds in Jewish learning and Jewish leadership. Among the nineteen members, one is a Jewish Theological Seminary drop-out, two are Seminary rejects, two are current rabbinical students at the Seminary, and one is a Seminary graduate. There are rabbinical students at the Jewish Institute of Religion, one has withdrawn, and one is on leave from that school. Others at one time or another considered applying to one of the seminaries. Thus, this group may exert a strong pull on present or prospective seminaries by providing a supplement or alternative to studies in "establishment" institutions.

At present, the New York Havurah represents the same anti-institutional and communal tendencies as its New England prototype, but differs somewhat from it. Both as a group and as individuals, its members are much more involved in liberal or left-wing political and social action projects. But it is not yet an all-encompassing framework. Generally, its members see the *havurah* as a supplement to other areas of study and community activity in which they are engaged— often together. For most, it is an attempt to build a religious community of people who share similar concerns—politically, societally, and religiously. As one member explained his dissatisfaction with "normal" Jewish life, "Why spend Shabbat with people with whom one wouldn't spend the weekdays?" Its members from the seminaries, upset with the matter-of-fact careerism and formality of their institutions, find that the *havurah* gives them a community in which they may truly participate. Ronnie Kronish, Brandeis 1968, and Arthur Ruberg, Haverford 1968, students at J.I.R. and J.T.S. respectively, hope that what is created at the *havurah* can be a paradigm for the Jewish community—more concern, more fellowship, more real religious learning. Not everyone shares these hopes. Rabbi David Sperling, J.T.S. 1967, has no illusions about American Jewry. "Its future," he quipped, "is at Kennedy Airport." But study and prayer with this fellowship have brought him renewed appreciation for religious study and for the religious life. "I got positively high on *tefillot*," he noted when speaking about a recent Shabbat service.

Less structured as to communal programs and less demanding in terms of study requirement, the New York Havurah has begun to build a spirit in which learning, prayer, community and social action are embraced as vital norms. Nevertheless, it lacks a dominant and guiding voice like Green's, and the requirements for participation are so minimal as to be almost nonexistent. Most members feel that they should give more time to the fellowship, but since all are involved in other ventures, this is most difficult. The future of the New York Havurah is still questionable. It may develop a total community experience—or it may become an "after-hours" Jewish study group with the power to grant 4-D's.

Living Option—or Historical Footnote

At this junction both *havurot* seem remarkably successful, but they could break up at any time. They have little institutional structure and no real lines of authority. There are, as noted above, tensions between the socially committed who turn outward to the community and the religious seekers who turn inward to the self. Then again, the *havurot* may currently demand too much or too little. A knowledgeable observer told me that Havurat Shalom recently has been challenged by the possible resignation of a group of members who seek an even more total communal experience—perhaps in Israel—than the group now provides. Finally, there is the potential and real conflict between the full-time and part-time members. These problems may be more real for the Massachusetts fellowship which has a fairly clear-cut idea of its aims, than for the New York group.

Whatever their success, the *havurot* face recurring knotty questions. It is difficult to see how the *havurah* pattern could be followed in America, outside of a few centers where extra-institutional scholars and rabbis are fortuitously gathered. By cutting themselves off from the existing "establishment" institutions, the *havurot* may simultaneously limit the number of knowledgeable resource personnel available for additional groups. Surely, it is totally unrealistic to expect that *havurot* in other cities will have rabbis of the caliber of Green, Levine, and Swirsky available to them if they write off the synagogues and their professional leadership.

Most unsettling and most short-sighted of all is the facile way in which the *haverim* scornfully condemn the institutions of the Jewish community. Most had good Jewish backgrounds;

many were active in Ramah, U.S.Y., and Conservative synagogues; a much smaller number were active in the Reform
movement. Yet despite their positive experiences, few enter-
tain any real hope for the synagogue. For them, the congregation and the congregational rabbinate are not where the action
is. And perhaps, in view of the existing synagogues, the
haverim may be right. However, there is no law which says
that congregations cannot change, and no unwritten law
denying the possibility of *havurot* being formed within existing
congregations. Few of the *haverim* consider this to be a
realistic goal, for they seem to share a certain Puritan sense of
the corruption of the existing order and the concomitant requirement for a New Zion. With their generational obsessions
and their biases against buildings and budgets and the bourgeois, they refuse to grant that within synagogues one may
find small numbers of like-minded people, rabbinic and lay,
for whom study is important, prayer a challenge, and community a desideratum. They want little part in supporting this
group, in strengthening the content and quality of the synagogue program, in acting as the leaven within the larger congregation. Ultimately, they are acting out, in the Jewish
sphere, the broad generational rebellion. They want to study
with and learn from people of their generation or close to it
(the exigencies of serious Jewish study may demand that the
havurah members trust people until they're 40 or there-
abouts!), to pray with them, to live and interact with them.
Clearly, they think that they can't "do their thing" meaningfully
with the corrupted or deadened elders.

Havurah members are willing to work with Jewish youth
whom they, like the radical movements, consider good material
to mold. In this regard, it is incorrect to suggest, as Professor
Neusner does, that they exist in splendid spiritual isolation.
Most of the *haverim* in Somerville do sally forth regularly into
the community, nourished by their *havurah* experience, to
teach and to lead Jewish youth. However, they share with the
Lubavitcher Chassidim an exaggerated sense of the correct-
ness of their ways, an explicit condescension toward the insti-

tutions which engage them. Ultimately, this would seem to limit their effectiveness as builders, for to teach positively one must have some stake in the community in which one works. The *haverim* lack this, and thus it is difficult to expect that they will nurture the kind of creative rebels who will seek to improve the quality of synagogue life. Alternatively, if they do create revolutionaries who reject the establishment, they will lose their present entree into establishment circles.

How long can one remain a member of a *havurah*? For many members of Havurat Shalom, affiliation is considered a life-long enterprise. Yet Professor Neusner is probably correct when he questions the ability of *havurot* to continue to function with their idealistic assumptions about community and study once families arrive and full-time obligations are undertaken. (Rabbi Rosenblum notes that there are perhaps sixty or seventy people in his congregation who constitute a fellowship of sorts for study and worship, but who participate within the context of family life and a complete working week.) Furthermore, given the currents of our time, one cannot be sure that a twenty-five-year-old would care to participate in a *havurah* half of whose members might be over forty. Would there have to be *havurot* for different age groups; or more intensive groups for graduate students who have free time, and less intensive fellowships for family men? How would the programs of the latter differ from the best a good synagogue has to offer?

A real *havurah* must remain small—forty to fifty members at the most—and thus its potential for influence is limited. For many *haverim* this is not a paramount consideration. Some have written off the Jewish community except for the "saving remnant." Moreover, the continued survival of Israel the people, or Israel the state, is not a subject of major concern. The *haverim* have their own souls to worry about.

It is precisely the failure to value the religious component of the survival of the Jewish people that weakens the power of Havurat Shalom, and may destine it to become no more than an interesting footnote in the history of our time. This is not a necessary development. One wishes that the *havurah* would try to coordinate more of its activities with the creative elements in the "establishment." One would hope that with the Holocaust a scant generation behind us, the continuing existence of the Jewish people would be a concern to which all of the *haverim* would be willing to devote themselves. (Until recently, a course on the theologies of the Holocaust was given to interested members of New York Havurah by Rabbi David W. Silverman of the Jewish Theological Seminary. Although himself not a member of the group, Rabbi Silverman conveys the *havurah's* commitment to other faculty members, and attempts to inhibit polarization and stereotyping judgments on the part of each group.)

A Challenge to the Community

The *havurah*, then, is not without glaring faults and mistaken emphases. Nevertheless, its existence and its real achievements provide a challenge to the Jewish community. It emphasizes that there is a small but growing number of young people who want to study seriously and to worship intensely. Many of them have received their initial impetus in this direction through programs run by our synagogues or by the Conservative movement. As adolescents they found no place for their commitment in the synagogues, where prayer is rote-reading, community is expressed in suburban soirees, and learning is best described as a Harry Golden lecture. Large synagogues ghettoized the youngsters in the youth service, *de facto havurot*. Rarely did the adult service attempt to integrate youthful energy and creativity into channels of worship or education. Rarely did the youngsters feel that they really shared in synagogue activity. Thus was lost the ideal of the synagogue as a center which could bridge the generation gap and bring together Jews of all ages, as it had for centuries.

If the *havurah* does nothing else, it should remind Jewish leaders that, as successful youth services have indicated for years, religious creativity, fervor, and a sense of community have not passed from this earth. Business as usual at the *shul* is no longer acceptable. Rabbis will have to surmount their own inertia, the resistance of synagogue boards and ritual committees, and get youth involved in every aspect of synagogue life. They must make sure that services provide at least some modicum of informality, youthful participation, and creative study.

The challenge to the seminaries, and to the Jewish Theological Seminary in particular, is even greater. More and more students want to study in a setting in which relevance is at least as important as depth, where informality and openness are valued alongside scholarly attainments. Jewish *Wissenschaft* is no longer a necessary and sufficient cause of learning. Furthermore, the schools must acknowledge that as many students are interested in courses in *agadah* and mysticism as in Talmud. While the seminaries should not alter their curriculum merely to suit a current fad, they should expand their offerings to provide adequate courses in areas of Jewish study which they have undervalued and which attract vibrant students today. With the increasing number of alternatives currently available, the seminaries cannot assume that students will automatically flock to their admissions offices. If the establishment fails to respond to the request for new styles of learning, more and more students will find supplemental sources of enlightenment or bypass the seminaries altogether.

In sum, the *havurot* offer a strong challenge to the present shape of things in American Jewry. The *havurah* as an institution will not solve the malaise in the American Jewish community; it presents problems of its own and it may not even endure. But it has indicated that a way can be found to make serious study of Jewish sources more relevant, and religious services and the religious life more meaningful. By and large, the *haverim* evince great and genuine affection for their program. Would that the same were true of the students in our seminaries and the young people in our synagogues!

Hebrew and Yiddish Terms
(in order of appearance)

kipot	—	skullcaps worn by pious Jews
U.S.Y.	—	United Synagogue Youth, the mass youth movement of Conservative Judaism
davener	—	congregant
moreh d'atra	—	the local religious authority and judge
rebbe	—	Chassidic master whose authority is based more on charisma than on knowledge of religious law
agadah	—	Jewish lore and legend
cabala	—	Jewish mysticism
Chassidism	—	Jewish pietistic movement which swept Eastern Europe in the second half of the 18th century
epikoros	—	a non-believer
davens	—	prays
halakhah	—	Jewish law
Kabbalat Shabbat	—	service welcoming the Sabbath
seudat shelishit	—	the third meal of the Sabbath
hazzan	—	cantor
Shacharit	—	morning service
niggunim	—	melodies
Torah	—	the Pentateuch
Musaf	—	the additional service which follows the public reading of the Torah on Sabbaths and Jewish holidays
shtiebel	—	a small, traditional synagogue
kashrut	—	Jewish dietary laws
Siddur	—	Jewish prayer book
Chumash	—	Pentateuch
bet midrash	—	traditional center of study
Rashi	—	the greatest medieval Jewish commentator on the Bible and Talmud

baale halakhah	—	experts in Jewish law
yeshivah	—	advanced Talmudic academy
Kudsha B'rich Hu	—	The Holy One, Blessed Be He
mitnagdic	—	anti-Chassidic
Agnon	—	the greatest writer of Hebrew fiction in modern times; Nobel prizewinner
Zohar	—	the classic text of Jewish mysticism
Torah lishmah	—	Jewish study for its own sake
tefillot	—	religious services
shul	—	synagogue

Encounter with Chabad

Alan Smolover

4/13/78

"Can you believe President Nixon caring for each and every American's divine soul?" A Lubavitcher Chassid asked me this question with a skeptical twinkling in his eye. He and I both have our doubts about President Nixon, but his follow-up question was perhaps more plausible: "Can you believe the Lubavitcher Rebbe (may he live long and happily, amen) cares for each and every Jew's divine soul?"

Chassidism (or, in Yiddish, *Chassidus*) is two and a half centuries old, founded by Rabbi Israel Ba'al Shem Tov in the Carpathian mountain area, rapidly spreading throughout the Jewish world. While originally a movement identified with emotional mysticism at the expense of deep Jewish learning, *Chabad Chassidus* developed during the third generation after the Ba'al Shem Tov, reemphasizing the intellectual approach to mysticism. Leadership of the movement is vested in the charismatic authority of the Lubavitcher Rebbe, Rabbi Mena-

Alan Smolover, Honors B.A. in philosophy from the University of Pittsburgh, studied at Hebrew University in 1969–1970 and the Université de Dijon in 1968, and is currently crystallizing plans for graduate school in Israel. He is a free-lance writer, photographer, and plays lead violin with Gypsy Forest, a Renaissance, troubadour, street-minstrel, and honky-tonk/boogie ensemble. This article is reprinted by permission of the author from *Rock of Ages Review*, Winter, 1972, Issue No. 1, copyright © 1972 by Alan Smolover (Pittsburgh, Pennsylvania, 1972).

chem Mendel Schneerson, of the seventh generation of *Chassidus.*

On Shabbos Vayechi, 5732, corresponding to New Year's weekend, 1972, the Lubavitcher Chassidim sponsored an encounter with Chassidism at their movement headquarters in Brooklyn, which I attended with about eighty other college-aged, male Jews. During the preceding weekend, the Lubavitchers had hosted an encounter for college-aged, female Jews. Both meetings were open to anyone of either category who was interested and could come to Brooklyn for Shabbos.

I went to encounter Chassidism for a lot of good reasons, only one of which was salient to my host. Of course it was good to be intellectually curious, of course it is wonderful to see the Rebbe (*m-h-l-l-a-h-a*), but really, why did you come all the way to Brooklyn from Pittsburgh? I'll tell you why—and he did: You came because your soul was searching . . .

He was right, but I was right, too. I was curious, both intellectually and spiritually. But I went mainly because I was seeking the Answer. And not merely the Answer, but, of course, the Answerer.

There was every reason to believe the Answer could be found in the court of the Lubavitcher Rebbe, just as it was not to be found where I had been so far. Having set out to explore certain dimensions of the thesis "being human, nothing human should be foreign to me," I set out for Brooklyn to narrow the range of inquiry a bit: being a Jew, nothing Jewish should be foreign to me.

To begin with, Chassidim were not entirely unknown to me. For several years on Simchat Torah, I would go and dance with the local Chassidim at their *shtiebl* (synagogue), a practice which had come to mean more for me than dancing in the synagogue of my childhood. I knew about the Ba'al Shem Tov from various sources of my elementary Jewish education, and, on a college level, Gershom Scholem's work and Martin Buber's *Tales* had enchanted me long before I thought of going to Brooklyn to be encountered.

I had also enjoyed some less enchanting encounters with

Chassidism: on my first trip to Israel a few years ago, I ran into several Chassidim (of unknown denomination) in the Central Bus Station in Tel Aviv. These were the kind of fanatics who would grab an unsuspecting kid in short-shorts and sandals, even with a pack on his back, and bind him with *tefillin*, right there, between a man hawking Israeli girly magazines and people rushing to buy tickets.

The world-wide *tefillin* campaign introduced by the Lubavitchers since the Six-Day War seems to be more sophisticated. My next encounter was this past summer at the Greater London Lubavitcher *tefillin*-mobile, parked at Hyde Park Corner one Sunday afternoon, to which I was invited earnestly, but not dragged, by a young Chassid.

But to return to the Shabbos in Brooklyn—encountering the Lubavitchers, especially on their spiritual home ground (with the Rebbe, not in Jerusalem) makes for a warm and thoroughly joyous experience, full of the special love which is *ahavas yisroel* (love of Israel). Nevertheless, there is also a subtly sinister aspect of an "encounter"; by this I refer to the antagonistic connotation of the term; meaning a genuine confrontation of forces, to meet with and contend against.

For while the Lubavitchers are warm-hearted, loving, and generally pious people in their special way, they are also quite serious in their encountering. As one rabbi told me, the ultimate objective of Lubavitchers is nothing less than complete *teshuvah*, nothing less than the desire to revolutionize completely and irrevocably the life of the modern Jew by making binding upon him an authoritarian religious system.

By *teshuvah* the Lubavitchers do not mean its unfortunate translation as "repentance," but the ancient Jewish concept of "return"—for the Jew to return to his or her inherent goodness, the revelation of the inner, good self, however corrupted it has become. To the Lubavitchers the way is clear: Torah and *mitzvot*, plus the special mediation of the Rebbe. I went to Brooklyn to see what this was all about.

The weekend was laid out for us in convention format: a timetable (working on Jewish time, you should know it's the same for the Lubavitchers) ranged from an introductory "Confronting Chabad" to "Stepping into Prayer"; from various workshops on "Chassidic Expressionistic Art," "Original Chassidic Music," "*Tefillin:* 'Inside and Out' ", "*Tzitzis:* 'The Knots and Twists of It—Do It Yourself Course' ", to a discourse by the Rebbe himself on Shabbos afternoon (four hours, in Yiddish, without simultaneous translation); finally a midnight-to-dawn *Fabrangen* on the theme *Lechayim* (a less formal encounter, where anyone who asks a question must toast the leader's health with a straight shot of vodka, which the answerer must reciprocate before replying).

All of this activity was bordered by the traditional rituals in the Lubavitchers' methodology of daily sanctification, to borrow a phrase from Weber: morning, afternoon, and evening prayers; meals set off by prayer; ritual bathing in a *mikvah* (ritual bath) in preparation for the Sabbath; Shabbos-welcoming prayers, the special Shabbos meals; Shabbos-day prayers and Shabbos-departing prayers. Study and prayer, laced with doses of heavy eating, and heavy, segregated dancing and singing were the main activities of the weekend.

In introducing the ground rules for the encounter, besides the requirements of ritual observance, the Lubavitchers were particularly careful to emphasize the total freedom of discussion: ask any question at all, ask it of any lecturer or any of the Chassidim—all will be answered. I knew this was a necessary, if actually *false* orientation to a supposedly no-holds-barred encounter spirit, because it could not actually be carried out. For while the Chabad *male* Chassidim make no sacrifice of the intellect in their commitment to Torah, their ideology, as any traditional orthodoxy, necessarily subordinates the quest for truth to an a priori loyalty to a written and oral tradition, which bars certain questions altogether— about the reasonableness of the texts and the rules of interpretation—or at the very most, defines such questions as meaningless.

Going to Brooklyn I knew in advance what the closed system would be like, and so it was almost an intellectual game to sit back and let the questions be asked, and to wait for the answers to be shot back. I knew the questions that would be asked, and which answers would be given; for I had already asked them and been answered, not only by the Orthodox, but by the Conservatives, the Reform, the Reconstructionists, not to mention the secular humanists, Labor Zionists, communists, and Bundists.

Most of the people who asked questions at the encounter asked them, of course, because they did not know the answers in advance; perhaps because they had never before confronted themselves with meaningful questions about their heritage. Those who did most of the asking were predominantly young men with little or no Jewish background or Judaic education.

Then there were people of similar background to mine—people who have perhaps studied in Israel, who speak and read Hebrew, who know something of Jewish history, who have perhaps been involved in various Jewish movements, summer camps, or have been teaching in Jewish schools in one way or another. Those of us in this second category could only remain silent through most of the questioning, joining in with a sigh of relief when the Chassidim would break up the "dialogue" with moments of humming, singing, or wild Chassidic dancing. (Mixed dancing still means older male Chassidim with younger, or perhaps any of the Chassidim with us tourists.)

I refer to "dialogue" with quotation marks, because there was no real dialogue in the Socratic sense, to which I was accustomed as a student of philosophy in a secular university. The Socratic search for truth is an open quest, both enabling and encouraging the deepest questioning of any premise, any original text, or principle of exegesis. This is the essential difference between the searchings for truth of Socrates and Rabbi Akiba, as Walter Kaufman notes in *Critique of Religion and Philosophy:*

> Like Socrates, Akiba would sooner die than cease searching for truth in his own peculiar way. Like Socrates, he had a

sense of humor and realized that the search for truth was not altogether unlike a game but this game was his life. What he died for was not some one particular truth but his concern with truth, his determination to go on seeking truth—which he did by way of interpreting Scripture. About particular truths he was willing to argue and ready to be shown that he was wrong, provided it was done according to the rules of the game.

This is the critical principle I had in mind in listening to the "dialogue" of the encounter. It undoubtedly was good for those who needed basic knowledge to question and be answered, in what must have been for many their first exposure to any kind of intense Jewish experience. And the questions certainly were well answered—no mere reciting of a dogmatic, Jewish catechism, but at all times a sincerely intellectual kind of reasoning; if only on a plane bound by certain necessary assumptions; i.e., *Torah mi sinai*. (Torah, or revelation, from Sinai; a basic tenet of Orthodoxy, referring to both the written and oral tradition and laws of Judaism).

Indeed, this was the most impressive characteristic of *Chabad Chassidus:* the comprehensive integration of the *Halakhic* with the philosophic and mystic trends of Judaism. It was a well balanced, if closed, system that was presented during the encounter; even a beautiful multimedia system—for between questions and lectures we hummed, sang, and even got up and danced.

But many questions of interest to me lay beyond the reach of the encounter. For example, how could I ask seriously about such fundamentally important, antitraditional exigencies of today as the role of the modern woman, Jewish or otherwise, in a world of potential human liberation from sex-biased roles which all people have been forced to play traditionally, for countless generations? How could I ask this, even as a text question, after a Lubavitcher male refuses to hear a woman's voice in joyous, communal song, around a Shabbos table? Or when a Lubavitcher woman sincerely tells me that the *Chumash* (Pentateuch, Five Books of Moses) proves women are naturally and intellectually inferior to men? (Intellectually inferior, but, of course, "naturally" superior in certain "womanly" virtues, and so the cop-out goes . . .)

The system is closed, and this saddened me. There was no intellectual tokenism, for some of the lecturers were brilliant —the Rebbe himself holds a Ph.D. from the Sorbonne—but they could only go as far as their overriding loyalty to tradition allowed them to go.

One lecturer particularly impressed me: a professor of (Greek!) philosophy at a secular university, who was trained at Harvard before becoming a disciple of the Rebbe. He makes his living teaching philosophy, so of course I wanted to talk with him privately, to ask how he came to find the Answer here in Brooklyn; but anyone of such appeal to our audience was in constant public demand. But he did relate one beautiful story which seemed to draw the various seekings for the Answer into focus:

It seems there was a prisoner in a dungeon, whose sole function during all the many years of his bondage was to turn a wheel, embedded in the wall to which he was chained. Each day of his life in the dungeon, the man sought to assign some meaning to his turning of the wheel, some imagined connection between the rim of the wheel he could touch as he turned it and the world beyond the dungeon wall which he could not see.

At one time he imagined the wheel to be connected to the gears of a flour mill, and thus could think of his wheel-turning as a meaningful action, grinding the flour for the bread of the people who lived beyond his prison world. Another time he would think of the wheel being connected to a pump, so that his turning meant bringing water to irrigate life-giving crops.

The absolutely essential thing for the prisoner was for him to have meaning to his toil; to turn the wheel for no good reason would be to despair. Finally one day, after many years of imprisonment, the jailer came to release him. He ran from the prison and rushed to the other side of the dungeon to see why, in reality, he had been turning the wheel for all those years. And what do you imagine his shock to be when, upon reaching the other side of the wall he finds . . .

It was suggested that all there is on the other side of the wall of our personal dungeon is sex. (Freud says so, and he is a rebbe, too, for many people . . .) But if this is true, then isn't out wheel-turning utterly meaningless?

Ah, but the Lubavitchers reply, after the Torah and *mitzvot* were revealed to us, there is really no point in asking such a silly question. "You have been told, man, what is good; and what the Lord demands of you . . ." (Micah).

How can I come to terms with the conflicts that arise when I encounter Chabad? How do I answer their challenge?

Among the many dynamics of dialectical tensions in Judaism today, consider this possible matrix: The Lubavitchers, as a prime example of their genus, serve a role of keepers of the flame, or at least some of the more central flames in the burning bush of Jewish tradition. They thus become the necessary foil to the left-wing of the Jewish people, the unaffiliated hangers-on, the "Jews by birth." Perhaps we should see them as our priestly tribe, bearing the ark of our covenant with God, as we journey interdependently through the wilderness of life in the world today.

This is not to agree necessarily with the Lubavitchers, that the Rebbe is the Moses of our generation; for various other types of *rebbes* exist for many of us today. We live in this Jewish era after the Holocaust and after the State of Israel; but no less do we live in this human era after Hiroshima, during the liberation from bondage of another people in our American society, during Vietnam, Biafra, Bangladesh, etc.

One wholly other *rebbe* might be Elie Wiesel, who certainly speaks to us all. One certainly does not have to give over the direction of one's life to a charismatic, fundamentally authoritarian and necessarily male-chauvinist Rebbe to live a fully Jewish life of Torah and *mitzvot*.

Even as the Lubavitchers say, it was easy to be a good Jew at Sinai, while witnessing the miraculous acts of the living

God and hearing the Torah from the lips of God's greatest prophet. It was easy to answer with one collective voice of affirmation. *Na'aseh v'nishmah,* we will *do* and we will *listen.*

But it is not so easy today, as man hides his humanity and potential godliness from his fellow man, and contrives to bear witness to such self-made and such contradictory Sinai-events as the Holocaust and the creation of the State of Israel. It is not so easy now, with all the *rebbes* of Jewish origin competing for our attention—Marx, Freud, and Einstein, not to mention Jesus. So perhaps the best lesson of such an encounter is that, in our wheel-turning in the wilderness, there are just too many *rebbes* to take one, once and for all.

Part Five

Radical Jews and the Jewish Establishment

Who speaks today for American Jewry? In the past such dynamic personalities as Henrietta Szold, Rabbi Stephen Wise, Justice Louis Brandeis, Abraham Cahan, Louis Marshall, and Isaac Leeser gave depth and direction to their respective generations. Jews looked toward these individuals for leadership.

Is the day of the charismatic Jewish leader a thing of the past? Is the size of his check, or the wealth of his congregation, the measure of a Jew's importance today?

Can the young Jews of today identify with the philanthropists and professional bureaucrats who run the Jewish Establishment complex? Does Max Fisher, the Detroit industrialist, President Nixon's "Jewish affairs advisor," and a former chairman of the National Council of Jewish Philanthropies and Welfare Funds, represent Jews on the campuses and in the streets, to say nothing of the poor, working class, and aged Jews in isolated pockets of New York, Boston, Miami, and elsewhere?

Is combatting anti-Semitism and raising money the *raison d'être* of American Jewry? Why does the present system of Jewish education do so poor a job of transmitting the Jewish heritage to the young?

Is the Jewish Establishment so blinded by the trauma of the Holocaust, the founding of the State of Israel, McCarthyism, and the ghetto revolts that it cannot deal creatively with the dilemmas facing Jews in Israel, the Soviet Union, and elsewhere?

The writers in this chapter attempt to answer these and other questions in offering a critique of the Jewish Establishment.

Hillel Levine's speech scores the complacency and nondirection of Jewish leadership. Robert Goldman directs his assault against the pretentious efforts of world Jewish leaders to ease the plight of Soviet Jewry—and calls for more dramatic strategies.

Dr. Judah J. Shapiro knows the Jewish Establishment from the inside, having served as consultant and executive for several major groups. His article on the philanthropies is a damning view of Jewish fund raisers. In both its methods and its priorities, these charitable organizations are being pressured to change.

Everett Gendler, an unorthodox young rabbi from Boston, proposes a radical—and practical—alternative to the large, impersonal synagogue of today, a type of congregation that is communal, open, and dynamic; and in conclusion, Sherman Rosenfeld argues that Jews have been corrupted by values inimical to Jewish tradition.

To Share a Vision

Hillel Levine

It is said that when the Messiah comes he will turn the hearts of fathers to children and the hearts of children to fathers. In this age, one can understand how this might be his most difficult task.

At the outset, I must make one point clear. I am not a part of this convention; neither was I nor any young person asked to speak at this time. I stand here with a mandate from my friends hoping that what I say expresses the opinion of many other young Jews, but I stand here because of pressure that we exerted upon the planners of this conference to permit us to address you directly. Knowing that we were given this opportunity only through threats of a disruption, you might dismiss us as children of our times, bored with the battle of the campus and looking for a new stage upon which to plan our childish pranks of doubtful morality. But we see ourselves as more than children of our times; we see ourselves as children of timelessness. We see ourselves as Jews who know

Hillel Levine, graduate of the Jewish Theological Seminary and the New School for Social Research, is presently a teaching fellow and Ph.D. candidate in sociology at Harvard University. His essay is the text of a speech given to the Council of Jewish Federations and Welfare Funds in November, 1969, and is reprinted from *Response*, Winter, 1969, by permission of the author. Copyright © 1969 by *Response* magazine.

that when one has an urgent matter to bring up to the attention of the community, even the reading of the Torah in the synagogue may be disrupted. We see ourselves as your children, the children of Jews who with great dedication concern themselves with the needs of the community, the children of Jews who bring comfort to the afflicted, give aid to the poor, who have built mammoth philanthropic organizations, who have aided the remnants of the Holocaust, who have given unfalteringly to the building of Israel, who give more per capita to charity than any other group in America. We are your children and affirm this, but, to paraphrase the Rabbinic aphorism, we want to be not only children—*banim*—but also builders—*bonim*. We want to participate with you in the building of a vision of a great Jewish community. It is when we think of this that we become dismayed with the reality of American Jewish life which we cannot reconcile with what you have taught us to cherish.

We thought we understood you. You grew up during the Depression and always wanted us to have what you did not. You worked your way through college with great difficulty. You lived through the difficult years of World War II, knew of the death of six million Jews, for which we cannot envy you. You enjoyed the post-war prosperity, made it to the suburbs, built synagogues and centers. You want us to be a little Jewish and bring you a lot of *naches*.

But perhaps you would be more interested in knowing who we are. We were born during and shortly after the war. The Holocaust made a deep impression on our young minds, as did the new-felt pride in the State of Israel. We had the best set of blocks, the shiniest bicycle, and piano lessons. We did well in school. We went to Hebrew school and occasionally synagogue, but found them dull. There were fewer exciting models for us in the Jewish community, little opportunity to give expression to our youthful ideals. In contrast, the larger world was exciting, a labyrinth of mystery and challenge. The warmth of an old grandfather, the tranquility of a Sabbath at home, the moral indignation of a verse from the Prophets may have given us second thoughts about our Jewish identity, but on the whole we knew where the action was and where it was not. We went down to Mississippi for summers, marched against the war. The Jewish publicists spilled seas of ink bemoaning our alienation. Rarely, though, was an honest appraisal made of the source of our alienation. Perhaps it was a sign of our health that we were not attracted to a Jewish life devoid of intellectual and spiritual energy.

It took us several years to realize our confusion of form and essence and to recognize that there was more to Judaism than its poor expressions in the American Jewish community. For some it was a trip to Israel, for others it was the reading of Buber's *I and Thou,* for others an encounter with Chassidim, for others it was a traditional Jewish education redirected to confront existential problems, for others the exploration of self could not overlook the Jewish component. The Six-Day War forced us to reassess our attachment in deciding to risk our lives if necessary on Israel's behalf. The black awakening reminded us that the melting pot dream was a fool's fantasy and that differences were legitimate. We woke up from the American dream and tried to discover who we really were. For many of us this now means turning our concerns inward into the Jewish community because we are disenchanted with the crass materialism of the larger society. Yet where can we find inspiration in the multimillion-dollar Jewish presences of suburbia?

It is perhaps unfair to place the blame of a stillborn American Jewish life on the philanthropic organizations. Yet insofar as they are the closest semblance of an organized Jewish community, insofar as they assume the responsibility of planning for the Jewish community and establishing its priorities, insofar as they control the largest charity coffers, any statement on the lack of fulfillment of the Jewish community must begin with them.

In describing the history of Jewish philanthropy in America, the account inevitably goes back to the agreement concluded by the early Jewish colonists in New Amsterdam with Peter Stuyvesant, whereby they would be allowed to settle in a place which would later become the world's largest Jewish community, on the condition that they agreed to provide for their needy. I am always amused by the repetition of this story in that by making Peter Stuyvesant honorary founder of American Jewish philanthropies, one might imply that it would be conceivable for Jews not to provide for their own needy—as if there was not Torah and tradition which made the same demands. *Tzedakah* was always a primary obligation of the Jew and throughout Jewish history there have existed complex philanthropic organizations involving all Jews in the provision of the physical and spiritual needs of the community. Perhaps attributing secular origins to Jewish philanthropies in America is an attempt to justify its secular concerns. A cursory examination of organized Jewish charity indicates its two major concerns—adjustment to American life and the perpetuation of a vague sense of Jewishness.

Until the late 19th century, philanthropy was managed by synagogue adjuncts and local societies, but soon such management was found inadequate. Federations of charities were formed with wealthy benefactors maintaining controlling interest for pet projects with resultant inefficiency and duplication. Orphanages, health agencies, and settlement houses proliferated. Millions of immigrants were aided to make material and cultural adjustments to the new world. America was the golden land and it was accepted without second thought that adjustment had to be made in whatever ways demanded, particularly culturally. Like their emancipated coreligionists in Europe, American Jews were willing to leave their Jewishness behind as the entrance fee to the modern world. A labor force of Jewish civil servants and social workers was developed. Early in the history of Federated charities, concern was expressed for the responsibilities of Jewish philanthropies. One position on Jewish social service saw its purpose as perpetuating spiritual as well as serving physical needs. The opposite position was that the task of Jewish charities is to accelerate the process of assimilation and to help Jews become an integral part of the brotherhood of man. What was consistently characteristic of American Jewish philanthropies and what perhaps made them typically American was that they lacked direction and well-considered priorities. They shared the American malaise of favoring action over thought, regardless of its intrinsic value or the needs that it filled, a program was undertaken if it attracted the interest of sponsors. The response to discrimination against Jews was to reproduce that which Jews were excluded from. They did not allow us into their hotels, so we built our own. They did not allow our doctors to receive training in their hospitals, so we built bigger and better ones. As the Jew rose into a secure middle-class niche, he became more of a social and political being. Organizations multiplied which reflected the needs of adjustment and defense. Later these became euphemistically known as community relations. Settlement houses had suburban off-shoots of Jewish community centers closely modeled after Y.M.C.A.'s. These Jewish swimming pools and game rooms were to be instrumental in maintaining Jewish loyalties. Yet the philosophy of the Jewish community center, which is often alluded to in the literature, to the best of my knowledge never received a cogent exposition. Through Jewish group experience under the supervision of social workers, Jewish content would somehow be transmitted, perhaps by magic or osmosis.

Jewish education was the stepson of organized Jewish philanthropies. An occasional community school received support, but as the synagogues, which themselves aspired to be Jewish centers with denominational affiliations, began to develop as a force in the Jewish community, most Jewish education fell within their domain. The later developing day schools received even less support. The Jewish Federation, choosing to be "nonsectarian," refused to accept fully its responsibility to religious life and chose the recreational-oriented center of low Jewish content over Jewish education of substance. Ironically, constituent organizations had declared a holy war against government support of Jewish education while simultaneously refusing any aid themselves. Peter Stuyvesant, who was a good Christian, would have had something to say about Jews who refuse to support their Hebrew schools. The priorities of organized Jewish philanthropies favored a greater mobilization of resources to combat one crackpot anti-Semite than to deal with the Jewish illiteracy of millions of Jews.

But times have changed, changed dramatically, whereas these changes have not been reflected in the priorities of Federation leaders, many of whom are aware of these changes. As a prominent Jewish scholar has said, we are prepared to fight battles of thirty years ago—while the urgent needs of today receive little response. Jewish philanthropic organizations have proven their success at helping large numbers of Jews adjust to American life. They have maintained some Jewish loyalties through their centers and camps. But most of these efforts merely duplicate existing services in the general community. They are no longer a primary responsibility of the Jewish community. A vague sense of Jewishness can no longer compete in an open market of identities for Jews three or four generations removed from a substantive Jewish experience. Identities are based on ideologies and experiences, and neither can be offered by Jewish swimming pools and game rooms.

Changing notions of social responsibility and soaring costs of public health and welfare have forced the government to assume a greater financial responsibility in these areas. Yet again, Federation allocations reflect little response to these changing circumstances. The special services that such institutions under Jewish sponsorship could offer the Jewish community are either no longer necessary or no longer available. Jewish doctors are readily accepted for training in all hospitals and kosher food is often easier to obtain in non-Jewish hospitals than in Jewish hospitals. It is clear that Jews as individuals contribute to local health agencies. Federation allocations to such agencies now constitute a minor portion of the total budgets of these agencies, which if phased out over a period of several years would be replaced by government funds. Such freeing of a significant percentage of the Jewish charity dollar would allow its application to areas of Jewish life in dire need of funding.

We know of the historical generative powers of Jewish education and its stimulation of a meaningful Jewish life. In modern times we know of its ability to deter intermarriage and assimilation. We know that it correlates highly with participation in Jewish life and support of communal activities. Yet Jewish education in America can be spoken of only in litanies of despair. Its insipid and irrelevant content can often have counterproductive effects on young minds. You being closer to the scene know the situation better than anyone. Your 34th and 35th conferences were dedicated to the problem of bringing Jewish education out of the Middle Ages. Consistently you have passed resolutions which acknowledge the problem and its seriousness, call for creative responses for which Federations must assume a greater financial responsibility. Some Federations have taken this responsibility seriously and there have been hopeful responses. Yet there is no dramatic increase in the funding of Jewish education in most cities. Of the total budget of over $44 million of funds allocated locally in 125 communities in 1967, only $6,238,000, or 14.1 percent of the budget, went to Jewish education on all levels while $12,448,000, or 28.1 percent, went to Jewish community centers, camps, and youth services of low Jewish content. While 35 percent of the total budget for community relations in 1966 was covered by local Federations and Welfare Funds, less than 10 percent of the budget for education and only 2½ percent of cultural agencies' budgets was covered by the Federations. To be sure, the lack of funding is only one of the shortcomings of Jewish education. The shortage of qualified teachers and administrators and the absence of curricula development are crucial; but the problem is of such a magnitude that only innovation implemented by top-level planning and well-financed research will make an impact. From examining the response of most Federations and of the C.J.F.W.F. to the problem of Jewish education, one gets the impression that the situation is rather hopeless but not terribly serious—not serious enough to warrant concerted and creative responses. Federations which in soliciting funds exploit Jewish sentiments carefully imbued through Jewish living and education cannot be oblivious to these concerns. It is no secret that fewer people, and particularly fewer young people, are responding to Federation appeals. This should certainly be a warning. But the possibilities of Jewish education cannot be seen simply in terms of keeping Jews within the folds or training future *machers*. Jewish education must compensate for the shortcomings of the educational system in character building and stimulating moral sensitivity. Living in more than one culture can give young Jews valuable perspective. Quality Jewish education will help the individual remain whole in a society which denies sanctity to the human vessel.

How many best-sellers and Hollywood movies does it take to tell us that there is something seriously wrong with the Jewish family? When walking through the neat rows of split-levels in Brookline or Beverly Hills, Scarsdale or Highland Park, one gets a sense that the cumulative aspirations of millenia of civilization went into such push-button comfort. Yet what unhappiness is there to be found behind so many of those gold trim doors. We all know of this perhaps in intimate ways. Experimentation with ritual experiences in Jewish life and imaginative settings may ease some of the tensions that modern existence thrusts upon the family and may deepen relations in beautiful ways. Existing family agencies are simply not coping with such problems. Only funding and direction from the organized Jewish philanthropies could lead to any imaginative solutions.

And what about the campus, that wasteland of Jewish life, the one sphere that has been unresponsive to some of the awkward approaches of Jewish life? Yet we are told that young people are most open to challenges in life styles, most prepared to embrace meaningful ideologies. Why should the campus be a Jewish wasteland? No one has definitive answers but the situation encourages intelligent conjectures. What opportunity is there for young Jews to grow Jewishly commensurate with their general intellect? What overall plan does the Jewish community have to train Jewish scholars, to stimulate the growth of departments of Judaica in universities? The Jewish Culture Foundation, among its other responsibilities, is entrusted with these tasks of inestimable importance but awarded only $81,000 for its operations by Federations. Can any serious program be undertaken with such an amount? And there are those who would make solemn pronouncements about the efficacy of Hillel Foundations, saying, "What has it accomplished? How many lives has it affected? Whom does it attract on the campus?" Yet Hillel has hardly had an opportunity to demonstrate its viability with its desperately insufficient funds and shortage of manpower. Dedicated rabbis are overwhelmed by the demands made on them as the only knowledgeable Jews on campuses with thousands of Jewish students and faculty members. These men certainly cannot use their talents effectively under such circumstances. Less than $600,000 of Hillel's budget comes from Federation sources. This hardly represents a significant contribution on the part of Federations to campus life. In the last few years several new student groups, journals, and *havurot* or religious communities have been developed by young Jews, a clear sign of vitality. Yet little has been done to encourage them. Some of these projects, with a fraction of the amount of money that this conference will cost, could have a great impact on Jewish student life. There is one student project in the Boston area (Havurat Shalom Community Seminary) which has received most of its support from a Christian foundation. Gentlemen, what would Peter Stuyvesant have to say about that?

An important Federation leader once shared his disappointment with me over the lack of interest on the part of young Jews in Federation activities. With great sincerity he stated the resources that Federation is prepared to make available to students. "We have 256 agencies in this city where a Jewish student can have his appendix removed and a mental hospital where he can be committed. We truly care about Jewish students." This concern I do not for a moment doubt, and I appreciate it. But it is not our neuroses nor our ruptured appendixes that we wish to share. Coupled with your abilities and your experience, we want to build a Jewish community that is creative and not one that must concern itself with mere survival.

We don't want commissions "to explore the problems of youth." We do want to convert alienation into participation, acrimony into joy—the joy of being the possessors of a great legacy—a legacy which has meaning for today. This renewal can be accomplished only through a massive and personal rededication to Jewish study and meaningful Jewish existence. It is inconceivable for a Jewish community to be guided by Jewish principles and values if its leaders are ignorant of them. Surely some knowledge of Hebrew, of Jewish history and traditions should be a prerequisite. Leaders of Jewish philanthropies should not only solicit funds but educate benefactors to the needs of the community. This requires Jewish knowledge. Furthermore, participation of thousands of leaders in Jewish education will make them sensitive to the inadequacies of Jewish education and stimulate its creative development. Federations, as important benefactors to Jewish life, can set the pace by a reappraisal of their priorities by phasing out operations that can obtain support from other agencies or that no longer serve necessary functions, while retraining displaced personnel for more vital areas of Jewish life. Federations must seek not only the financial support but also the guidance and leadership of a broader constituency from the American Jewish community. It can no longer be run by a few generous men or the patrons of particular projects whose concerns do not transcend their project. Rabbis, people involved in Jewish education, Jewish scholars, students, and concerned Jews should participate on all levels of decision making and allocations. Our philanthropic organizations must again view their work as holy. Philanthropy must again become *tzedakah* righteousness, soliciting the personal involvement of the community. The operation may not be as streamlined but it will itself be a source of spiritual renewal.

I cannot propose a detailed architectural design for the new Jewish community, only a sketch. The details will be filled in through careful deliberation, but we must begin immediately. I know that it is easy to criticize and hard to create. I realize that each suggestion involves countless intricacies of implementation but we must overcome institutional inertia which has made the community stagnant. There must be recognition that *ayn zu haderech,* this is not the way. I will spare you the predictions of doom for Jewish life in America which will be inevitable if we do not start.

You will see some of us here in the next few days. We hope we will have a chance to speak to you. We, our peers, and other Jews disenchanted with the Federations of Jewish Philanthropies will be at all your future meetings, hopefully in affirmation and not in dissent. We will be present at your offices and conferences and vociferously will demand the changes we know to be necessary. We will not be pacified, co-opted, nor compromised with vague resolutions. We want action and not delays. We want a change of the order of allocations and we want more equitable representation in decision making.

Your response to us could be, "You pampered kids, if you want things done differently, why don't you do it yourselves and leave us alone? This is the way *we* want the Jewish community." If that would be your response, then with much pain and disappointment we would indeed be forced to do it ourselves. It would take us longer and be more difficult, but we have already begun, the processes which have been set into action will not come to a stop. *Revach vehatzalah yavo memakonacher,* help will come from somewhere else; in that we trust. And the organized Jewish philanthropies which have given aid and support to generations of Jews will fade from our spheres of concern. And then it will only be the coming of the Messiah that will turn our hearts to yours.

Brussels: The Politics of Futility

Robert Goldman

The World Conference of Jewish Communities of Soviet Jewry, held in Brussels, February 23-25 [1971], has been compared to the first Zionist Congress as a watershed in Jewish history. The comparison is absurd. The Brussels Conference was perhaps the most telling evidence of the moral bankruptcy of world Jewish leadership since the Holocaust. For three days almost a thousand delegates from thirty-eight countries could observe behind the show the reality of organizational self-aggrandizement, bureaucratic buck-passing, cowardice, and cynicism. In three days world Jewry could undertake no substantive efforts to aid three million of their own. For three days the world Jewish establishment bickered in the face of crisis, displaying to 255 accredited journalists the same penchant for disunity which paralyzed Jews while six million died.

The idea for a conference had originated in 1965–66, during the last international uproar over Soviet anti-Semitism. Inter-organizational suspicion delayed planning until 1970. In the

Robert Goldman, graduate student in Jewish history at Brandeis, founded the New England Student Struggle for Soviet Jewry, and at the time this article was written, was a member of the steering committee of the North American Jewish Students' Network, an affiliate of the World Union of Jewish Students. This article is reprinted by permission of the author.

end only Israeli insistence prevailed on feuding Jewish groups to put the issue before their private interests.

The struggle to take credit for the Conference was heroic. At various points major groups (including B'nai B'rith and the World Jewish Congress) threatened to boycott the gathering in protest over the makeup of the presidium. In the end Nahum Goldmann, head of the World Jewish Congress, refused to attend (Rose Halprin of Hadassah and the Jewish Agency sat in for him when his vice president, Rabbi Joachim Prinz, begged off sick) after publicly blasting it in a statement he later retracted. Nominally the presidium ended up representing all world Jewry through seven voting members and a few observers (representing less consequential constituencies, such as Australia and, through the World Union of Jewish Students, the youth who have to date carried the brunt of Soviet Jewry action).

Four umbrella organizations purported to represent all Jews concerned with Soviet Jewry in North and South America, Europe, and Israel. None of them were functioning bodies. The only one that came close to being a legitimate agency was the American Jewish Conference on Soviet Jewry, a seven-year-old *ad hoc* subcommittee of the Presidents' Conference, staffed by one professional out of a single room, unfunded, and without significant support or influence.

Aside from these "territorial bodies," the American Presidents' Conference, the World Jewish Congress, and the Jewish Agency made up the presidium and called the shots.

The Conference was only successful before it began. Few delegates seemed to realize that one price the Conference had paid for "unity" among its sponsors was a general agreement not to undertake any substantive action, not to form any new organization, not to vote on plenary resolutions, and not even to reconvene the body at a future date. The conference was planned as a demonstration, no more, no less. What the delegates did know was that Jewish dignitaries were present, that the occasion was laden with importance, and that they themselves were somehow important dignitaries by being there.

The procession of dignitaries began Tuesday evening and continued Wednesday morning until a delegate rushed to the podium demanding "to know who ordered Meir Kahane's arrest." In fact, no one had. Since Kahane's Jewish Defense League was not one of the twenty-eight member organizations of the American Jewish Conference on Soviet Jewry, he, along with representatives of other dissident groups interested in Russian Jews, had not been accredited as a delegate. With much publicity he flew to Belgium nevertheless.

The presidium, however, had already decided that Rabbi Herschel Schacter would be the scapegoat and should validate the credentials of each American delegate. He assured them that he would not accredit Kahane.

The decision to exclude Kahane was certainly not democratically reached nor did it satisfy all delegates. In fact, several J.D.L. members, including Kahane's lieutenant, Steven Zweibon, were able to gain entrance and remain in the Conference. What kept Kahane out was cowardice, the fear of a Jewish Establishment of little men that one dissident voice might expose them to contumely for their inaction. That J.D.L. is, in what philosophy it has, neofascist does not alter the fact that it is a populist movement and that Kahane enjoys the personal confidence of more Jews than virtually any other organizational leader in Brussels had.

Most delegates would have been interested in hearing Kahane, but American Jewish leaders, who had long sought to read Kahane out of the Jewish people, could not tolerate him.

The Conference proceeded through several workshop sessions which produced some interesting proposals that, in the absence of any organizational structure to implement or even consider them, were ultimately pointless.

The sessions ended up with the reading of a timid declaration, worked out behind closed doors by the presidium, the appearance of David Ben-Gurion, and a performance of a play purporting to relate somehow to Elie Wiesel's *Jews of Silence*. Those delegates who came hoping to accomplish something left in deep disappointment. Most had expected nothing and departed only a bit more cynical or trusting than they had come. The Conference was painfully symptomatic of the plight of world Jewry, reflecting all the defects of its leadership and the basic failings of its organizational life.

If column inches are a measure of success, then Brussels succeeded. Yet poor planning and presentation diffused the central issues and left the press to carry confused and confusing accounts, dealing more in emotion than fact. The Conference had no focus, no spokesman, no symbol, and only the barest theme: "Let my people go!" It never tried to set policy or even come to grips with such basic issues as Jewish cultural rights in the U.S.S.R. as opposed to emigration, the meaning of Jewish nationality in *galut* (so glibly espoused for Soviet Jews by armchair Zionists), priorities of concern, international tactics, or mobilization of resources.

It adjourned sine die with one crucial question remaining on its tacit agenda: what now? No one was empowered to follow up anything. There was not even a central address, let alone a central body, to turn to.

If the Conference organizers take credit for any increase in emigration from the U.S.S.R., they must grant that it could have been due not to any real threat or accomplishment of the Conference but only to the publicity it stirred, and, as a one-shot affair, the Conference lost all publicity value the moment it adjourned. Whatever its impact on non-Jews, however, Brussels deeply affected Jews. For all the predictable plaudits, the meeting drew astonishing criticism, both in the Jewish press and from Jewish communal activists, particularly younger Jews. The distress which Brussels elicited severely shook confidence in Jewish leadership.

Certainly it was the flashiest international gathering of Jews in memory. Yet for many of us there—young and old— it was deeply disillusioning, disappointing in a terrible intimate way that reflected on our faith and hopes in our communal identity as Jews as well as on the people whom we blindly believed might lead us.

Some of us had refused to admit that power corrupts. We indulged a fantasy that the petty claimants to Jewish leadership in our own cities were perversions of the true Jewish leadership which must prevail, if not on a national, certainly on the international level.

Brussels reminded us that our *macher*archy has no one to offer as a personification of Jewish values, no model of Jewish living, none to inspire us to seize our destiny. Nor could we expect more of most Jewish functionaries, paid to relieve the communal conscience of all sense of obligation or personal responsibility. Outside the Jewish state, Jewish leadership has reached a nadir of mediocrity and petty politicking.

But our worst disillusionment in Brussels was with Jews, Jews who tolerate such shallow, timorous, and ultimately unworthy men as leaders. Those figureheads reflected *galut* Jewry, not very Jewish and, as such, unable to be desperately concerned over the plight of kinsmen who no longer seek assimilation but Jewish lives in a Jewish state. Diaspora Jewry can hardly be expected to commit itself to the struggle of Jews for rights which it does not value enough to exercise in freedom. What can the dreams of Soviet Jews mean to those who have no Jewish aspirations of their own, who can but choose not to live in Israel, who ignore real opportunities for Jewish culture and education, who do not lack but do not value rabbis, scholars, religious articles, or synagogues? Jews who care too little about being Jewish to live Jewishly will not sacrifice for others seeking such a life.

While two dozen incredibly brave Moscow Jews defied the wrath of Russia by staging the first sit-in at a Soviet office, a dozen participants in the Conference's presidium were worrying about the wording of the "Brussels Appeal," a craven documentation of moral mongolism. The momentous announcement of world Jewry to an expectant press was the daring pledge to "continue to mobilize the energies of all Jewish communities." How and to what end, our visionary leaders could not say. Two hundred Soviet Jews sent a public appeal to the Conference. It did not reply. The Moscow demonstrators telephoned us the news of their daring. It was not announced. Recent escapees from Soviet oppression—prisons and mad houses—implored the assembly. Yet we ultimately ignored the purpose of our gathering.

What did that bathetic gathering teach us? We learned that Jewish organizations were hypocritical enough in their protestations of concern not only to prevent an international instrument to aid Soviet Jews but even to refuse to empower and fund existing bodies, like the American Jewish Conference on Soviet Jewry.

Since Brussels almost all Jewish help for Soviet Jews has come from Israel, the Joint Distribution Committee, H.I.A.S., and similar Jewish relief services (almost all supported by U.J.A.). Political action has been invisible. In America, the American Jewish Conference on Soviet Jewry has made no practical progress in tearing loose from the restraints of the Presidents' Conference, despite the efforts of concerned Jews who have met with, petitioned, and picketed major Jewish organizations. Rank and file dissatisfaction with organizational efforts grows daily. The Brussels Conference, for all its apologists, may yet become a symbol and rallying cry for a revolution in Jewish life, against bankrupt institutions and corrupt leaders.

When a Russian Jew asks us what we are doing to free his family and friends, we must know that no one "up there" will assume the responsibility for us. After Brussels we must know that the tasks are for each of us, to learn, think, cooperate, work, to use any means that are effective in freeing our Soviet brothers, to encourage them not to despair, and to hope for divine favor.

The Philistine Philanthropists:
The Power and Shame of Jewish Federations

Judah J. Shapiro

For somewhat over thirty years now, Jews throughout the world have distinguished themselves in their expressions of solidarity and have provided vast sums of money on behalf of those Jews who found themselves in a variety of intolerable and desperate situations. This has been an era during which Nazism not only decimated German Jewry but expanded to oppress and destroy Jewries throughout continental Europe. Programs of rescue and relief, beyond any prior efforts of this kind, were undertaken and carried out. The war added to the number of sufferers and also inhibited the programs of assistance, but upon its conclusion in 1945 the enormity of the destruction of European Jewry became evident. To rescue and relief were added programs for those incarcerated in the D.P. camps of Germany, Austria, and Italy on a seemingly indeterminate sentence, and efforts also were made at reconstituting the Jewish communities, especially in Western Europe.

Soon after, the vast movements of migration, the redistribu-

Judah J. Shapiro, journalist, radio news analyst, and consultant, is a Professor of Sociology, Graduate Division, at the Jewish Teachers Seminary in New York and lecturer in contemporary Jewish thought, School of Jewish Communal Service, Hebrew Union College, Los Angeles. This article is reprinted from *The Jewish Liberation Journal*, October, 1969, by permission of its editorial board and the author.

tion of Jewish populations, began reaching to Australia and South Africa, to Latin America and North America, as well as to Israel. And the State of Israel itself required substantial assistance in its earliest years when grain was imported, discharged at the port of Haifa, and supplied to bakeries by truck, town by town, along the roads out of Haifa. Populations from Moslem countries were not merely transported but rehabilitated. Orphans and aged, the lame and the halt, the sick and the dispirited, all required attention and received it. Recurring shifts in several countries—political and economic —produced new clients for the tremendous welfare efforts of Jews. American Jews were part of this effort and in the main, they acquitted themselves admirably in their responsibilities to their fellow Jews.

Most of these programs of relief and rehabilitation were financed through the central Jewish Federations and Welfare Funds. There was a readiness of most agencies to stand aside, to accept the discipline of centralization of fund raising and distribution so that the priority of stricken Jewry elsewhere could be observed. Originally charity agencies acting in concert to raise their funds locally, the Federations now expanded into broader bodies concerned with all the community's responsibilities, except the religious ones, within the Jewish field at home and abroad.

In the spirit of the modern sociology, we should shift our vantage point from considering the poor who are served, to an examination of who is on top. This will lead to the fruitful approach whereby we can understand the Jewish community by knowing the nature and distribution of power in its midst. It is within the Federations that we discover the *top* of the Jewish community.

Beautiful and innocent people are the mainstay of these Federations, making contributions to their annual campaign for funds in the conviction that their support is their tangible identification with fellow Jews in need of financial assistance at home and abroad. This annual pledge and its payment is the modern equivalent of being a card-carrying Jew. Theology, ideology, value systems, and ritual are all secondary to the support of the Jewish Federation and Welfare Fund as evidence of one's Jewishness.

In these circumstances, the innocence of the contributors is the gelatinous culture in which the germs of the power disease incubate and grow. It is not unlike the fallacy of "peoples' capitalism"* whereby widely scattered ownership of industry gives power to a managerial class, undreamed of in the days when one really had to own a business with one's own money to exercise so much power over others. So, in the realm of Jewish philanthropy today, largely centralized by Jewish Federations and Welfare Funds, power is the province of those who manage the contributed funds of the numerous well-intentioned individuals who provide their money as an expression of Jewish solidarity and concern for fellow Jews.

The new role of the Federations during these past twenty-five years has produced many new problems, mainly pertaining to the way in which the local Jewish Federations function as the final and ultimate arbiters of Jewish communal affairs. A distinguished record of fund raising in dire circumstances for European Jewry and in support of the risen State of Israel has unfortunately made obscure the pressing issue of Jewish communal viability in this country, and the need for the participation of individuals other than the rich; as well as the requirement of this society for a community which permits democratic participation of its constituents, makes leadership accountable to its adherents, and provides opportunities for dealing with aspirations of the group as well as urgencies of welfare clients.

In a comparison with industry, the Jewish Federations come out a poor second, even with respect to the superficial aspects of democratic procedures. By law, shareholders in industry have opportunities to vote on policy and administrative matters, at least by proxy. In Jewish Federations there is no

---

* Michael Harrington, *The Accidental Century*, Macmillan, New York, 1965.

election in which the shareholders have a voice with respect to the selection of leadership, the approval of policy, or the choice of alternatives. There is not even a poll of sentiment with respect to actions taken. This means, in fact, that there is no accountability of the leadership to the contributors, to the Federation's constituency. It is sometimes difficult to believe that these Federations function in the U.S., where no undertaking by the leadership of a union, for example, has validity without the vote of the union's membership, as a matter of law; and where a variety of public opinion polls are constantly assessing the satisfaction of the electorate with the performance of elected officials.

There is an explanation of the studied avoidance of hearing the voice of the people. It is too obvious that the goals of the people and of Federation leadership are by now far apart, and being a *voluntary association,* the leadership would not long support a program other than its own, even if the program were that of the majority of the people. The *leadership,* therefore, is really without a following, nor does the Jewish population of any locality really have an organized community recognizable by any of the usual definitions of social and political science.

Until the late 1930's the Federations were the limited instrument for maintaining the charitable enterprises, mainly in the health and welfare category. They had no awareness and little concern for the Jewish community as an entity with common aspirations among its individual adherents, involving such matters as cultural identity, Jewish education, ideological positions, and political viability. The annual campaign of the Federation was generally in support of the sick and the poor, and later, the psychologically disoriented. Other and separate campaigns pursued the goals of overseas relief, Zionism and its quest for establishment of a Jewish state, education, and cultural movements. The overseas events and their consequences required financing and it was generally conceded that the greatest hope for maximum financial support was the centralization of all Jewish fund raising.

No one should detract in any way from the value of the massive assistance which was provided by the high-powered campaigning within the context of Federations and Welfare Funds. The questions to be considered and acted upon are the methods and processes for the disposition of the funds.

There is, first, a basic question about the appropriateness and competence of welfare-oriented personalities to deal with educational and cultural matters. As one social scientist has expressed it: "The policy conclusions that can be reached by a factual analysis of the problems of education are not as specific and indisputable as those arrived at by surveying the current health situation in the light of modern knowledge."* Yet in Jewish Federations, the *ad hoc* quality of decisions in the health field are imposed upon programs whose implications are long-term and of generational significance.

There are also deeper aspects of the new definition of the Federations' communal role. The managerial class is best defined by the title of a recent volume on the social work profession, *The Professional Altruists.*† It is in itself a commentary on our society that "having regard for others," which is the dictionary definition of altruism, is a profession. But in the complexities of modern society one must discard the 19th century abhorrence of bureaucracy and accept that we must be bureaucratic. The real question is whether we have good or bad bureaucrats.

In the Jewish Federations, the test of a good executive is his contribution to the raising of funds, rather than his identification with group aspirations. One listens to a new language, by which an executive claims the distinction of having gone "from 3.8 to 4.2." This means that his claim to fame is that the city where he worked has advanced from raising $3,800,-000 to the sum of $4,200,000 during this executive's incumbency. This is so good a record that he becomes eligible for

---

* Gunnar Myrdal, *Asian Drama* (Pantheon, 1968), vol. III, p. 1629.
† By Ray Lubove, Harvard University Press, Cambridge, 1963.

assignment to a larger city where he can start with "5.1" in the expectation that he will be moving towards "6." In the nature of things, this executive is responsible for the bulk of the fund raising in his city for Israel, but may despise Zionists. He is seen to be the executive of the Jewish communal interests but is himself without Jewish education or prior Jewish identification.

The lay leadership, in contradistinction to the professional altruists, has become the ultimate in amateur egoism. It does not buy itself out of participation in Jewish affairs by making a contribution, as used to be the style of the rich; it makes its contribution with the understanding that it will have a role in the decision making. Its amateur status in Jewish affairs is a contradiction of the very meaning of modernization in the political science sense, whereby one's status is by achievement rather than by ascription. The recognizable achievements of this laity is in every field—business, law, and government—except the area of Jewish affairs. Entrance into Jewish leadership begins with the size of one's financial support of the Federation, and once there, the criteria of the individual's success in other spheres ascribes to him similar competence in the Jewish field. The Jewish Federation becomes for such individuals a club, exclusive and personal, rather than a communal instrument for the Jews of the locality in their pursuit of group goals.

There are many dilemmas now faced by American Jewry which ought to be matters of public discussion and group decision. Were the Federations democratically constituted, these might be occurring within that context. For example, all Jewish organizations enjoy sending telegrams to the Soviet Union protesting the treatment of Yiddish writers, but a Yiddish writer could starve in the major cities of this country without the same organizations doing anything to alleviate the situation. The protests to the Soviet Union would come with better grace were it possible to say that in the country of the protesters, Yiddish writers have the support of the free Jewish community.

What is one to do, and who is to decide about keeping the Jewish historical record? The Philistine attitude towards Jewish cultural enterprise has several reputable and competent agencies in the direst circumstances. The employees of certain Jewish cultural agencies earn considerably less than these who remove the garbage from the streets of New York City. Newspapers, letters, and books of the greatest historical value, at least for those who may later compose the history of earlier periods, are inadequately protected and their accessibility is limited. Efforts are afoot to get the project for the Great Yiddish Dictionary out of this country and to Israel to assure its ultimate completion because there is no recognition here of the value of such a *magnum opus* in the cultural-intellectual life of the Jews. No major enterprise for updating text materials; for translations from Yiddish, Hebrew and other languages into English; for programs for youth designed to make them competent for leadership participation. No such enterprises get the ear of the Federations except in pious but ineffectual terms..

There really is no leadership in Jewish affairs in this country today, for those who rule justify the existing programs as the ones the givers are ready to support. Leadership is not that element in our community which formulates programs for which money should be given, and then convinces supporters. That is why we have a Jewish chapel at John F. Kennedy Airport which no interpretation of the Jewish tradition or ethos could justify, but those who provided the funds wished to do it for reasons utterly extraneous to Jewish communal needs. That is why health is the number one priority in Jewish affairs in this country, where Jews are citizens and beneficiaries of whatever health protection the country offers.

The Federation answer to the questions about this priority is inevitably—that's what the givers are ready to support. That is why there are over 30,000 volumes on the Civil War in the Library of Congress, but a request for support of a scholarly undertaking on the history of the Jews of Warsaw obtains a Federation response that there is *a* book on this subject already. Examples of Philistinism are too numerous to record here.

The inhibition to reorienting the Jewish Federations in this country is rooted in the fact that everybody gets something and is not ready to forego the pittance. Zionists know that they have no standing within the top leadership of Jewish Federations but accept the reality of the support of Israel by Federations as reason enough for avoiding any conceptual or ideological conflict with them. And so the Jewish Federations are, in fact, the treasury and the budget bureau of a nonexistent Jewish community.

The road to change is two-pronged. There is the possibility of asking out loud all the embarrassing questions about the denial of democratic rights to the Jews of every community where a Federation functions. There is the second possibility of undertaking some research, even if by polling, on what the people think is important and comparing that with what the Federations do. There is no question about the gaps, but they should be recorded with precision and they should be publicized.

There are some exceptions to the distortions in Jewish communal affairs as represented by the primacy of the Federations in the support of Jewish causes. Those exceptions are either in the individuals of given communities, lay and professional, who truly exert themselves on behalf of the concept of community against the pressures described here. They should be supported and have the right to expect encouragement from any who undertake the correction of the present situation; and there are the exceptions in particular communities where enough individuals rise to challenge the powers-to-be, and in such instances more consistent programs of challenge must be formulated and implemented. It would all seem worthwhile, for a Jewish communal reality in an American society, undergoing so much change, requires more than ever a democratic polity. And what we have to lose is a Jewish communal future.

Yesh B'rera?
Is There An Alternative?

Everett Gendler

(A Preliminary Proposal for An Alternate Religious Structure)

Author's note: As I prepare to send off this somewhat personal proposal for wider circulation, I feel a certain temptation to depersonalize it and make of it a more objective model. Yet that would be rather misleading and perhaps presumptuous at this stage of the experimentation.

So far, I've had the opportunity to meet with only three or four nuclei, and these are at various stages of development. But in each case there has been some response to the proposals as here submitted. Why not, then, share this beginning point? It is clearly presented as suggestive, not definitive, and it invites critical treatment and modification, not imitation.

If there is some wider interest in this proposal, others will surely try it out in various ways. Several of us here in the Boston area will be involved as well, and later in the year we may well want to compare reactions and results.

Everett Gendler is a graduate of the University of Chicago and the Jewish Theological Seminary; he has served congregations in Mexico, Brazil, Cuba, and Princeton, New Jersey; presently rabbi (part-time) of Temple Emanuel, Lowell, Massachusetts, a teaching member of Havurat Shalom Community Seminary near Boston, and resource person for a couple of Yesh B'rera groups in the Boston area. This article is reprinted by permission of the author from *Response*, #11, Fall, 1971. Copyright © 1971 by *Response* magazine.

For now, however, with all its loose ends and ambiguities,
the following preliminary formulation is the most honest for
wider sharing.

E.G.

When Havurat Shalom Community Seminary was established three years ago, its founders felt a keen sense of the
crisis both in the United States at large and within the Jewish
community in particular. The draft, Vietnam, racial and
economic injustice, and personal disorientation were evident
to all. These issues persist today in perhaps aggravated form,
while the deterioration of cities and the massive environmental
threat join the list of urgencies. As for the Jewish scene, there
was little within organized Jewish religious life in the U.S.
which adequately related the resources of the tradition to the
problems faced at the time; and that has not changed significantly during these three years.

Havurat Shalom has provided an important alternative for
some concerned Jews of the college and postcollege age group,
but it has not addressed itself to the religious needs of many
other Jews, including those with young children. Neither has
it been particularly satisfying for Jews with a socialist activist
bent; nor has it related to comparable religious experiments
in non-Jewish segments of our society. In short, Havurat
Shalom, for all its accomplishments and value, has not concerned itself with the needs of many Jews whose present
alternatives seem either to be established synagogues or non-
affiliation, with consequent religious isolation. Are there other
conceivable alternatives?

Personally, I do not write off the synagogue as a potential
resource, but there are some basic problems with the institution in its present form which make it an unlikely agency for
religious involvement of a kind appropriate to the coming age.

The present synagogue depends on a full-time professional
staff whose income needs are constantly rising. The present
synagogue also presupposes a sizable building which, however modest, is still costly to construct, finance, and main-

tain. Together, these factors tend to make the synagogue captive to an affluent life style which is ecologically untenable, economically unjustifiable, and religiously questionable. Even a slight economic recession threatens its solvency, and it has a built-in tendency (like all institutions) to become self-preoccupied, financially and institutionally.

In addition, for economic reasons, it must grow to a size which precludes the very intimacy and warmth which people rightly seek from religious involvement.

The religious professionals, especially the rabbi, both enjoy and suffer from being the primary focus of the institutionalized religious activity. On the one hand, the rabbi enjoys great personal gratification from his creative work with services, teaching, preaching, counselling, and pastoral functions. On the other hand, his hierarchical position is a burden as well, making enormous demands on his time and emotions, leaving little time for his family, and tending to routinize his contact with people.

As for the congregant, his own opportunities for personal gratification through such significant religious activities as planning and leading services are few. However talented, however learned, the structure tends to place him in passive relation to the religious life of the synagogue, with few opportunities to share his personal gifts of religious sensibility.

The religious education which students receive often bears little relation to their homes or lives outside the synagogue. They often find little meaning in the instruction; they retain little; the burden of additional formal class hours added to overly-demanding school days pressures them further, and their indifference to Jewish learning quickly becomes active resistance and hostility.

Synagogues are almost never selective in membership. Financial needs combine with a commendable spirit of hospitality to make the synagogue open to all who can afford it. This means, in practice, however, that each synagogue tends to have such a mixture of people in it that, attempting to meet the needs of all in this quite random grouping, there develops a distressing uniformity among the institutions. Given the rich individual diversity among Jews today, it is sad that particular synagogues do not represent particular emphases and outlooks so that those so inclined might find fuller satisfaction of religious expression in them. Furthermore, in this situation each rabbi must moderate many of his own particular gifts and tendencies in order to be as "fair" as he can be to all involved. This, too, contributes to a lack of distinctiveness in the institutions, and what the rabbi pays in loss of genuine selfhood is hard to calculate.

What I have mentioned should be sufficient to suggest that the plight of the synagogue today is not basically due to egotism, greed, or personal inadequacy, but rather results from characteristics of the institution as we know it at present.

Before attempting to outline a possible alternative, a brief speculative word about the general U.S. scene might be in order, for it is within that context that any alternative must function.

Most likely, some modifications will be made in the draft policies of Selective Servitude (S.S.) in order to reduce popular political protests against U.S. policies in Southeast Asia and elsewhere in the world. It also seems likely that political repression will increase. Economic injustices domestically will almost surely be aggravated, as economic policies seek stability through devices which favor the already well-off; and internationally the appalling gap between us and the "underdeveloped" nations will continue to widen. Environmental corrections here may already be beyond our means; it is certainly beyond our will at this point. Hence congestion will increase, local travel become more and more difficult, essential services continue to deteriorate, costs increase, frustration increase, and a sense of helplessness grow as over-centralized, exploitive, industrial gigantism continues slowly to disintegrate in nervous convulsions of varying degrees of intensity.

Given the present situation in the United States and in its Jewish community, what significant alternatives to the present synagogue structure might be imagined? There are already some in the process of emerging, with the model of the Jews for Urban Justice especially suggestive. However, this model presupposes a communal life style which most of us are either unable or unwilling to adopt at this time; or else it requires a physical relocation which again many of us are not able or willing to make. Our own search, then, should be for an alternative which could help us grow toward changes in our life styles without demanding, as the starting point, an impossible and immediate break with where we are now.

Such a model should be modest in its use of resources, minimize regular travel, be intimate yet not insulated from the larger society, be respectful of all the people involved in it, and utilize the capacities of all. It should relate to the traditions of Judaism but to other traditions as well, and therefore be a possible agency for whatever religious development and change may be appropriate at this period of history. It should also offer maximum possibilities for distinctiveness and spontaneity of expression. In yet other terms, it should offer us some support for our own lives while helping us direct ourselves to other lives as well.

What, then, might such an alternative be like?

Formally, Yesh B'rera? would be a buildingless network of regionally grouped nuclei which would meet regularly in homes of the members for various functions. For example, let us assume that there are three to twelve families* in a given area of the city, the suburbs, or the countryside who feel that they share certain religious/societal/communal interests.†

---

* Family is the unit I select by way of example, but this is to illustrate, not to exclude nonfamily units. Single people should not feel excluded, nor students; hopefully, the tradition of *hachnasat orchim* (hospitality) could be practiced with some ease. In fact, a broad age and status range would be desired, since there are serious questions to be raised about the increasing age-and-other segregation in our society.

† These people might be Jewish but need not be. Judaism would be the religious resource consulted at the beginning, but need not be the only one.

These families would arrange to meet on a weekly basis. There could be considerable individual variation, but one possible cycle might be the following: One week a Shabbat evening pot luck supper at one home, with the hosts assuming special responsibility for the religious atmosphere, table ceremonies, singing, a home service, etc. Other weeks, Shabbat morning services in someone's home (or lawn or at a park) which, meeting at different times of day, might produce quite different moods. ("The raiment of morning is not the raiment of evening.") Still another week, the group might meet for a sunset *Havdalah* service with yet a different mood and focus.

From such involvement, we might find ourselves using space differently in our homes. A corner, a fireplace, or a room might come to have a special sense of the sacred, with certain meditative objects concentrated there. Differentiated space within the house might make all of the space more significant. (*Cf.* Japanese interiors, wooden synagogues, Mircea Eliade on sacred space, candelabra, oil lamps, samovars, earthenware vessels, *kiddush* cups, incense holders, etc. Add to the list and we'll sanctify together.)

We might also find ourselves collecting and sharing with one another meditative material, selecting appropriate expressive music, using artistic talents to design pages for loose leaf prayer books, writing new material, etc.

Combined with this would be a program of religious-cultural-social learning centered primarily in homes and related directly to the weekly coming together of the entire group. After exploring in a preliminary way some of the religious sensibilities and inclinations of members of the group, both adults and children—N.B.: adults first; no cop-out via "it's

---

In addition, crucial to the experiment, would be the slow combining of various significant elements of our lives and outlooks so that there might begin to emerge genuine and whole expressions of our real religious commitments today. This setting might be especially helpful to couples who are trying to achieve a respectful synthesis of differing birthright traditions, i.e., the "intermarried."

only for the kids"— a relevant program of activities for learning would clearly suggest itself both for the children and for the adults, and this could be assisted in several ways.

First of all, we should hope to have a regular weekly session for children of each group, with an innovative curriculum which could be assisted, led, or taught by parents of the group, students from Havurat Shalom, or students from other colleges in the area. The rabbi would be one resource person for leaders of the various learning groups, and the imaginings of all of us might provide interesting stimuli for our children's expressive learning activities (though, in all likelihood, the children would soon provide a good bit of their own curriculum).

Secondly, in order to avoid the segregation of religious education from the rest of life, a sharing of resources with one another could help the religious material flow in and out of the children's experiences easily and naturally, becoming part of the texture of life rather than an element isolated from it. What I have in mind are some records of Hebrew, Israeli children's, and holiday songs which, played at home among other records, quickly become part of the children's natural frame of reference; simple but colorful Hebrew letter projects out of felt or wood, with flannel boards; some charming, easy, and bright Israeli children's books (the Hebrew version of Dick Bruna's series, for example, in which *Tilly and Tessa* becomes *Tzili v'Gili,* is a delight to our children); the Columbia Israeli recording, with Hebrew narration, of *Peter and the Wolf* (with word lists, etc.; I've done this once before and the kids loved it, at least those who weren't afraid of the wolf!); *z'mirot;* and various other songs. The list will be a long one, and all of us will have ideas to contribute which, day by day, at story hour before bedtime, or at other shared times during the day, will help desegregate the "Jewish" and the "religious" from the rest of life.

Thirdly, for those who feel unsure of their own resources in these areas, support and instruction should be provided. After knowing what we're after and why, we can become very specific in ways of sharing such material and experiences naturally and comfortably with our children. It's important to remember, after all, that children are delighted to learn *with* as well as *from* adults, and that not everything has to be done immediately. It's also important to remember that it's not a matter of sitting down and summoning the kids to order. If the music is right, the sounds will themselves invite attention and interest; the same applies for colors, shapes, objects, movements, and occasions.

As for the adults, besides the discoveries about ourselves which we shall be making from our involvement in the religious education of our children, there ought to be another kind of relating among ourselves. This will surely vary from nucleus to nucleus, but could be seen as an exploration which draws upon intellectual resources without being intellectually bound. Thus, to share feelings, problems, and concerns of a personal kind, and to follow these wherever they might lead, could be aided by our various learnings and competences as well as by elements of our own and other traditions. To determine a course, a study, or an exploration by internal promptings and personal concerns rather than by external classifications of subject matter would be our point of departure.

One other formal element should be mentioned: periodic gatherings when the various nuclei could share concerns and celebrate together. These gatherings might take place at camp or retreat facilities in the Boston area, and could be either for a Shabbat or for an entire weekend. The timing might be related either to special Shabbats, holidays, new or full moons, or to occasions in the growth cycle of either vegetables or humans.

Substance has to do with social and religious emphases as well as with agents. A word about the latter first.

If this buildingless synagogue is truly to function, it will require a certain time investment on the part of both parents. A good beginning might be Urie Bronfenbrenner's *Two Worlds of Childhood,* a study of contemporary child rearing patterns in America and in Russia. In important respects, this volume, together with some of the issues raised by women's liberation, are central to this whole scheme of communality, study, and worship. If "the system sucks" (and it does!), it sucks the best of our time, our energies, and our attention outward toward production, professions, profits, and power—one goal of this buildingless institution must be to help us redress the imbalance of our lives.

A Personal Statement

For a variety of reasons, among them ecological considerations, religious tendencies, and personal preferences, we will be living on a small acreage not far from Boston. Part of our time, especially during the growing season, will be spent raising vegetables, planting fruit trees, and preserving. On the other hand, we hope to combine this with significant contact with people further in the city; Mary (Gendler; see page 261) through her involvement in T-groups and women's liberation, I through some parttime congregational involvement, and both of us through *Yesh B'rera?*. By sharing time and tasks rather differently from the way we used to, we hope that each of us can find some fulfillment while relating in mutually rewarding ways to the lives of others.

I would like briefly to state some of my own particular religious inclinations, which might perhaps help some of you evaluate how compatible with your interests and inclinations mine may be:

—*the prophetic:* This must be singled out for special mention since it lies at the heart of the Biblical adventure both in time and meaning; it is a difficult, essential category of awareness for our lives in relation to society, and one which must be made specific for all of us.

—*women in Judaism:* Male dominance must be corrected, and the tradition of Miriam the Prophetess leading the people in celebration of the Crossing of the Sea must be reclaimed; the need for feminine religious leadership is great within Judaism today for obvious and varying reasons.

—*theology:* The supposed split between "nature" and "history" has been a disaster environmentally and spiritually; to reclaim the nature elements of Judaism while retaining the prophetic emphasis on redemptive history is an urgent priority.

—*prayer:* Rather more meditative and celebrative than petitionary, with a central purpose of helping us integrate ourselves with the cosmic rhythms which manifest *chei ha-olamim,* the Life of the Universe, God-in-Creation.

—*Hebrew:* A fine sound of a language, expressive and powerful, some relation to which is almost essential to a genuine religious service.

—*Israel:* A focus of deep personal concern for Jews today and one vital aspect of contemporary Jewish life; not, however, the center of Jewish life as I understand it, but one pole of it; also, the power-political reality which is the State of Israel should not be identified with the religious ideal of Zion; hence, critical sympathy is appropriate, together with a concern for all the human beings and peoples involved in the Middle East.

—*Jewish identity:* The predicate "Jewish," like all predicates today, is problematic; furthermore, new religious conditions and developments suggest that there are possibly some new religious formations in the making, related to the traditional ones and drawing from them, yet very likely having their own distinct characters; part of our task is to assist with this process of transformation.

—*interreligious relations:* An area to be explored not by goodwill clichés, nor by institutional defensiveness, but by interpersonal religious experiments of various sorts; these might include study of the meaning of shared religious symbols (e.g., bread, wine, candles) to the various traditions, considerations of new religious developments, sharings of particular holiday celebrations, and so on.

—*Jewish survival:* A by-product, not the goal, of religious involvement; self-preoccupation is both wearisome and self-defeating; religion should be mainly a lens for viewing the world, not primarily a mirror for viewing the group self; those aspects of the tradition which genuinely contribute to the vanity of our lives *will be preserved,* whatever the fad of the moment; our job is to live the tradition, not focus so overwhelmingly on preserving it.

How to Proceed

Organization: I should imagine that we begin by individual expressions of interest, see where the interested people are, bring them together with other interested people in the area, and work from there.

Personally, I would hope to meet with each nucleus to help explore the particular possibilities and problems at the beginning, and if it were helpful and not intrusive, I'd like to continue to meet personally with the various nuclei in some regular way.

Financing and personnel: Hopefully, with time, each individual nucleus would draw increasingly on its own resources, and even at the beginning much would depend on the personal involvement of members of the group. This, of course, would help minimize costs.

On the other hand, it does seem to me that the assistance and coordination of a rabbi would be important, at least at the beginning of such an alternative. This may simply reflect my own clerical training and bias, but it is also possible that it reflects the reality of our relating to the resources of a rich historical tradition such as Judaism. If the latter is so, then the rabbi as a resource person, teacher, and guide might have a valid transitional role in *Yesh B'rera?.* However it would work out in practice, it seems to me that the rabbinic involvement should in principle be defined as "part-time" rather than "full-time," and that the maximum salary be anticipated at $7500 for the year.

In addition, it seems desirable to have the services of at

least some student-teachers, and funds should be available for them also. How many teachers will be needed will depend, of course, on how many nuclei form, each nucleus probably needing a teacher for one session of a couple of hours each week. Assuming the present remuneration for teaching of this kind to average $10 per hour, assuming weekly sessions of two hours extending over forty weeks, and allowing extra hours for regular meetings between teachers, the rabbi, and parents, each nucleus should envision a teaching budget of approximately $1000.

As for Shabbat and weekend gatherings at camps or retreat centers, the costs of these could be shared by the participants on each occasion.

Were we to assume seventy-two families involved, say six nuclei of twelve families each (with the twelve perhaps splitting into two sections for the weekly Shabbat home get-togethers), the budget for rabbi and teachers would be about $13,500 for the year. If each family could assume the responsibility for $18 per month (*chai* is a fine number), this would yield $15,552 per year of twelve months, leaving a margin for expenses of mimeographing, phoning, mailing, etc.

However, no one should feel excluded if these costs were too high. Who knows, after all, precisely what the figures will be? Perhaps some will be able to contribute more. Perhaps some concerned agencies or individuals will want to contribute towards this experiment (though ideally it should be self-sustaining). In any event, *no one* should hesitate to express interest because of financial considerations. Unquestionably, deficits, if there were any, would be met somehow. Personal commitment must be the determining criterion for participation in *Yesh B'rera?*.

Relation to the Present Synagogues

How essential is a building to religious involvement? How centralized must worship be? How professional must be the leading of services? How much equipment, and what kind, does education need? To what extent will home involvement prove more effective educationally than almost any conceivable developments in curricula, materials, and techniques?

To what extent does the synagogue as institution release religious energy, insight, and involvement? To what extent does it repress them? Do the formal religious institutions help or hinder people's involvement in social issues?

Can the function of the rabbi become different so that the present dissatisfactions with congregational work will be reduced, and defections from the pulpit decrease? What changes should take place in the rabbi's role? Should it be redefined or superseded altogether? If the latter takes place, will there still be a need for some specialized ministering to pastoral needs such as weddings, funerals, *bar* and *bat mitzvahs,* and so forth? By whom? What about maintaining contact with the resources of the tradition, and of Jewish learning? What changes, if any, in the directions outlined in this proposal can or should occur within the present synagogue structure.

The above questions are not meant to be rhetorical; they are genuine. The answers are not clear to me, but I think they are important in relation to the future of the synagogue and the future of Judaism. *Yesh B'rera?* may cast some light on at least some possible answers.

Yesh B'rera?

The term includes a question mark at this point. Perhaps in a year it can be removed and stand as a tentative affirmation. Perhaps in three years it might be replaced by an exclamation mark. On the other hand, it may well be that the removal of the question mark will follow the erasure of the slogan altogether, at least as it relates to this particular model. Then we shall know that if there is an alternative, this is not it.

Shall we at least explore the matter together?

The Struggle for *Shalom*

Sherman Rosenfeld

4/13/78

Shalom is a Hebrew word which means "completeness, wholeness." It does not mean "peace" (i.e., absence of war). Such a concept connotes a dynamic, well-integrated whole and implies that considerable energy is required for both its acquisition and maintenance.

There should be no doubt in anyone's mind that although we may have an absence of war in the American Jewish community, we certainly have no *shalom*. It would be more worth trying to understand how this concept of wholeness was traditionally incorporated into the lives of Jews and their communities than to analyze what has presently gone wrong and why, and finally to outline a plan for bringing *shalom* into contemporary American life.

* * *

The value of wholeness and integrity has traditionally been a supreme value in Jewish life, permeating all study, ritual,

Born in Los Angeles in 1948, Sherman Rosenfeld studied at the University of Chicago and the Hebrew University in Jerusalem before graduating with a B.A. in ecology from Berkeley, where he was active in the Radical Jewish Union and city director of the Jewish youth group Young Judea. From 1971–72 he worked as teacher and counselor at an Israeli high school in the Negev kibbutz of Sde Boker. This article is reprinted from *The Jewish Radical*, Winter, 1971, by permission of its editors and the author.

and action. In fact, these three mechanisms for transmitting Jewish values form a unity in themselves.

For the traditional Jew, the realm of all holiness and art was the realm of human conduct. A sacred relationship existed between the matrices of words and action, so that study was as vital and necessary to the Jew as food and air. Once the rabbis debated what was better—study or action. They chose this answer—study that leads to action is best. The "People of the Book," as they were called with derision by surrounding civilizations, through analysis of men's lives and laws of ethical conduct, used the study of Torah both as a vehicle for transmitting values and as an indispensible guide for their own behavior. The lessons of the prophets repeatedly called for the fusion of politics with ethics. Talmudic study sharpened the student's own powers of analysis and problem-solving, which could be applied frequently to the demands of everyday life.

Implicit in this approach were the dual dangers of over-verbalization and overconceptualization, which could easily turn the concern with ethical action into an ivory-towered scholasticism, divorced from life. The deterrent to this undesirable fate was clearly recognized and is best summarized by the rabbinical dictum to "say little and do much," and by Judah Ibn Tibbon's advice to his son: "Let conduct be the end of all thou learnest."

Rituals were models of action, where explicit and hidden values were ingrained in each individual Jew by force of habit. These values could then be applied and injected into every possible living situation. For example, the ritual of tasting the bitter herbs at the Passover meal as a reminder of what it was like to be a slave in Egypt was intended to make Jews more sensitive to the condition of oppressed peoples. A *mitzvah* meant not only "commandment," but "good deed," i.e., an inwardly satisfying act. Holidays infused life with a sense of continuity, community, and joy, the latter always being regarded as a *mitzvah*.

The goal of all study and ritual was the most effective

mechanism for transmitting values. Action was the ultimate language, for values were meaningful only if lived.

Traditionally, the individual and the community were seen as interrelating and interdependent aspects of a common whole. Each individual was important to the community since everyone was recognized as a unique being capable of unique contributions. Conversely, the community was valuable to each individual since it provided diversity, social contact, and a secure environment for growth.

Particularism and universalism were inextricably connected. The importance of Jewish collective responsibility ("All the members of Israel are responsible, each to the others.") was mirrored by the imperative for Jews to respond to other peoples of the world ("Love the stranger, for you once were a stranger in the land of Egypt.").

The Jewish way of life traditionally aimed at completeness in human relations and behavior by stressing in every conceivable area—by study, ritual and action—the complementary relationships of study and action, the individual, and the community, the particular, and the universal.

* * *

The most obvious reason why there is no *shalom* in the American Jewish community is that traditional Jewish values have been divorced from action. Such division can be seen on all levels.

The social institution most responsible for the decadence of American Jewry is the traditional greenhouse of human values —the family. Most American Jewish parents don't seem to give a damn about living Jewishness in their houses, yet they get angry with their kids for choosing non-Jewish spouses. Ignored at home, the transmission of Jewish values is delegated to the Hebrew school. Children of such irresponsible parents, seeing the split between daily life and what they learn in Hebrew school, conclude that the one is unconnected to the other.

With such lack of support from the home, study is automatically isolated from action and the Hebrew school is given a near-impossible assignment. Still, it aggravates the situation with a sterile and infantile approach that insults students and leaves them cold. The curriculum is full of discontinuities and lack of direction: the teaching staffs are poorly trained and ill-motivated; enormous areas of tremendous depth and enthusiasm are neglected or deprived of their intrinsic vitality. However, students who do stick it out seem to develop something of value—a sense of camaraderie forged by common suffering.

The contemporary American synagogue seems to intensify the split between Jewish values and action. A wall exists between the pulpit and the congregation; the latter comes as members of a passive audience to "services" (literally, *tephillah* means "self-judgment"). Members of the Board of Directors are chosen on the basis of their bank accounts, not integrity; the issues they discuss are overwhelmingly financial. Extravagant buildings, Friday-night fashion shows, *bar mitzvah* exhibitions and weddings smothered in wealth betray the traditional concern for community and deep feeling with a concern for money and status.

Similar values are reflected on the "community" level, the priorities of which may be summarized in two words: public relations. Unlike traditional Jews, to whom it was inconceivable to question the value of Jewish education, the leaders of the Jewish Establishment do all they can to "combat anti-Semitism and Arab propaganda," but have no deeper commitment to Jewish education—neither for the community nor for themselves. Those who support Jewish studies must make *demands* on Welfare Federations, since these organizations often side-step their basic responsibility. A recent weekend conference of Jewish community center directors in Monterey had no plans to even mention the Shabbat; an Israeli visitor had to point out this error, explain to them the meaning of Shabbat, say the appropriate blessings, and teach them some elementary songs—none of which any of them knew. Internally weak and externally competitive, the countless Jewish organizations, run by incompetent leaders, shatter the Jewish community into pieces. Only something as dramatic as the Six-Day War seems to bring these pieces together, if only for a brief time.

The stereotypical product of all this is the neurotic, self-hating, guilt-ridden, and joyless Jew best popularized in the character of Alexander Portnoy. To ask how he got that way is to ask how the American Jewish family, Hebrew school, synagogue, and Establishment came to practice the schizophrenia of saying one set of values while living another set.

The Jewish immigrant saw in the New World a place where he and his set of values could finally be accepted. His children (and to a greater extent, their children) found that compromise was the surest road to their own acceptance, especially when their values clashed with those of the larger society. To facilitate change, the Enlightenment and the scientific revolution had helped to discredit religion and ritual. Other powerful forces (e.g., technology, urbanization, mass-media) worked in concert with this trend.

With compromise, Jewish institutions began to take on a constellation of foreign values that substituted traditional Jewish ones, specifically in three areas: 1) an intense individualism that thrived on a competition ethic and isolation replaced the traditional concern with community; 2) the concern for "making an impression" and superficial images replaced the concern for depth; and 3) money and status replaced study and action as the measure of human worth.

But the most fatal compromise of all was made when American Jews, wanting to believe in the dream of the melting pot, defined themselves solely as religious beings, trading in their political souls in the process. Now they were really split in two: Jewish in "thought," American in action.

Such a definition denying the crucial link between Jewish thought and action fragmented the Jew into a severe schizophrenia, where inner and outer, spirit and body, value and action were set apart. The resulting confusion, self-doubt, and shame of the Jewish American reinforced his impotent and apologetic posture, making the whole scene all the more difficult for Jewish youth to accept.

Just as no healthy person has consciously desired to take on a disease, no healthy Jewish youth consciously accepted this schizophrenic Jewish identity. If he accepted this identity unconsciously or without knowing what it really was, when he found out, he hated himself the more for what he was and rejected it all, vowing never to return. Such reactions are reasonable. But the deep tragedy is that nobody was around to point it out.

So the question becomes: Why are there any committed (and healthy) Jewish youth at all? The answer, I believe, is that such young Jews have been exposed to organic-living approaches (e.g., in a Jewish home, a *havurah,* a summer camp, a Jewish youth group, Israel) where there was no split in the Jewish personality. These various experiences, I believe, somehow integrated—rather than fragmented—their lives. If these positive experiences occurred after they received the stereotypical American Jewish experience, then they realized just how much they had been cheated.

Such a realization obligates us to undo the mess around us by working for wholeness in our communities. First, we must restore the unity between Jewish ethics and our own politics, between what we believe and what we do. To do this, we must search to our roots for sources of strength and affirmation, which is why Jewish education—not assimilation—must be seen as our number one priority for survival. Second, we must work to build a sense of community and joy, replacing apologies with an identity based upon positive commitment. Because these actions go to the root of our problems which are ignored by the Jewish Establishment, they are radical in the true sense of the word.

All over this country, grass-roots radical Jewish movements are beginning to develop. They are basically *organic,* meaning that they affirm the total Jewish personality within a *living* context. In this way they are trying to discover living answers to questions that have been forgotten or ignored by most of American Jewry.

The rabbis were quick to point out that the gap between *matzui* (the way it is) and *ratzui* (the way it ought to be) is filled with *mar* (bitterness). The struggle for *shalom* is just that—an intense and bitter struggle. But knowing the task at hand is half of the battle.

Part Six

The Plight of Soviet Jewry

In 1971 almost 14,000 Soviet Jews were permitted to emigrate to Israel, more than the total for the previous ten years. The harsh terrorist repression of both Czarist and Stalinist Russia has given way to a more subtle "cultural genocide" in which any open expression of Jewish identity can result in loss of basic political, social, and economic privileges. Dissenting Jews who demand their rights are labeled "Zionist spies" and spectacles such as the winter 1971 Leningrad Trials are the result.

Is the recent easing of visa restrictions by Soviet officials, then, a smokescreen to keep world attention away from the continued internal harassment of Jews, or is it truly a sign of a new policy in response to the pressure of outside world opinion and dissent within the Soviet Union itself?

The nearly three million Jews who remain in the Soviet Union are prisoners of war—prisoners in the cold war policies of both the United States and Russia. The Soviet Jews are a pawn in the chessboard of international diplomacy. Soviet and American interests in the Middle East dictate their policy toward the Jews in Russia.

How many Jews would leave if Russia initiated an "open-door" policy? It is impossible to say. The risks of being an open Jew in Russia have caused a great many to abandon their Jewish identity. Yet, as in the United States, the Six-Day War shocked many young Russian Jews into a realization that they could not completely forget the legacy of a once-great Russian Jewish culture. Young Jews are openly speaking out today, agitating for a more lenient policy toward both Jewish emigration and Jewish cultural and religious freedom. Efforts to dramatize their plight have run the gamut from quiet diplomacy to the violent tactics of the Jewish Defense League.

New Left spokesmen such as I. F. Stone, Noam Chomsky, David Dellinger, and David McReynolds signed an appeal on behalf of the victims of the Leningrad Trials, a healthy sign that the right will not be allowed to monopolize the issue in the name of anticommunism. Yet there is a danger that anticommunist appeals will rally people to the Soviet Jewry cause— perhaps at the expense of enlightened domestic policies. The Jewish Left has had to walk this tightrope and combat these Cold War sentiments while developing an alternative strategy to save Soviet Jews.

The pieces in this chapter shed some light on the "Jewish question" in the U.S.S.R.

A Russian Jew Cries Out

Boris Kochubiyevsky

Boris Kochubiyevsky has dared even more than other Russian Jews, and has consequently paid a greater price. From the Six-Day War onward he repeatedly and publicly defended Israel's position, which brought down upon him enormous hostility and pressure, which ultimately forced him out of his engineering job, and his wife out of her pedagogical institute and the Young Communist League. In September, 1968, in the face of provocations, he staunchly insisted, at a memorial meeting for the scores of thousands of Jews slaughtered by the Nazis at Babi Yar in 1941–43, that this was a unique tragedy for the Jewish people.

A week after he wrote this letter he was arrested. Ultimately, he was brought to trial in Kiev from May 13–16, 1969, on charges of disseminating anti-Soviet slander. He was found guilty and sentenced to three years of forced labor. Recently, he has been released and is now in Israel.

November 28, 1968

TO: The Secretary General of the C.P.S.U. Central Committee —Brezhnev, The First Secretary of the (Ukraine C.P.) Central Committee

Boris Kochubiyevsky was released from a Soviet prison and now lives in Israel. This article first appeared in *Fourth World*, January, 1971, and is reprinted by permission of its editorial board.

COPY TO: The Investigator of the Prosecutor's Office in the Shevchenko Region of the City of Kiev—V. V. Doroshenko.

FROM: The Accused of Slander of Soviet Reality—B. L. Kochubiyevsky, Jew.

I am a Jew. I want to live in the Jewish State. This is my right, just as it is the right of a Ukrainian to live in the Ukraine, the right of a Russian to live in Russia, the right of a Georgian to live in Georgia.

I want to live in Israel.

This is my dream, this is the goal not only of my life but also of the lives of hundreds of generations which preceded me, of my ancestors who were expelled from their land.

I want my children to study in a school in the Hebrew language. I want to read Jewish papers, I want to attend a Jewish theater. What's wrong with that? What is my crime? Most of my relatives were shot by the fascists. My father perished and his parents were killed. Were they alive now, they would be standing at my side: Let me go!

I have repeatedly turned with this request to various authorities and have achieved only this: Dismissal from my job, my wife's expulsion from her Institute; and, to crown it all, a criminal charge of slandering Soviet reality. What is this slander? Is it slander that in the multinational Soviet State only the Jewish people cannot educate its children in Jewish schools? Is it slander that there is no Jewish theater in the U.S.S.R.? Is it slander that in the U.S.S.R. there are no Jewish papers? By the way, no one even denies this. Perhaps it is slander that for over a year I have not succeeded in obtaining an exit permit for Israel? Or is it slander that nobody wants to speak to me, that there is nobody to complain to? Nobody reacts. But even this isn't the heart of the matter. I don't want to be involved in the national affairs of a state in which I consider myself an alien. I want to go away from here. I want to live in Israel. My wish does not contradict Soviet law.

I have an affidavit of invitation from my relatives; all the formalities have been observed. Is that why you are instituting a criminal case against me?

Is that why my home was searched?

I am not asking for mercy. Listen to the voice of reason: Let me go!

As long as I live, as long as I am capable of feeling, I shall devote all my strength to obtaining an exit permit for Israel. And even if you should find it possible to sentence me for this —I shall anyway, if I live long enough to be freed, be prepared even then to make my way even on foot to the homeland of my ancestors.

A Russian Jew Speaks

Dov Sperling

To understand what is going on in Russia with the Jews, it is vital to understand that the entire regime is against the Jewish people. It is not a question of whether Brezhnev is anti-Semitic or whether Khrushchev was anti-Semitic. The regime wants to destroy our people.

Before Lenin got to power he wrote "the only solution is that the Jews must assimilate among the other nations and the Jews are not a nation." When he got the power he started to do what he wrote and after him Stalin continued and Khrushchev and, today, other leaders in the Kremlin are continuing the fight against the Jewish people. Why? Because the communists can't understand what the Jewish people is—how the Jews, living among all the nations, not having a common territory, or a common language—survive. For them, the Jews are something mystic and they understand that some day, even if Jews supported the Russian Revolution in 1917, the Jews will be against the regime because Jews were against all regimes that wanted to destroy them.

Dov Sperling was born, raised, and educated in the U.S.S.R. In 1968 he was allowed to emigrate from the Soviet Union and went to Israel where he now lives. This article is based on a speech given by Mr. Sperling to a student audience at York University, Canada. It appeared in *Fourth World*, January, 1971, and is reprinted by permission of its editorial board.

Who Am I?

I'll give a couple of simple examples of what they did to our youth. Until 1956 I didn't even know that Israel existed, that there exists a Jewish state. We get a communist Russian education. We go to Russian schools. We don't have any culture, any Jewish school or Hebrew school—nothing at all. We are Russians as any other Russians, but in our identification card is written *"Ivri*—Jew." We know we are Jews, but what does it mean to be a Jew? I wondered, "Who am I?" And when I looked around me I saw the Jews are something less than other people are.

Before 1956 I believed in Stalin. There was no doubt for me that every word that Stalin said was right—completely right. And when I saw that the Jews have no culture, have no schools, haven't anything, I couldn't imagine that the regime is fighting against us, because the regime is the best regime in the world. But when I saw that even gypsies have a big theater in Moscow which goes abroad and gets all the support of the government, I understood that we were worse even than the gypsies. So I felt like every young Jew—humiliated. I got an inferiority complex. I had nothing to answer against other people when they spoke against Jews, because I didn't know.

I don't know what the image of Russia is in Canada, but I am afraid the people here think that the Soviet Union is one great family of many nations and every nation has its rights and everything is all right. It's not so.

The Russians occupied many territories, like Latvia, the Ukraine, and Georgia. And every small nation hates the Russians because they don't need the Russians and can't be independent. They speak about their pride in being Georgian, Ukrainian, or Latvian, and we live in a chauvinistic surrounding. We hear the Georgians say, "My people are the most beautiful," the Latvians say "My people are the most courageous," and so on.

Only we had nothing to answer; we didn't have anything to

say. And it was a terrible thing for us that the regime destroyed us as a nation.

First Heard of Israel

The first time I heard about the State of Israel was when an Israeli football team came to Russia. I accidentally turned on the radio, I was in Riga, and I heard *Hatikvah* on the Soviet radio. It was the first time I had heard *Hatikvah*. I didn't know how the anthem of the State of Israel sounds. But I am not ashamed to tell that when I heard that anthem, I cried. Because for me, as for every young Jew, who lived with an inferiority complex, it made us free. It pointed out the very existence of Israel, of a Jewish state, and made us free from our inferiority complexes. And this is the biggest difference between us, the Jewish youth in Russia, and the American Jewish youth or the Jewish youth in the free world. Because you know about Israel and sometimes you don't care. If you want, you can go to a synagogue, if you want, you can live here like Jews.

The Sinai campaign broke out and suddenly we opened the radio and we heard that Israel is fighting against poor Arabs, millions of Arabs, and it was terrible for the Arabs, of course. And it was great for us. We saw that not only do we have a land, but that it is a big country, a great country, not according to the number of citizens in the country, but all the world was against Israel—the U.S.A., England, and France and all the world said to Israel, "You must withdraw from Gaza!" And Israel said, "No," because Israel believed she was right. Israel withdrew after four months, but it showed us that it is a great country.

After that I went to a cinema—it was in 1957. And suddenly I saw a documentary film of what happened in 1956. Suddenly I saw Jewish soldiers. The commentator said that they are fascists and . . . it is not important what he said. You can take the newspapers of the New Left and you will understand what they said in 1956. But I suddenly saw Jewish soldiers and I suddenly saw a Jewish general. I didn't know what his name is but I saw a young general with one eye. It was very important that he had one eye. It shows us that he himself fights. He lost his eye in battle. We didn't know where, but this was not like Soviet generals who sit a thousand kilometers behind the lines and send their soldiers ahead to die.

You must realize that for us it is a big thing to see many Jews together. In Russia there are only two places where you can see many Jews together—in the few synagogues that still remain in Russia or the Jewish cemetery. You don't have any club or any place to see many Jews. And suddenly you see Jewish soldiers. And you suddenly hear the gentiles around you in the cinema saying, "They are Jews? Jews look like these soldiers?" And I heard and saw that they have respect for these Jews, not like for us, the Russian Jews.

Jewish Underground

There does exist an underground in Russia—a Zionist underground among the youth—because the elderly people are afraid. They had enough—they saw Stalin. The fear is in their blood and they can't act as the young people can. Now what did we do? We got the book, Leon Uris' *Exodus*. We translated it into Russian and we typed it, because we have nowhere to print it, we can only type it in the houses. And we studied Hebrew, and sometimes Yiddish. We listened to the Israel radio and we printed Zionistic literature. Because it is our war. We want to survive; we want to go to Israel; we want to be Jews. And to be Jews you need to know something.

We were sitting in our houses and studying and suddenly we saw after the Sinai campaign that there was a little liberalization. We started to look for books such as Dubnov's *The History of the Jewish People*. We found that Bar Kochba exists and the Maccabees and that the Jews fought against Rome when Russia was swamp and woods and forests and wasn't a nation. So we found out that we are a nation.

I would like to emphasize again and again that the problem now is not Jewish schools in Russia. We don't want to go to Jewish schools where the communist regime will teach us anti-Zionism, anti-Jewishness, anti-Israel. We have enough of that in Russian! We don't need it in Yiddish!

Now I was a student and every student in Russia must study Marxism-Leninism. We study the question of nations according to Stalin, and according to him only a group of people which has a common language, a common territory, a common country and history and so on, is called a nation. And Jews are not a nation. I started to argue. I had already read Dubnov and I heard Israel radio. I said, "You are wrong, because we had a country before you had," and so on. I argued so long until they came to my house in the morning and took me to jail. I had a trial. I got two years in prison.

When I arrived in prison I met a lot of Jews from all parts of Russia—young and old, mostly young. They were in prison for a simple thing—love for Israel. One of them was an old Jew who knew Hebrew and I started to study with him. When I came home I found that the Jewish youth knew almost everything about Israel. Every day they listen to Israeli radio.

When we get a postcard from Israel, and such things do reach the Soviet Union, it is the best gift for a Jew. A postcard from Israel, or something small from Israel, is a holy thing.

Effects of the Six-Day War

When the Six-Day War broke out we were in a terrible situation because we couldn't speak openly for Israel. Here you will be hated by the New Left if you speak for Israel. But there, if you speak for Israel, you will be sent to prison. But when the Jews met in the streets, they said to one another: "*Mazel tov,* we liberated Jerusalem." We didn't say "somebody occupied Jerusalem." Such a question didn't exist. Jerusalem is ours even if we didn't get a Jewish education. We didn't say, "they liberated Jerusalem," but "we liberated Jerusalem."

After the Six-Day War, together with the actions of the underground—printing literature, etc.—you can see every year—tens of thousands of young Jews coming to the few synagogues still remaining in Russia and shouting "Long live Israel," "Long live Dayan," and dancing dances and singing songs like *David Melech Israel* and *Eretz Zavat Chalav Udvash*. Short and simple songs because they don't understand what the words really mean and it's not important. It's only important that the song came from Israel.

Release Troublemakers

When the Soviet government sees young Jews going crazy in the capital of the Soviet Empire and young Jews identifying themselves with a hostile land, they want to destroy us immediately. But they can't. The regime is weak. Khrushchev destroyed the image of the regime among the population and they don't have a new Stalin in the government. Stalin knew what to do and he was a strong man. They must look for a solution. They decided in September of 1968 to try to give the Jews permission to go to Israel. Only, of course, for the unification of families. You must get an invitation from Israel, from your uncle or aunt, or someone else, and you must come to the Interior Ministry and say "I want to go to my aunt because I can't live without her. I have a passionate longing to see my aunt, whom I have never seen."

The Soviet official understands that you want to go to Israel, not because you want to see your uncle, but because you want to join the Israeli army, to join Israel.

The government decided it can't send all the tens of thousands of Jews because it is weak, so they will allow a small number of troublemakers to go to Israel. They think that in this way they'll solve the problem.

They quickly saw that they were wrong. It is not a thousand troublemakers, not two or three thousand. It is hundreds of thousands of people asking permission to leave for Israel.

Now they continue to give permission to go to Israel for a hundred people every month. They are trying to buy us cheap.

They want to destroy us. Maybe in half a year we will not have a chance to act because a new Stalin may come and destroy our people.

Part Seven

The Jewish Woman

"Are Jewish women oppressed?" asks Judy Timberg. The pieces in this chapter attempt to answer that question. More precisely, is the oppression of Jewish women quantitatively different from that of, first, Jewish men, and second, non-Jewish women?

There is little question that Jewish culture is patriarchal and "sexist." Traditionally, sex roles in Jewish culture were rigidly defined. It seems that in the Old Testament women "begat" only males!

There are, of course, heroines in the Bible—Esther, Ruth, and Deborah, for example. But here the exception proves the rule. Jewish women were almost always supposed to be in the home with the children. In fact, the prayer men recited in the synagogue every day unabashedly revealed her position: "Blessed art thou, O Lord . . . for not making me a woman."

The "Jewish mother" and the "Jewish princess"—popular stereotypes in recent American fiction (Marjorie Morningstar, Mrs. Portnoy, Brenda Potemkin)—are symbols of the special kind of image Jewish girls are offered as they mature and attempt to develop a positive identity. (For another viewpoint, see Zena Blaus' "In Defense of the Jewish Mother," in Peter Rose, ed., *The Ghetto and Beyond*, Random House, New York, 1969).

Jewish women's "consciousness raising" groups have

emerged to deal with their plight. Women's liberation, an attack on rigid sex roles, is ultimately the liberation of men. Perhaps Jewish men's groups will emerge as well, for there is no doubt a special oppression of Jewish men—the anxiety of achievement and failure, their socialization into intellectual rather than physical roles (why are there so few Jewish soldiers, hunters, and athletes?), and the awkward relationship between Jewish men and non-Jewish women. This chapter opens up fresh questions to age-old problems.

Are Jewish Women Oppressed?

Judy Timberg

Recently, an article in *Brooklyn Bridge* considered the condition of Jewish women, past and present. It applied a familiar women's liberation analysis to the Jews: "precisely like the sexual division of labor that occurs in all cultures, the men do what is considered important and significant, while the women do everything that men do not want to be bothered with." This easy formula distorts the meaning *to women* of their role in the community. I would ask how women themselves felt about their lives, in Eastern Europe and America, and then ask what their experience can mean for us.

There is one indispensable book, *Life Is With People* by Zborowski and Herzog (Schocken Books, New York, 1962), about the Eastern European *shtetl,* and it gives a fairly complete picture of the woman's world. From this book it is clear that in religious terms, women of the *shtetl* were considered inferior. In a culture which placed the highest value on the mind, study, and education, women were barely literate in Yiddish, read Hebrew without comprehending it, and spent a

---

Judy Timberg graduated from Carleton College and spent two years in graduate school in sociology at the University of California, Berkeley. Her involvement with the Berkeley Radical Jewish Union stems from its early period of growth in 1970. This article first appeared in *The Jewish Radical,* Spring, 1971, and is reprinted by permission of the author.

minimum amount of time in school. In the synagogue they had no religious duties.

Most of the negative aspects of a woman's life involved exclusion from the male sphere, but I would agree that this was offset by her free rein and often dominance in other valued spheres of community life. I do not think that the woman's *formal* religious status deprived her of a sense of importance, accomplishment, or power. Her *informal* status as complement to the scholar-husband in all things, woman of practical affairs, and emotional center of the family required her to be strong in ways that were well-appreciated by the family and community.

Moreover, nothing in the culture supported the idea that she should be strong in a man's way—that is, in religious learning. Since that was considered peculiar, I doubt she felt frustrated in the modern sense of not developing her potential; more likely she complained of having too much responsibility. To see the difference in men's and women's roles as inherently oppressive is to think in terms alien to the *shtetl*—a dangerous practice if you're trying to understand people's feelings about their lives.

In the *shtetl* a woman really was fulfilling her destiny by doing what all acknowledged she ought to do, whereas in America a woman often feels cheated of her destiny if she is *only* a wife and mother. America, I think, does not honor its standard women's roles as much as the *shtetl* did. Nor does it give women the same sense of power.

Zborowski and Herzog present a picture of the "functioning balance of power between the sexes": "The woman's informal status is more demanding and more rewarding than that formally assigned to her, for in actual living the complementary character of her role is always to the fore" (p. 131); and "to a comfortable degree, in the day by day rush of life, each sex is oriented to its own reality. If one's world revolves around the activities of the *shul*, the domestic economy is seen as an indispensable but secondary adjunct. If home is the hub of the universe, the *shul* and its activities become a necessary luxury, sometimes classed as a burden and sometimes as a privilege. In either case, one can feel—mine is the real work of the world." (p. 141)

It is clear that the *shtetl* woman had an active rather than passive role. She was likely to support the family as well as sustain it in every other way, and she notoriously did not do it quietly. Her life was home-centered but not home-limited; since she was the one to deal with merchants and peasants, she was (more often than men) familiar with the local language, and was likely to travel away from the *shtetl* to neighboring towns. She was expected to be outspoken, physical, expressive: "in behavior the model man is restrained, poised, laconic. It is taken for granted that women are far more expressive, ready with tears, laughter, and volubility . . . (in appearance) a woman should, in short, be a solid, healthy body, whereas a man should be a strong, transcendent spirit . . . (pp. 138–9)"

It was mostly into mothering that the *shtetl* woman poured her energies, received her satisfactions, and found her problems. "The stereotype of the *Yiddishe mammeh,* familiar in many lands, has firm roots in the *shtetl.* No matter what you do, no matter what happens, she will love you always. She may have odd and sometimes irritating ways of showing it, but in a hazardous and unstable world the belief about the mother's love is strong and unshakable . . . The mother's love is manifested . . . by unremitting solicitude about every aspect of her child's welfare . . . worry is not viewed as an indulgence but as an expression of affection and almost a duty. If you worry actively enough, something may come of it" (pp. 293-4).

We all know about the dangers inherent in this style of mothering—it can be intrusive and smothering and demanding. *Portnoy's Complaint* portrays the Jewish mother at her worst. But who could mistake an extreme example, a distortion of the normal, for the whole picture? Every kind of typical behavior has its pathology if circumstances thwart its normal expression. At her best, the Jewish mother did extremely positive things for her children—she gave them a security nothing else in *shtetl* life could offer and a sense of confidence and ability that they assumed by being *her* children.

However, in America, circumstances do not support the *shtetl* style. Not much is made of the immigrant mother's powerful part in getting the Jews out of the Lower East Side in one generation. I suspect that she was crucial in accomplishing this partly because her role in the family had not changed as drastically as the man's in the move to America. He lost the prime source of his dignity and joy as the *shul* ceased to be the center of life, and as the Jewish community opened up to secular American values when the children went to public school. The family was desperately poor, as in the *shtetl,* but the man no longer had refuge from the definition of himself as simply a poor man. Moreover, he was now in a society where not everyone was poor, and being poor was not so accepted. It was important for his self-esteem in America to have money, but he was often ill-equipped to get it.

The woman, however, still was the center of home life, still poured her love and hopes into her children, and often worked to support the family; the *shtetl* strength was still required of her. There was probably a difference in the satisfactions of her life, between the *shtetl* and the Lower East Side, because the roles that complemented hers in the past didn't work in the same way in America. Most importantly, the father's status didn't enhance hers and her own work didn't enhance his religious life. This may have caused many women to invest even more in their sons, who already bore the traditional Jewish boy's load of parental hopes. The sons had to recapture the father's lost dignity—in an American way. And they did. Their mothers' intense involvement with this process—the distortion of a *shtetl* pattern—may well have contributed to the caricature of the overinvolved Jewish mother in America.

The Eastern European Jewish woman's style didn't fit American middle-class ideas of motherhood or femininity for the second or succeeding generations. It was embarrassingly lower-class and ethnic. The reaction to it is documented, after a fashion, in *The Jewish Wife* by Wyden and Schwartz (Peter

Wyden, Inc., New York, 1969). Their book is *not* reliable as proof for anything, since it gives no idea of how many people responded in what way, or how their answers compared with those of the non-Jewish women interviewed. However, it is useful in a suggestive way because it portrays some very familiar characteristics that second- and third-generation women share with immigrant and *shtetl* women.

We see first the reaction *against* the immigrant Jewish mother's style: in contrast to her ample figure, desirable in a culture where a woman should be a "solid, healthy body," the American Jewish woman fights fat like the plague. She markedly dislikes and avoids manual work. She travels first-class when she can. She probably doesn't work, much less support the family.

But her acceptance of the *shtetl* pattern is more basic than her rejection of it. She is extremely active, values practical competence highly, and organizes everything so she can get more done. She has high expectations of herself—things don't happen to her, she happens to them. Although she probably doesn't work, she is more likely than non-Jewish women to have activities outside the home.

The Jewish wife described in this book is intensely involved with her family. The husband-wife relationship is seen by both as a partnership, and the husband leans heavily on the wife for advice and support. The husband and wife operate in different spheres and most women are not competitive in the work world. She reads all the psychology books and knows the theories about child-raising, but in the end she is more confident about her own ideas and her own ability to handle a situation. She expects a lot of her children, praising them at every opportunity and encouraging them into activities and accomplishments. Just as in the *shtetl,* she often worries and feels guilty, but she believes also that these feelings spur her on to do more and better. She is expressive—laughs, quarrels, cries freely—and pours her feelings into her family. *Naches* from the children means a great deal to her; each one has to be a *mensch,* and she has to make him one. The sociologist Marshall Sklare says that one of the great things she does is give her children self-confidence in the possibility of achievement. By a process of clutching and pushing away she sends them out in this world without abandoning them.

* * *

Are we oppressed now? I think that insofar as we feel embarrassed or uncomfortable about the idea of the Jewish mother, we are letting others define us. The only judgment I think we really do have to face down comes from the negative aspects of the Jewish mother stereotype, and I think it is often presented with affection as well as dismay. If we know where the Jewish mother came from and what she accomplished, we can understand her sense of self, her gift for sustaining a homeful of people.

But there are other problems with the mother role in America and they can have an extra intensity for Jewish women, who invest so much in family life.

It is a universal American problem that women live longer than they used to and the last of their children move out of their sphere when the women are at the peak of the powers they have been developing for twenty years. I suspect that this problem is particularly acute for Jewish mothers, who, like other women, need to invest themselves in other viable roles.

It is ironic that in America, where women are supposed to be more "free" than women of a traditional society like the shtetl, the options she is free to choose all have something wrong with them. In America there is no feminine role that is truly honored, and women are very often torn between the low self-esteem that comes of being "only a housewife" and the dissatisfactions of ill-paid, ill-valued work which takes her almost completely away from her family. In America, self-esteem requires "achievement." Naturally, women are trying to liberate themselves from a role the society only half values. This is not a specifically Jewish problem, but again, given the Jewish woman's traditional investment in the family, it could be especially demoralizing to her.

A slightly more Jewish problem in America is the recompense Jewish mothers have traditionally gotten from their children that makes their devotion worthwhile—*naches fun kinder*. Children are no longer considered to be extensions of their parents, with obligations to them. It's harder to get them to come up with some *naches*. They don't play the game as readily as *shtetl* children did. So the equation doesn't work out as it used to; it's the generation gap problem, of course, but again with an extra twist for Jewish women.

You may say that these are middle-aged, middle-class problems and you don't expect to be a "Jewish mother" (certainly you may not be concerned with that now), but I think most of us have more "Jewish mother" in us than we imagine. These things go very deep, and have rather little to do with religious belief or life style.

Somewhat connected to the hollowness of the mother role in America is the question of women's exclusion from the orthodox religious realm. It is a religious problem that the world doesn't divide up between men and women as it used to. Young women have more education now, and they are not trained for the life that traditional women knew; they will not be as well compensated for being subordinate in the religious sphere. Women want to explore their Judaism more intellectually than women have done in the past, and they want to play a more central part in the religious life of the community. Their liberation will involve exploring new forms of religious life in a way that respects Jewish tradition.

Thus, the problems I see for Jewish women today come from three situations: mixed feelings about the "Jewish mother" stereotype, the problems of the mother role in America, and the exclusion of women from religious life.

But I think we should also realize our assets and make the most of them. Most obvious is our tradition of strength. Jewish women may worry, they may feel guilty, but they get things done. Even when they adapt the "Jewish mother" style to the American middle class, they keep this sense of being an active personality, of impressing themselves on events.

And in what is this strength? Much of it goes into giving, because ideally Jewish women feel they're strong enough to give. Doormats they aren't, but give they do. Having a sense of self means you can afford to liberate your energies for others beyond yourself.

Along with this strength goes the Jewish partnership in marriage. The Jewish wife is a full partner—a valued counselor and an equal contributor. Both members are active in this relationship, both give *and* take.

Finally, Jewish women often do expand their world beyond the family—it has been in the past and still is a Jewish thing to combine devotion to a family with outside activities.

I conclude that it would be a mistake to concentrate too heavily on our "oppression"—better to understand our past and make the most of its legacy of female strength.

National Liberation and the Jewish Woman

Sheryl Baron

It is very chic today in liberal circles to discuss women's liberation. And apparently it is even more chic to discuss it in Jewish liberal circles. The liberal literati of the American Jewish community have taken a few misplaced stabs at the topic, only to turn out a tiring discussion of the quantity and quality of orgasmic responses in middle-class Jewish females. Consequently, one has to consider whether or not a point is being stretched when the topic of "Jewish women and women's liberation" is discussed. Outside of a political context, this topic suggests only a sociological study or a survey, neither of which is crucial to the development of ideology in that anti-ideological stronghold called the American Jewish community. However, if we choose to deal politically with the topic of women's liberation as it relates to the condition of the Jewish nation, we can begin to pull ourselves out of the abyss of liberal ideology that the American Jewish condition has created.

Since the women's movement in this country started (as a middle-class phenomenon), it has expanded its thought and

Sheryl Baron is a student in history at U.C.L.A., a member of the Jewish Radical Community in Los Angeles, and a member of the National Steering Committee of the Radical Zionist Alliance. She has been active in the women's liberation movement since 1968. This article originally appeared in *Davka*, Summer, 1971, and is reprinted by permission of the author.

action into the area of women in oppressed national minorities. What at this point sounds rather hackneyed to the veterans of the radical feminism still rings true: women of oppressed national minorities are doubly oppressed; they are oppressed as women and, in our case, as Jews. Both of those contentions must be defended since many would debate them.

The fact that women are oppressed in this country and elsewhere should not continue to be disputable. However, a myriad of interpretations abounds from the egalitarian "piece of the pie" noises of the National Organization for Women to revolutionary feminist ideologists such as Ellen Willis of Redstockings. For the most part the "piece of the pie" feminist ideology is useless to us, it has no link up to wider social ills (not to mention oppressed national minorities) nor does it even consider working-class women in its analysis.

Radical feminist ideology which links the liberation of women to the struggle for socialism provides the only viable and political explanation for the oppression of women. The primacy here is of an economic base: most women do nonpaying, but socially-necessary work in an economy based on wage-labor. This condition is a one-way ticket to second-class existence. What most feminists attack, however, is the ideology and social practice that society has developed to maintain that condition, i.e., the glorification of housewifery and motherhood, the training of women to accept subordination to men as a natural condition, etc. However, in order to eliminate the problem, the base of it must be attacked. Everything points to the fact that women are private property—socially necessary machines that are used in an individual consumption unit, the family. Such demands as free child-care for working mothers provided by the state and large corporations attack this, as do demands for paid pregnancy leave from work. Ultimately, the socialization of home labor is desirable as is the elimination of the economic system which created this condition in the first place.

It is unnecessary here to reiterate in detail the other conditions of women's oppression—the ideology of male supremacy that attacks us at every turn from television to our own radical organizations. Those who claim ignorance of those conditions are, at this point, not to be excused.

Therefore, we will continue with the defense of our claims of oppression by attempting to analyze the position of the Jew in American society and to describe the Jew's general malaise. Primarily, the American Jew has found himself rising and falling with the tides of American capitalism. The Jews who immigrated to America in the 1840's walked right into an expanding country in need of merchants to link the industrial East with the developing West. Those Jews having a great deal of mercantile experience filled that need. Consequently, they prospered. They were, however, unlike their more unfortunate brethren who immigrated a half century later into an America that was in need of industrial workers to expand its economy. These people, our grandparents, were those who out of a response to some of the cruelest industrial working conditions created a large sector of the labor movement in America.

And in the next great change in American capitalism—the technological revolution—Jews have elevated almost entirely to the ranks of the petit bourgeoisie. And that is their social position today—albeit an unstable one with the growth of monopoly capital.

The social consequences of this progression have been enormous. The American Jew has lost all recollection of this national identity, he has instead been forced for purposes of social acceptance into the safe but illusory role of the third "Great American Religion." We must realize that this in itself is a very perverse form of oppression—the erasure of a nation's identity as a nation. When you have no national consciousness, you can neither sense national oppression nor can you fight it.

The American Jew, like his Western European counterparts, lives a marginal existence—abnormally concentrated into the most economically and politically tenuous sector of society, forced to renounce his national identity in order to maintain his economic position. He is neither present in the strongholds of the large bourgeoisie—nor is he conspicuous in the ranks of the working class. Marginal to the class struggle, he is forced to walk a tightrope, unable because of his class interests to work for a socialist society, nor able to realize his own dilemma. Consequently, the Jew without the homogenizing benefits of national consolidation in the homeland finds himself in a marginal position—marginal to the progress of his own process of national liberation—as Memmi points out in *Liberation of the Jew*—for the Jew to engage in a process of self-affirmation would be for him to admit his oppression, and he is unwilling to do this.

Now that we have resolved that both women and Jews are oppressed, how do we deal with people who fall into both categories? The imperative for both is to resolve the contradictions inherent to their respective conditions. For the Jew, the contradiction of marginal economic and social existence is solved by national reconsolidation in the Jewish national homeland and the building of a socialist society in that homeland.

For Jewish women, however, there is the question that faces women of every oppressed national minority. We are confronted with the primacy of the national struggle. The elimination of national oppression as the precondition to the elimination of the contradictions internal to that national, and to the creation of a socialist egalitarian society; and, consequently, to the elimination of all male supremacy.

This tends to suggest that Jewish women must repress any movement toward women's liberation and subordinate it to national liberation. This, however, is not the intent. Rather, the point is that Jewish women can be most effective in their fight for women's liberation in the context of national consolidation—that is, in Israel.

The struggle for a socialist society is an essential component to the achievement of women's liberation and Diaspora Jewry is, for the most part, marginal to that struggle.

The answer then for Jewish women in the Diaspora is to

struggle in a Socialist-Zionist context. They must fight for equality in their organizations. They must work in general women's groups and they must maintain the integrity of their own interests, so that their struggle for women's liberation will not be quashed by the larger problem of Jewish national liberation.

This is an essential problem—women must always fight in their own interests even in the context of a national or social revolution. Jewish women are no exception. As Jews, they must free themselves from the contradiction of Diaspora existence—an existence which has forced them to be more "womanish" than other women for fear of appearing outside of the American cultural fold (the "Jewish mother" is in reality every other frustrated housewife-mother in Western culture, multiplied tenfold). And as women they must fight for the same things as all other women—the right to develop their full human potential free from undue social, political, and mythological encumbrances.

The discussion of women's liberation in a Socialist-Zionist context is not "me-tooism," a polite afterthought, nor an excuse to talk about one or the other. It is the recognition of two major problems that demand solution and it is the recognition that the two are quite complementary if not inseparable. Women are not going to fight for Jewish national liberation at the expense of their own interest and struggle. Nor can women fight for freedom from sexual oppression while ignoring their own national oppression. The course for the Socialist-Zionist-feminist (a rather rare species) is to build antimale supremist Socialist-Zionist organizations in the Diaspora and to work for socialism and women's liberation in the homeland, never losing sight of either goal.

If I may quote the great French intellectual and feminist Simone de Beauvoir:

> Simply from the fact that liberty in women is still abstract and empty she can exercise it only in revolt, which is the only road open to those who have no opportunity of doing any-

thing constructive. They must reject the limitations of their situation and seek to open the road of the future. Resignation is only abdication and flight. There is no other way out for a woman than to work for her liberation.

(*The Second Sex*. Alfred A. Knopf, New York, 1953)

Women and Judaism – Time for a Change

Mary Gendler

I am a woman. I am a Jew. I am a Jewish woman. I am both and I want to be both. I have only one problem. I am not quite certain what it means to be a woman; I am equally unclear about what it means to be a Jew. That leaves me especially puzzled about what it means to be a Jewish woman. This may sound flippant, but the question causes me much conflict. For I have, on the one hand, the traditional view of woman, and especially Jewish woman, and on the other hand inner thrusts which take me far from this image. How am I to reconcile the two? Can I be "liberated" and still be a "woman"? Can I be "emancipated" and still be "Jewish"? But let me be more specific.

Since the triumph of the patriarchy, thousands of years ago, women have been unmistakably second-class citizens in almost every tribe and country and culture. Simone de Beauvoir, in her book *The Second Sex* (New York, 1953), traces brilliantly and in depth the historical development of the role of women, a feat which I will not attempt here. Certain highlights, how-

Mary Gendler, an ex-teacher and ex-housewife, lives in Andover, Massachusetts, with her husband and two young children. Besides feminism, her chief involvements are with the human potential movement, organic gardening, and educational alternatives. This article is reprinted from the *Response* Symposium, Winter, 1970–71, by permission of the author. Copyright © 1971 by *Response* magazine.

ever, might prove helpful in elucidating my dilemma. Except for a few places in the ancient world, women, at least in the Western and Near Eastern countries, have until quite recently been regarded as weak, inferior beings. (I do not wish to consider the Far East or places like Africa because I know almost nothing about their cultures.) That this is so is evident from even a cursory glance at the laws and social customs in the various cultures. Women, deprived of legal, social, and spiritual rights, have been forced to undergo such indignities as polygamy, harems, confinement to the home, veils over their faces, exclusion from education and training other than home-making, lack of legal recourse, etc. And, in general, women have accepted this inferior position. (Why they have done so is a good and fair question. I do not know the answer, but I do not believe that it is possible to oppress without some measure of acceptance from the oppressed, certainly in this sort of relationship.) And even when they have not been forced to suffer *great* indignities such as the ones just mentioned, they have accepted legal and social arrangements which locked them in the home and granted them the privileges and status of pampered and not-so-pampered children. This pattern, of course, has and is still changing a great deal. But although in most Western countries the legal and social opportunities for women are theoretically the same as those for men, custom and psychological barriers are very difficult to break down.

It is often argued that, despite the discrimination, there have been outstanding women throughout history who have broken through these huge barriers and prejudices to attain unusual accomplishments. I do not deny this, but I reject this particular argument for women on the same grounds that I reject it for blacks or for other oppressed groups. Why should we (or they) have to overcome unnatural hurdles? What would happen if we all really competed equally? Why have such a disproportionate number of men been the political leaders, artists, musicians, philosophers, poets, etc.? Women, to state the obvious, comprise 50 percent of the population, but nowhere near 50 percent of its creative geniuses. From this we could conclude one of several things: women really *are* inferior to men and here is the very proof (which I reject); women's creativity is fully encompassed by and expressed in child bearing and rearing (which I also reject); something has happened historically in the cultural arrangements of societies which has prevented women from fully developing and realizing their potential.

Here I would like to interject an important cautionary note. I do *not* feel that women and men are or should be the same. We certainly are not the same biologically. To state the obvious: men are, in general, physically stronger and therefore able to do certain kinds of work which are very difficult for women; only women, on the other hand, are able to bear and give suck to children. Thus, *to a certain extent,* our roles *are* biologically determined. But men have never been limited to nor bound solely by their biology. Their intellect and imagination have enabled them to leap and thrust into new beginnings, constantly enlarging the boundaries of their world and their experience. The most recent example of this is the penetration into space which defied all bounds of gravity and opened the possibility of almost limitless reshaping. (This restlessness may, of course, lead to the extinction of us all, and it may be that what man needs is a renewed sense of the wonder of the earth more than conquering new worlds.) Women, it is true, have benefited from these advances, but with few exceptions (Marie Curie comes immediately to mind) they have remained much more closely bound to their biological destiny than have men. In saying this I would like to emphasize that I am *not* denying the worth and dignity of childrearing and homemaking. I feel, however, that it is an unfair limitation when the woman is so overburdened with these physical aspects of life that she has no opportunity to push towards the kind of intellectual and spiritual transcendence which has enabled men, for better or for worse, to shape history. The male, on the other hand, by moving as far away as he can from biological demands, denies and is thus denied an opportunity to develop the softer side within himself. It is this softer, more passive, more rhythmic side of man which, recognized and cultivated, might add a measure of humaneness often sorely lacking in his dealings with the world. For men, in their mad desire to control everything about them, have lost touch with the intimacies of birth and growth; they have lost the sense of the incredible fragility and preciousness of life which women, through nurturing their children, experience daily. The effects on the world of this polarization of roles have been devastating!

* * *

And what of the Jewish woman? How does she fit into this overview of women in history? Unfortunately, her fate has been no better than that of her Christian and Moslem sisters. Jewish law reduces her to the level of a child or servant. For example: she is not a valid witness in legal proceedings; she cannot initiate divorce proceedings, but must be "granted" a divorce by her husband. If he disappears, refuses, or goes insane, she has no recourse and may never remarry. Custom reflects this basic attitude toward women. Socially and religiously she was never the equal of men. For many centuries she was not sent to school, and this in the midst of a culture which valued education very highly. She is not counted in the *minyon*. She cannot officiate at a service or read the Torah. For that matter, she is not even permitted to sit among the men in the synagogue. (It is as if the men were afraid that women would distract them from the more serious matters of prayer and the soul. This seems to say that they [women] were regarded solely as "body." Their removal to a balcony frees the men's spirits of the fleshly temptation and thus permits its expansion or purification. But what of the woman's soul? Why was it not considered? Why not seat the men in the balcony?) She has no special garments for prayer. Indeed, she is really not expected to pray, and is excused from it because of her "home responsibilities." And when she does come to the synagogue, she sits and gossips in the balcony, thus confirming the male's suspicion that she is not inclined towards prayer anyway. (But why not gossip? Hidden in a balcony, excluded from any real participation in the service, what meaning could it have for her? Her gossip was merely a confirmation of her alienation.)

And so emerged the story-book picture image of the Jewish mama, face red from the heat of the stove, loading the creaking table with goodies for the men as they returned, bodies freshly scrubbed from the *mikvah* and souls washed clean by prayer in the femaleless *shul*. Their spirits refreshed, they were now ready to satisfy their bodies. But what of the woman's spirit? When was she given the opportunity to soar and delve into the outer and inner spaces? Burdened with many children and household duties, she profited little from the Shabbat: she rarely received an opportunity for true renewal.

This, I believe, is an accurate portrait of the Jewish woman, at least until a hundred years ago. With the advent of the Enlightenment in Europe and the subsequent freeing of Judaism from the rigid exigencies of orthodoxy, the woman's position, especially in Western Europe and North America, gradually improved—somewhat. As industrialization and secularization proceeded in these countries, many found themselves forced to have much more interaction with the surrounding society than they had ever had before. Legislation making schooling compulsory for all children up to a certain age was the rule. And so, more and more Jewish girls went out into the world and discovered that its boundaries were broader than they had ever guessed. More and more they (as did their brothers, of course) began mixing with the *goyim* and learned that their girl friends had more freedom than they. One by one they started to rebel against the restrictions and burdens of a tradition which asked much of them and granted little in the way of true rewards in return. *Kashrut*, separate dishes for Pesach, festive meals for the many holidays—these things meshed less and less with the kind of lives they wanted to lead. Some, as did their brothers, rejected Judaism completely. Others chose to try to maintain some contact with it, and the tradition accommodated itself somewhat to the changing times and attitudes. And so women were, for example, gradually permitted to sit, first, downstairs on a special side in the synagogue and, finally, in Reform and most Conservative temples, to join the men. They gave up the *sheitl* and dressed in modern, stylish clothes. They mixed more and more with the outside world, received an education, and entered the professions.

In the final analysis, however, the Conservative and Liberal (European) movements have made shockingly few basic changes. Women are still not counted in a *minyon,* generally not called to the Torah, and rarely permitted to lead the service. The Reform tradition, to its credit, has eliminated these arbitrary distinctions between men and women, but even there unfair *de facto* distinctions remain. For although women are taking a more active role in the temples and synagogues, and although religious involvement plays a smaller and smaller part in the lives of nonorthodox men, the latter still retain most of the influential positions. For example, no woman, as far as I know, has yet been ordained a rabbi (although this *is* possible in the Reform seminaries and may occur this year). There are no female cantors. How many women have been president of their congregations?

The other side of the question is, of course, why so few women have taken advantage of the opportunities available to them. And why have they not pressed harder for more change? The answer, for me personally, is tied up with the questions I posed at the beginning of the paper: What does it mean to be a woman, a Jew, a Jewish woman?

* * *

In the first part of the paper I tried to give a general overview which might suggest what some of the answers to these questions have been in the past. Very briefly, being a woman meant submitting yourself first to the dictates of your father and then to those of your husband. The woman, in essence, "belonged" to the male. He may have adored and worshipped her (at best), but she served him. Being a Jew, if you were a male, meant an intense involvement with the laws and spiritual life of Judaism. But if you were a female, it meant exclusion from most of the spiritual aspects of the religion and bondage to the myriad legal taboos and restrictions.

Times, as I tried to indicate, have changed; but it is my contention that they have not changed enough. Inertia, custom, the natural inclination of little girls to follow in the paths of their mothers, the social ostracism which often accompanies attempts to break into new patterns, all these things press hard against the forces of change. We can see this within Judaism. Having been "excused" from prayer (public, community prayer, that is), we have become habituated not to think of ourselves as spiritual beings. And so it is that most of us, as was the case with our great-great-grandmothers, still never even dare to dream of becoming a rabbi ourselves, but sublimate any conscious or unconscious yearnings we might have in that direction into a desire to marry or to bear one. The result is a denial of a legitimate thrust which may lead to destructive, vicarious living. This is not to say that I feel that all, or even most, rabbis should be women; rather, it is to press for the option that this be psychologically and socially as well as legally availabe to those women who are so inclined.

I realize that the factors which enter into the rapid secularization of Jews in the United States are many and complex. I would not attempt to catalogue them here. I would like to suggest, however, that insofar as women have, in the past, been the principal bearers of Judaism to their children, the drift away from involvement in it may be a reflection of their conscious or unconscious rejection of a tradition which assigns them such an inferior status. (These inequalities are more likely to be visible to her now than two hundred years ago because she is more involved in the "outside" world and so can compare and contrast. Also, I am speaking here mainly of Conservative and Orthodox Judaism, less of Reform.) I feel that if women were not only permitted but encouraged to take a more active role in the service, to enter more power positions in the synagogue so that its direction could directly reflect their interests and thrusts, to enter seminaries, to develop their spiritual resources—then, perhaps, the tide away from the synagogues might begin to be stemmed. For women who feel themselves to be "really" a part of something at a very deep level would be more likely to communicate an enthusiasm of Judaism to their children. Perhaps an example from my own life would help to explain what I'm saying.

As a modern woman, I am finding the old definitions of my role and status inadequate. I do not like being confined solely to mothering and nourishing, although I take great pleasure in both. I find that this aspect of myself must be balanced by enough time and freedom to permit other parts of me to grow. So, for example, I enjoy going to school, planning services for a house synagogue, writing papers and articles, reading books, picketing and petitioning, planting and tending a garden, talking with adults, listening to music, going to movies and theater, etc. But for me to have the time to do these things requires rearrangements and adjustments within the home. Our two small children still need to be tended and the housework still has to be done. The process of change is, as I indicated earlier, slow and sometimes painful, but as my husband and I grapple with growth towards a new balance, we are both finding that each of us and the children are benefitting.

How does the reevaluation of my role as a woman affect my life as Jew and Jewish woman? Formerly our religious life was very highly polarized. My husband is a rabbi and had a congregation for a number of years. Thus, he was very involved in spiritual matters in a beautiful and inspiring way. I have never attended services which I enjoy more than his. On the other hand, it was often difficult to enjoy the services because, first of all, I was frequently so tired from the holiday preparations that I almost fell asleep; secondly, because of the customs and stratifications of the synagogue as well as my own cultural conditioning, there was little opportunity for real participation in the service.

Many things have been changing for us in the last year. Since he no longer leads a congregation, the actual physical demands on my husband's time are much more flexible. This has given us an opportunity to experiment with new arrangements within the home. So, for example, we both prepare for holidays together. This means that we both participate in the cooking and cleaning, and from this we have found that many things follow almost automatically. First, I am no longer too exhausted at sundown to enjoy or participate in soul-elevating experiences. Secondly, I feel considerably less resentment about doing the work now because we are doing it together, and work done "with" someone always has a different feel, for me anyway. This, in a strange way "frees" part of me, for as he shares in my work, I am released to share in his. The provinces are no longer "mine" and "his." Thirdly, my husband is no longer isolated from participation in the physical preparation which provides a lovely setting for and accompaniment to the spiritual uplifting of the holidays. He, therefore, is more in touch with the "body" of the experience while I am freed to reach towards its "soul." Both of us gain immeasurably from this.

* * *

I insist on the right to be a woman, a Jew, and a Jewish woman. I will not relinquish my tradition, despite its rigidities, until I am absolutely convinced that no efforts can make it bend. But neither will I stand passively by while the Conservative and Orthodox movements continue to consider me a second-class citizen. Change is always hard, and the familiar is comfortable, even if it is unjust. It is especially difficult to relinquish power and privilege. But this must come within Judaism, I am convinced, or else the religious commitment of women, as well as of men, will continue to wither. Children whose religious involvement is solely outside the home seldom develop a deep feeling for it. But perhaps, just perhaps, if women become more conscious of their exclusion from certain aspects of religious life and press for change, if men will begin to exchange some of their power-in-the-world for some participation-in-the-home, if men and women begin to develop a kind of sharing which will enable each to develop a generally neglected other-side of himself, perhaps this might just be the revitalizing spark which could rekindle the dimming light of religious commitment to Judaism.

The Jewish Wife

Traditional Orthodox Jewish Prayer

The Jewish husband traditionally recites this poem to his wife on the Sabbath evening before Kiddush *at the dinner table.*

A woman of valor who can find?
For her price is far above rubies.
The heart of her husband doth safely trust in her,
And he hath no lack of gain.
She doeth him good and not evil
All the days of her life,
She seeketh wool and flax,
And worketh willingly with her hands.
She is like the merchant-ships;
She bringeth her food from afar.
She riseth also while it is yet night,
And giveth food to her household.
And a portion to her maidens.
She considereth a field, and buyeth it;
With the fruit of her hands she planteth a vineyard.
She girdeth her loins with strength,
And maketh strong her arms.

From the Orthodox Jewish prayerbook, Jewish Publication Society translation, 1917.

She perceiveth that her merchandise is good;
Her lamp goeth not out by night.
She layeth her hands to the distaff,
And her hands hold the spindle.
She stretcheth out her hand to the poor;
Yea, she reacheth forth her hands to the needy.
She is not afraid of the snow for her household;
For her household are clothed with scarlet.
She maketh for herself coverlets;
Her clothing is fine linen and purple,
Her husband is known in the gates,
When he sitteth among the elders of the land, she maketh linen
    garments and selleth them;
And delivereth girdles unto the merchant.
Strength and dignity are her clothing;
And she laugheth at the time to come.
She openeth her mouth with wisdom;
And the law of kindness is on her tongue.
She looketh well to the ways of her household,
And eateth not the bread of idleness.
Her children rise up, and call her blessed;
Her husband also, and he praiseth her;
"Many daughters have done valiantly,
But thou excellest them all."
Grace is deceitful, and beauty is vain;
But a woman that feareth the Lord, she shall be praised.
Give her of the fruit of her hands;
And let her works praise her in the gates.

—*Proverbs* 31:10–31

Part Eight

The Jewish Defense League and Its Critics

Since the Jewish Defense League made national headlines in October, 1968, Rabbi Meir Kahane and his followers have been the subject of continuing debate within the Jewish community. While active J.D.L.ers are predominantly young, working and lower middle class, and residents of transitional neighborhoods (once all Jewish, now increasingly black and Puerto Rican), Kahane receives standing ovations from adult suburban audiences of lawyers, doctors, and corporate executives.

Does Kahane represent the silent spector of "Jewish *machismo*"? Is it the suburbanites' guilt feelings which respond to "Never Again"—a nostalgic thirst for the rich traditions of their parents which they have abandoned for an antiseptic middle-class culture?

Despite all the hysteria, the J.D.L. is responding to Jews with real problems—the break-up of old settled neighborhoods, the increasing violence of the inner city, and the indifference of the Jewish Establishment to the Jews "left behind" there.

People struggling to survive day-to-day seldom are able to respond to long-term solutions; they see little victories and little defeats as their daily diet. It should therefore have surprised no one when Kahane organized a band of Jews to patrol their local area against what they perceived as harassment by blacks and Puerto Ricans. Neighborhoods were losing their ethnic character. Small-time Jewish merchants were losing business. Jewish children were getting beaten up in the streets.

Many Jews found Kahane's militant appeals appealing. *Nice Jewish boys get beat up.* For too long Jews have been nice, quiet, acquiescent, ready to flee, and had no "balls" to fight. Never again!

With a following of a few hundred on Halloween Eve, 1967, Kahane made the headlines by "standing guard" with clubs and chains at a local Jewish cemetery which had been vandalized for several years. Some blacks showed up and the J.D.L. swung into action. The J.D.L. membership reached several thousand by the following spring when Kahane led his followers to "downtown" Temple Emmanu-El on Fifth Avenue in Manhattan. James Forman, a black leader, was rumored to be on his way to demand reparations for white oppression of blacks, and the J.D.L. was prepared to see that he wouldn't. Forman never came, but the ensuing publicity was a gold mine for Kahane and the J.D.L.

By late 1971, the J.D.L. had organized chapters in nearly every city with a large Jewish population—although none as large as the New York chapter. A J.D.L. summer camp in upstate New York teaches young members—dressed in paramilitary uniforms—Hebrew, karate, and riflery. A new international headquarters has been set up in Israel. Though its future is unclear, the J.D.L. is definitely growing as a movement.

To some, the charismatic Kahane is seen as a martyr-savior; to others, his very name is anathema. The reaction of the Jewish Establishment was predictable—the J.D.L.'s antics were bad for the Jews, not "respectable," and would only result in an anti-Semitic backlash. The response of the Jewish Left was more complex and more ambiguous—more sympathetic and more hostile at the same time.

Here we present both sides. An interview with Rabbi Kahane is followed by two critiques by radical Jews.

Right On Judaism...
J.D.L.'s Meir Kahane
Speaks Out—An Interview

Zvi Lowenthal and Jonathan Braun

QUESTION: *With the campaign on behalf of Soviet Jews, J.D.L. received more publicity and recognition than it ever did in the past. What do you feel was the major importance of the campaign—and still is, if it's still going on?*

KAHANE: It is. The important thing is that we helped Russian Jews. What else is there? That is why we started; that is why we're doing it now—to help Russian Jews. I think very very few people really realize why J.D.L. began. This Soviet Jewish campaign is nothing different from anything that we did in our very first days. We were not formed just to help Jews in Brooklyn, not just to help Jews in Crown Heights. We were formed to help Jews wherever Jews had to be helped.

If in 1969 we didn't organize anything for Soviet Jews it's not because we didn't realize then that this had to be done. But we were a small group and you don't start something like this until you are ready to finish it . . . But there are no boundaries when it comes to Jewish pain.

That's interesting, because one of the main criticisms of

Zvi Lowenthal and Jonathan Braun interviewed Rabbi Meir Kahane. Zvi is a New York-based free-lance writer and former editor of *The Flame*, where the interview first appeared in the Winter, 1971, issue. Jonathan is a free-lance writer and a student at the Columbia University Graduate School of Journalism. This article is reprinted by permission of the editors.

*J.D.L. is that it tends to view everything as part of the same
problem. In other words, missiles on the Suez Canal, threats
to the Soviet Jewish community, and an attack on a Jew in
Crown Heights are all seen with the same intensity.*

Exactly right. It's called Jewish pain. If one has pain in a
finger it may not be quite as serious as, perhaps, a heart attack.
The fact is, however, it's pain, and a little pain has to be eased
also. No one is that paranoid to believe that the immediate
threat to a Jew in Crown Heights is quite as urgent as the
threat to Russian Jews. Nevertheless, for that Jew in Crown
Heights it is a threat. For that Jew his problem is a very real
problem. While we certainly don't pour the same effort and the
same amount of energy into Crown Heights as we do for the
Jews of the U.S.S.R., the fact remains that the Jew on President Street who cannot walk safely has a problem. That problem has to be solved. We solve it on the same basis of love
for Jews that we apply to the Jews of the Soviet Union.

*Is it possible that the Jewish Defense League could be more
successful in dealing with local community issues than in dealing with international issues?*

There's no question that the smaller the problem the easier
it can be solved. And there is no question that we can certainly
solve smaller problems while the Soviet Jewish problem remains as a tremendous thing. But I really cannot find it in my
own heart to say, "Well, look, we don't have enough people
to solve all these problems so we'll solve just this one problem." I really cannot find it in my own heart to tell Soviet
Jews to wait politely while we solve a problem in East Flat-
bush.

*Do you think that the activist program of the J.D.L. has
been the decisive factor in attracting so many youth to the
J.D.L.?*

I think that's probably the key to everything that we have
done. The bankruptcy of Jewish leadership is manifested most
clearly in the results that we see with Jewish youth. I don't
always like to use the term "Establishment" but the fact is that

it does exist. Our Jewish leaders carry the sin and the crime of negligence when it comes to Jewish youth.

How do you think they've failed the Jewish youth community?

They have not given the young Jew any reason to feel Jewish. When I speak in synagogues and temples out in the suburbs, the adults come there expecting me to agree with them when someone gets up and attacks the Jewish New Left youth as lousy kids with long hair, and so on. They're usually very stunned when I say—and all our people say—that, on the contrary, our great hope is not so much the apathetic youth but the radical leftist who at least marches for something and feels something. If someone feels something he's alive.

And now, of course, you have to change them to the right way. How do you resurrect the dead? Both the dead Jews, the apathetic young Jews, and those who have gone into foreign fields, into strange fields, and marched with all sorts of non-Jewish and anti-Jewish causes—they have all done so because they've never received any reason for being proud to be Jewish. Everyone knows the incredible kind of training the young Jews get. A kid of eleven or twelve is brought to Hebrew school, not to be Jewish but for a *bar mitzvah*. If I had my way, I'd bury this entire ritual because it has buried us. A *bar mitzvah*, my God! That's not the beginning. That's it; that's the end of everything.

Judaism in this country is hypocrisy. It's a fraud. And when we come, we say to young people, "We don't want to give you anything; we demand of you something. You've got to help. You've got to march. You may even get arrested; you may have to fight police—but for something Jewish."

So you would say that the activism of the J.D.L. presents a viable alternative to the so-called Portnoy Judaism or the bagels-and-lox Judaism of the Jewish Establishment?

No question about it. I believe that there are only two meaningful Jewish trends at this moment on campus. They are the J.D.L. and the radical Zionist trends. These are two groups which offer sacrifices, which offer substance, not form. I feel very close in many ways to the Radical Zionist Alliance and to the Jewish Liberation Project. I differ with them strongly on certain issues. But I know there is substance there, and meaning and sincerity which young Jews sense both in them and in us.

You have indicated that you feel a closeness to the Radical Zionist Alliance and to the Jewish Liberation Project. Do you also feel a possible closeness toward other militant ethnic groups, such as the Young Lords and the Black Panthers?

There is no question that despite the effort to paint us as racists—which is incredible nothingness—we certainly do feel and understand a great many of the things that, for example, the Panthers say. We differ with them on a number of things— for example, branding all police as pigs. But there are pigs. No one has to teach me that. I've seen cops charging and shouting, "Lousy kikes!" I've seen and heard those things. I myself, in the 90th precinct in Queens, when I was arrested last June, saw one of our people handcuffed, both hands cuffed to a chair as he was beaten by a cop. I've seen the anti-Semitism. So there are pigs, and if they can do this to us you can imagine what they can do to some poor black guy.

So we don't differ with the Panthers on that. And we don't differ with the Panthers in the sense that if after asking for 300 years for things from the government—federal or local— it becomes necessary to use unorthodox or outrageous ways. There is no question. On this we don't differ. We don't differ on their wanting to instill in their young people ethnic pride. Not at all. Where we do differ with them is where we think that nationalism crosses the boundary line and becomes Nazism; instead of just love of our own people, hatred of others.

What I believe is clear evidence of anti-Semitism on the part of Panthers is not just anti-Zionism. This is a cop-out. This is nothing. I remember reading the April 25, 1970 issue of the Panther paper where they attack those three well-known Zionists—Abbie Hoffman, Jerry Rubin, and William Kunstler. They're not Zionists. They're Jews. This is a code name, the kind of thing the Poles used two years ago to expell their Zionists when they meant Jews. So we empathize with the Panthers and sympathize with them; but we get turned off when they suddenly deviate from what we feel to be a legitimate nationalism and go on to hatred of other people.

What about their revolutionary goals and their revolutionary analysis of American society? You differ with them there also?

Yes, I believe that this country has a great many faults, that's for sure. I believe that nevertheless, at this moment still —and maybe this will change in a year or two years or a month—nevertheless, this country still affords a chance for democratic change. It may be slower than most people want. It's slower than I want it. Sometimes you have to pay a certain price in speed. But the only right thing that any group has the right to ask is, "Is there change possible and is change taking place?" I mean, this country is not the Soviet Union. No matter what one may say about Agnew, Agnew is not Brezhnev. He's not a good guy. He's not one of my favorite people in this country. There could be a great many worse people in this country. And unfortunately, I'm afraid that you'll see them yet.

Does that mean that you feel that the American Jewish community may be endangered in the near future?

There is no hope for the Jews in this country. I'm going to say that quite clearly. I've said this over and over again to adults in the suburbs. I'd go for 40 minutes and they'd eat it up and love it, and then I'd say, "Remember, the only place for a Jew to live is in Israel." That's it. Goodbye. But again, I'm not out to score points with people. I'm out to deal with what I honestly believe to be a serious, physical crisis for Jews arising in this country.

I think that I love Jews enough to say things to them for what I think is their benefit, without having to make points. This is why we did take the stand that we took on Vietnam. We didn't have to say that. We could have gotten—I know we could have had at this moment—thousands and thousands

of new members on campuses if we didn't take that stand. I
believed then and I believe to this day that any time there is
a conflict between what I think is good for Jews and for J.D.L.
there is no conflict. Jews come first.

Recently, The New York Times *published an article stating
that you wrote the book* The Jewish Stake in Vietnam, *and
that you had access to certain intelligence information. Is
there any truth to the article's implication that you once belonged to the Central Intelligence Agency? What did you
think of the tone of the article?*

Well, it was a hatchet job. I know where they got their
facts from. They got them from A.D.L. I did some work for
them while I was in Washington on the radical right,
which did involve infiltrating the Birchers. And we did
a good, good job on the Birchers ferreting out sources of funds,
and so on. Much of what *The Times* said was true, much of it
was not true. Most of it was put in a context which was totally
false. It was a hatchet job. When someone throws mud at you
and you throw mud back you get dirtier. So, I had no contacts
with the C.I.A., that's for sure. Neither did I ever work for
H.U.A.C.; that's a bald lie, a total lie. The only contact I
ever had was when I was asked to testify before them on the
Soviet Jewish question . . . It was the first time since 1948
that any committee of Congress had the Soviet Jewish issue.
That's the first time I ever saw them and the last time.

*Why do you feel that the Vietnam War is in the Jewish
interest?*

I know that there would not be 20,000 Soviet combat
troops in Egypt today if not for the peace movement. And I
say that the peace movement was made up of a vast majority
of honest and decent and sensitive people who sincerely wanted
peace. They have emasculated the U.S. will to fight—anywhere,
just wars or unjust wars—so that the Soviets have correctly
gauged American opinion and they know that America is not
going to war, anywhere again, for a long, long time.

Vietnam is not an island unto itself. I have no use for Ky
and Thieu and no use for Saigon, not the slightest. But in

1939 there was a little country, a fascist country called Poland, a dictatorship where they used to rip Jewish beards out by the roots, and had I lived then I would have been overjoyed to see France and England go to its aid. Not because they liked Poland but because they could understand what would happen it the Nazis were not stopped. The Viet Cong are not Nazis; but the weakening of the U.S. will to win in Vietnam meant that the same will to win will be stopped anywhere.

Rather than setting up the choice between total intervention- ism and total isolationism, isn't it possible that the U.S. may find some course in between?

I don't think so. Especially not in Israel. Because now, not only are many of the non-Jewish doves still doves . . . but the hawks, when it comes to Israel, say, "Those goddamn Jews wanted us out of Asia, well, we're not going to help them in Israel."

Speaking about the hawks, you said that they might say, "Those goddamn Jews got us out of Vietnam." You've often said that the ultimate threat to the Jewish community in this country comes from the radical right—that the radical left may appear threatening at times, but that they don't really have the guns or the power that the right has. Do you still believe this to be true?

Much more so today. As the economic crisis has begun to grow in this country there is no question that for the first time since 1938 you have a significant number of white blue-collar workers out of work. A significant number. And it's much more dangerous now than in 1938, because for twenty years these people have tasted the good life. Anytime anyone tastes the good life for a long time he is much more dangerous than some peasant that has never had anything. He can't go back to poverty. He'll do anything not to go back to poverty. He'll kill and he'll use ovens just not to go back again. It's especially true in the same country where no one wants to be a worker; and it's the same kind of thinking which sent many lower- and mid- dle-class Germans to Hitler rather than to the communists. So the great erosion of the middle will be to the right not to the left.

If that happens, what hope can there be for the Jews even if they do go to Israel?

I'm an Orthodox Jew, and I don't believe that the fate of Israel depends on Rogers, on America, on Russia, or anybody else. Israel has come into being; that itself is a fantastic miracle. That miracle will not die. Israel will live. Israel does not depend upon this country . . . It's here to stay. I get upset with Jews of such little faith who don't believe in Israel. You don't have to be an Orthodox Jew to have faith; it's something you have to know—the Jewish story, the Jewish cycle. You know that the Jewish people are here and that they will always be here—that Israel is here and that Israel will always stay here.

What would you recommend for the Jews who do not go on aliyah?

One of the reasons why J.D.L. differs from other groups is that the average Zionist group says we're going on *aliyah* and if you people are too stupid to realize it—then, goodbye. I think that's immoral and un-Jewish. We preach *aliyah* and all of our kids are talking about *aliyah;* but we say that while you're here you have an obligation, and indeed you may have a greater one here. We tell our kids that they may have to stay here a while longer because there are six million beautiful, stupid Jews who need help. That's how we differ from other groups. We work on a sort of double plane. We try to alleviate Jewish pain here and at the same time try to convince Jews that their only future is in Israel.

It's been reported that you are going on aliyah *and that in Israel you intend to set up an international Jewish Defense League. Are these reports true? What would the purpose be of a world J.D.L.?*

Yes. On February 28th [1971] I'll be in Brussels, both for the Conference on Russian Jewry (see page 195) and also to meet with people from several Western European countries— England, Ireland, France, Belgium, Holland, and West Germany—to set up chapters in these countries. The demand from these countries and from every Latin country has really been overwhelming. So we do see that we're becoming a really world-wide movement; and if so, there is only one place for its main office to be—Israel.

The second reason why I'm going is because I've always tried to practice not telling members of J.D.L. to do something unless I do it too. "Go out and get arrested." They won't do it unless you do. You can't tell them to go on *aliyah* unless you do it.

Can you tell us why you were arrested tonight?

I was charged with harassing the Second Secretary of the Soviet Mission to the U.N. I wasn't really. We were simply engaging in a dialogue on Soviet Jews.

With the Second Secretary?

With the Second Secretary. It was a very short evening . . . While I was in the station house for about an hour, Secretary Rogers called the station; Lindsay called; Police Comissioner Murphy called. Apparently, the Soviets lodged a formal protest right then and there. It was a wild evening.

How do you answer the critics who say that perhaps the harassment tactics and some of the other militant tactics may be doing more harm than good with respect to Soviet Jewry?

There are supposed to be so many things that have been going on so secretly—so quietly that nobody knows about them. I remember when S.S.S.J. began . . . It escalated the campaign at a time when it was nothing. I remember when Yaacov Birnbaum did the revolutionary action of getting some young people out in the streets with signs, "Let My People Go," in 1960. That was the first time in 47 years that anybody had ever gone into the streets for Russian Jewry. And I remember what the American Jewish conference said about Yaacov Birnbaum. "He's making things worse for them!" That's the classic cop-out of all people that do nothing and try to rationalize their methods. How do you rationalize your nothingness? By saying the reason why you don't do anything is because it makes things worse. It doesn't make things worse, not at all. People like Mendell, Sperling, and Kazakoff cried out, "Don't be so good to us! Make it worse!" That's why

Kazakoff's family is out now. That's the only reason why Dropkin is out now. Because Jews here screamed and did what they didn't do thirty years ago.

If we don't see any results in the Soviet Jewry issue, is it possible that J.D.L. may escalate its tactics? Harassment campaigns may not continue to keep Soviet Jewry on page one.

First of all, we do see results. We do see families being let out. So we do see something. However, we do not in any way place any limitations on what we might not do. It's that simple.

So you have resumed the harassment campaign?

Oh yes.

What else do you hope to accomplish with this tactic?

Getting the Soviet Jewish question on page one is only part of the problem. The next thing is keeping it there. We paused for a month; and in that month what we saw was an almost total death of every other action on the part of every other group, which to me was very disturbing. It showed that we hadn't done what we thought we had done . . . We thought that there would be a certain impetus; there hasn't been really. Our basic purpose is to make the Soviet Jewish problem Richard Nixon's problem because Richard Nixon does not care about the Jewish problem. He does care about the Nixon problem. And we make this Nixon's problem by shaking the foundation of U.S. foreign policy. And that is building bridges to the East. And they will not build these bridges—at least not at Jewish expense.

Getting back to J.D.L.'s youth appeal. In your campaign to attract more students to the organization you've spoken on a number of campuses. What do you think is the value of these meetings?

I speak at an average of three or four campuses every single week, which in itself tells something about the change in attitude on campuses to J.D.L. . . . . I spoke at Syracuse where Israeli Ambassador Rabin had spoken a month earlier and drew 800 people. We drew 1200 people. I believe that Jewish youth sense something in J.D.L. It's more than one more Jewish group. It's not just different in quantity. It's not the one-hundred-and-first Jewish group. There's a qualitative difference.

They probably admire the J.D.L. image—that of people who place their lives on the line.

I think so. I think that above all young people like honesty, and no one is as honest as the one who practices what he preaches. Even those people who walk in here and really think that they differ with us strongly—even they have a certain fascination for any group which has done what we have done. And I can only tell you that the response has been tremendous . . . I think that we have seen perhaps the turning point on campus for Jewish youth. I think there's a hunger, a thirst for Jewishness.

I don't blame young people for not wanting to go to the more traditional things. I don't blame them for being turned off by Hillel. I really don't. I was turned off by Hillel, and even in the 1950's when it took a great deal to turn off Jews. And I don't blame them for being turned off by Hillel or by the average synagogue or the average rabbi. And if the American Jewish Congress has no youth it deserves it. Maybe they're looking for that which once was. I've always stated that we're not out to form any new Jew. We're out to resurrect that old Jew that once was. And the new Jew is a product of the *galut*. He's insecure, full of complexes. We'd like to bury that new Jew and resurrect the old one.

Jewish Militancy in Perspective

Debby Littman

Last year the Jewish Defense League placed an ad in *The New York Times* showing a group of boys brandishing lead pipes and baseball bats. The caption asked, "Is this any way for a nice Jewish boy to behave?"

Whether or not we agree with the affirmative answer given by the J.D.L., the question is an important one. Militancy and passivity have been equally recognized forms of Jewish response. In recent times there has been a movement away from the attitude of resignation and fatalism which long dominated Jewish tradition. The Jewish Defense League is only one manifestation of this new orientation. To fully understand the J.D.L. we must place it in the perspective of Jewish militancy in general, as well as examining the specific causes which gave rise to it.

The beginning of the 20th century saw Jews disillusioned with what had seemed to be the bright hope of "emancipation."

The Dreyfus Case in which a French Army Officer of the Jewish faith was falsely convicted of treason with the con-

Debby Littman, a graduate of McGill University, was an active member of Montreal's radical Jewish student community and a staff member of *Otherstand*. Presently, she is a graduate student in sociology at the London School of Economics. This article appeared originally in *Otherstand*, February 24, 1971. It is reprinted by permission of the author and publisher.

nivance of the general staff rocked Europe. Dreyfus, being Jewish, was considered expendable in order to save the honor of the French Army. If such plots could exist in enlightened France, the country which first proclaimed Jews full citizens, then the promise of protection by law was a myth. The program since the Czar's empire compelled many intellectual Jews to believe that anti-Semitism was a permanent, ineradicable symptom of Christian society.

Some began to argue that only when Jews had a country of their own, a territorial base, and the power to pass their own laws and have their own police, army, and navy, only then could Jews live "normally." Such were the beginnings of the Zionist movement which eventually grew into a world-wide movement to create the State of Israel as a national home for Jews.

Indeed, Israel is a special form of Jewish militancy. It represents the casting aside of Jewish patterns of submission which compelled Jews to grovel before mindless enemies. Israel is the insistence on the right of Jews to defend themselves against hostile nations; even to conduct a preventive strike if the threat makes it necessary.

Prior to World War II, many Jews had doubts about the validity of a Jewish nation reconstructed in the ancient homeland. However, with the extermination of six million Jews by the Nazis during the war, doubts ended. The calamity was of such proportions that it was impossible to imagine that God had consented to the slaughter. If such barbarism could emanate from the most cultured, scientific, and musical nation in Europe, there was no possible assurance that similar reversals could not occur in the most democratic and seemingly secure settings.

Militant Jewish defense organizations proliferated amongst America's Jews. Approximately fifty-five years ago the American Jewish Committee and the Anti-Defamation League of B'nai B'rith were founded. They were shortly joined by the American Jewish Congress, the Jewish War Veterans, the Jewish Labor Committee, and several others.

Anti-Semitism in the United States is different in character from that of Europe. The U.S. government has never promoted anti-Semitism. What prejudice exists lies in a free state brought to the surface by ancient myths, misinterpretations of religious dogma, and the compulsions of psychologically-disturbed persons.

In this atmosphere Jewish defense agencies operated on a level of militancy unknown in Europe. They fought discrimination against Jews and other minorities in the fields of employment and housing. They challenged the quota system generally used by American universities to limit Jewish enrollment, they campaigned for legislation on behalf of civil rights for all minorities. They joined as friends of the court in many key cases involving human rights. They contributed to the exposure of the Ku Klux Klan, the American Nazi Party, and the radical right. They scolded, they persuaded, and they demanded that America live up to its democratic ideals.

The race to realize ideals was, however, rapidly outdistanced by the constantly proliferating problems of the city and its urban poor.

Poverty is rarely genteel. The poor and the near-poor are frequently given to violence. In America's cities, newly arrived Jewish immigrants from Eastern Europe in the early 1900's encountered recently arrived immigrants from Ireland, Poland, Scandinavia, and Italy. Living side by side they frequently taunted and bruised each other in the streets. Most of the violence between America's ethnic groups disappeared as Jew, Irishman, Italian, and Pole got better jobs and moved into the middle class.

The Jewish Defense League gained its first impetus from the anxieties and fears of lower-middle-class Orthodox Jews trapped by the shifting residential patterns in New York City.

Blacks have lived in America for close to three hundred years. However, before 1920 they were Southern rural sharecroppers and now they are predominantly Northern and urban. The black ghettos spread as blacks became 30 to 45 percent of the city's population. The whites fled to the suburbs. Behind them they left people for whom flight was more difficult. Ofttimes those left behind were old and could not make the shift. Sometimes, as in Williamsburg, New York, a whole community of devout, Orthodox Jews was immobilized in a neighborhood surrounded by a black community. On the fringes of these areas violence grew.

Blacks are, in fact, the latest immigrants to the American city. Each of the previous waves of white immigration had brought violence and increased crime. This held true for the blacks as well, yet the sense of desperate hopelessness of the black in the United States intensified the level of violence. Most of the anger is directed by one black against another. Mostly blacks themselves are the victims of this violence, making life in the black ghetto "nasty, brutal, and short." Part of the violence is spent on "whitey," regardless of whether he is Jew or Christian. With increasing frequency, because blacks were moving into neighborhoods vacated by Jews, the nearest whites were Jewish.

Black radical organizations, such as the Black Panthers, in seeking to ally themselves with the forces of the Third World have chosen to support the Arabs and to denounce the Jews, thereby reinforcing the feeling of many Jews that they were the preferred victims of black hostility.

The 1968 strike of New York school teachers was a watershed of Jewish-black relationships. Many Jews claim that the strike clearly revealed that black militants had learned to use anti-Semitism as a weapon to gain their ends. At the same time, many blacks felt that the hitherto undeclared racism of Jews was painfully exposed. Groups of black youngsters standing at their school gates shouted anti-Jewish obscenities at the school teachers. A few of the teachers asked the Jewish Defense League to escort them to work.

The high rate of crime produced by the black ghetto has meant that storekeepers, both Jewish and non-Jewish, are vulnerable to robbery and attack. Elderly men and women have been violently mugged, children intimidated and forced to hand over their lunch money by schoolyard toughs.

Crime has become a national tragedy in the United States. The police seem to be unable to make the streets safe or to prevent the demoralization of youth. The cities are experimenting in a variety of directions in the hopes of supplementing police efforts. In some communities there are citizens who volunteer to serve as auxiliary policemen, thereby increasing the effective size of the police force. Because large apartment projects have proven susceptible to invasion by rapists and robbers, security guards are being hired and closed-circuit television is being installed to observe entrances, exits, corridors, and stairwells.

Here and there, communities are expressing their despair and their impatience by organizing neighborhood patrols which cruise the streets after dark.

One such neighborhood, in Crown Heights, Brooklyn, contained a mixture of highly Orthodox Jews, blacks, and some Italians. Driven to despair by the muggings and beatings in the neighborhood, and feeling that the police were either unable or unwilling to help, they organized such a patrol. The leader of the Maccabees (as the patrols in Crown Heights called themselves), was a rabbi who resided in the neighborhood. He answered charges of vigilantism by pointing out that his patrols would be unarmed, and would attack no one in the streets. The cruising cars containing interracial crews were equipped with two-way radios with which to reach the police, with whom they would be working closely. When the police improved their patrols in the area, the rabbi disbanded his without seeking to make political capital of his project. Many people, vaguely recalling the Crown Heights patrols in 1965, assume that they were organized by Rabbi Kahane, leader of the Jewish Defense League. They were not.

The Jewish Defense League was founded in 1968. In his speeches and writings that year Kahane sought to discredit the major Jewish organizations, which he labelled "the establishment," by accusing them of cringing before black anti-Semitism.

Kahane talked of patrol cars manned by J.D.L. members

which would cruise the streets of Williamsburg and Boston and prevent Negro attacks against Jews. It is doubtful that such patrols were sufficiently organized or persisted long enough to make any difference in neighborhood behavior. Sending out an occasional car full of young men armed with baseball bats is hardly a sufficient response to urban crime.

There were karate classes and a summer camp at which youngsters were taught close-order drill and physical conditioning. Kahane offered to escort teachers during the course of the strike. Most teachers spurned his offer and made their own way. A few chose a J.D.L. escort. However, the police were also on hand in large numbers and the effects of Kahane's forces is doubtful.

One incident is especially instructive. A coalition of black and white religious civil rights leaders, meeting in Chicago in 1968, issued what became known as the "Black Manifesto," demanding that Catholic, Protestant, and Jewish groups contribute to a billion-dollar fund to finance ghetto self-help projects. This call for "reparations" to compensate for three hundred years of indignity imposed on America's blacks was taken up by James Forman, former S.N.C.C. leader. In the company of one or two companions, Forman interrupted services at several churches and announced that he would be at Temple Emmanu-el's Friday night service in New York City.

Kahane boasted in a speech at McGill University, last year, that he telephoned James Forman on that Friday and "threatened to break both his arms and legs" if the black leader appeared at the Temple. While Kahane was making his threats, Temple officials were conferring with Sanford Garelick, Chief Inspector of the New York Police. They had agreed that if Forman came to the synagogue and insisted on interrupting the service, he would be escorted to the door by a police officer. If, however, he waited for the completion of the service, he would be invited to read his manifesto without interruption. That Friday night forty J.D.L. members armed with clubs and bicycle chains paraded in front of the Temple

Emmanu-el, miles from the black ghetto, waiting for a lone
black who wished to read a statement. Forman did not show
that night and Kahane claimed credit for saving Temple
Emmanu-el from black militancy.

In his speech at York University, Toronto, on January
21, 1971, Kahane claimed for the J.D.L. the major credit
for dramatizing the plight of Jews in the Soviet Union thereby
compelling the Soviet government to release two thousand
Jews a year and permitting them to emigrate to Israel. Kahane
claimed that the major Jewish organizations failed to act
aggressively to relieve the plight of Soviet Jewry, as they had
failed to save European Jewry thirty years earlier.

The major Jewish organizations are in a state of anguish
over such claims. They point to the years of intensive activity
on the issue of Soviet Jewry. They recall the years of research,
the hundreds of articles, pamphlets and books which have
been written on their urging. They point to the world-wide
series of demonstrations and petitions initiated over the past
eight years. Above all, they recite the delicate balance of
world opinion necessary to nudge the Soviet gates open and
express fear that the J.D.L.'s tactics may slam them shut
again.

The J.D.L. has identified its movement with that of the
Stern gang in pre-1948 Israel. They insist that had their
tactics been followed in the 1940's, many of the six million
who perished would have been saved. They insist that only
their organization recognizes threats to Jewish life and that the
J.D.L. alone is determined that such calamities shall never
happen again.

The validity of the J.D.L.'s claim is highly doubtful. Their
followers have not stemmed the tide of urban crime, intimidated ghetto toughs, protected storekeepers, or contributed
to the salvation of Russian Jewry.

The J.D.L.'s program will not solve the problem of urban
violence. Obscenities and garbage will not persuade the Russians to change their policies, and their claim to a monopoly
on Jewish militancy is a distortion of the realities of Jewish

life and history. Jews have rejected the passive response to persecution. They refuse to believe any longer that they are powerless. But Jewish militancy will never accept the abuse of power as a tactic, nor the persecution of other peoples as a goal.

A Radical Zionist's Critique of the Jewish Defense League

David Mandel

Jewish Defense League: The name alone conjures up various images in the mind; no doubt many have a strong reaction one way or the other. I would brashly say that just in its controversiality the J.D.L. has done some good, and has awakened many of our Jews from their ambivalence about themselves. It has seriously questioned in public and on a large scale the priorities and values of the Jewish Establishment and its institutions. We hear many praises and severe criticisms of the J.D.L. I would like to crystallize some of my feelings about them, from a socialist Zionist point of view.

J.D.L.'s analysis of the American Jewish community is almost completely the same as that of many radical Zionists. Recently in Brooklyn I heard Meir Kahane lead a discussion in which he presented a very accurate Marxist analysis of the economic position of America's Jews as a people-class—middlemen in the economic world, neither in control of major segments of the economy nor displaying potential for active participation in any socialist workers' movement; in short, marginal to the major processes of the society. And this role carries over into the political-social spheres. As James

David Mandel is national chairman of the Radical Zionist Alliance. This article was written especially for this book.

Sleeper of Boston has written: the American Jew is "a civil rights worker to southern whites, a slumlord to urban blacks, a capitalist to communist propagandists, and a communist to rednecks, a radical to Birchers, and an establishment businessman to the left." The answer, according to both the Radical Zionist Alliance and the J.D.L., is *aliyah*—immigration to Israel—in order to build a positive Jewish life where Jews as a people are liberated from their middleman role and freed from the even greater danger of assimilation. The pressure to conform is strong on any Jew in America, whether he conforms to the left, the right, the middle, or *anything* outside of a Jewish context.

J.D.L.'s attacks on the Jewish Establishment in America are almost totally valid. They can join other Jewish activist groups in demanding more money for education and the everyday needs of the Jewish communities from Jewish philanthropic organizations and less for non-Jewish hospitals and meaningless institutions that attempt to smooth the road to assimilation for American Jews rather than develop positive Jewish identity.

J.D.L.'s militancy has come under strenuous criticism as un-Jewish, racist, and fascistic. This isn't necessarily so. I do not believe that J.D.L.'s leadership is racist, although many of that type are attracted to the J.D.L. and little is done to discourage their participation. Militant defense of one's life and one's people is sometimes called for, and I am in favor of very drastic action against the Soviet Union's anti-Jewish policies.

I draw the line, however, before stupidity. Strong action in support of Soviet Jewry is taken for the dual purpose of harming the Russian government's prestige and getting favorable publicity for our struggle. Harassing families of Russians does neither. Verbal red-baiting does neither. In fact, the most effective protest against Russian treatment of Jews is that done from a leftist viewpoint, so that the protestors cannot be called "right-wing hooligans." Yes, militant protest is called for, but not stupidity.

This kind of stupidity, however, is only a symptom of the two basic problems I see in J.D.L.: one, placing "defense" before true Zionism, and two, a lack of political and ideological content.

As I said earlier, Kahane claims to be a true Zionist and I believe him, in private or with his own people. But a true Zionist organization must really put its Zionism "up front," and here the J.D.L. is almost as guilty as the Zionist Establishment (like the Zionist Organization of America, Hadassah, etc.), who rarely mention *aliyah*, and never *galut* (exile). Despite what Kahane might really believe, "defense," and not *aliyah*, has always been and still remains the main thrust of J.D.L. It is the image Jacob Feuerwerker's recent article in last April's *Hashofar* (newspaper of the Northern Ohio Union of Jewish Students) portrays when he says that "the Jewish Defense League stands for exactly what its name says—Jewish Defense"; and there is no mention of anything Zionist in the whole article! American Jews have always given high priority to "defense" organizations—the American Jewish Committee and the B'nai B'rith Anti-Defamation League are notorious examples. J.D.L.'s only real difference from these groups is a tactical one. None of them recognize any answer beyond "defending" the *status quo,* and maintaining a false unity of all Jews. Even when the J.D.L. does occasionally encourage *aliyah,* it, too, is seen as a strengthening of Israel's present position, and not as a step towards a more socialist, democratic, or peaceful Israel.

I have nothing against intelligent militancy nor anything against intelligent self-defense. It should be a given for every human being and certainly for every Jew, that he will defend himself, his people, and his homeland. However, when defense becomes an ideology unto itself, it becomes self-defeating. It is a manifestation of the mentality of exile when one makes defense of that exile the highest priority. It is not only non-Zionist to encourage an ideology of exilic self-defense, but anti-Zionist. Kahane would criticize these words as ignoring the "here and now problems" of the Jews in New

York. But no, the best thing that could happen to American Jews, already under increasingly great Israeli cultural influence, would be the development of a stronger, more vital, and more progressive Jewish community in Israel. J.D.L. has fallen into the same trap as the Jewish Establishment, of trying to identify Jews' interests with America's rulers' interests, rather than a true spirit of moral, cultural, and political independence centered in Israel.

My second major objection to J.D.L. is one of politics, or rather J.D.L.'s stated lack of *any* politics, left or right. J.D.L. claims that their only yardstick in determining response to a given political issue is a judgment of "what is good for the Jews." This statement, though not intrinsically wrong, narrows one's vision so as to make impossible any larger utilitarian judgment. But setting utilitarianism aside, neither politics nor Jews can exist in that kind of self-enclosed vacuum. A principle basic to Judaism is the idea of moral reciprocity, the golden rule, recognizing as an equal right for others that which we demand for ourselves. Of course we demand self-determination for our people in our homeland, and will fight to defend it. However, moral reciprocity demands that we recognize the same right for the Palestinian people, and that we struggle for our own rights only if we are totally committed to peace, to coexistence, and to compromise with another right. Moral reciprocity demands that we lend active support, at the very least our verbal support, to the struggles of the many other oppressed peoples of the world, the Vietnamese and the American minorities most visible from here. There is no need for this to detract from our own people's struggles for liberation. Furthermore, our adherence to the principle of moral reciprocity and at the same time our demand for such recognition from others is what is really "good for the Jews." The vacuum I have been talking about is not only an ideological one that sounds uncomfortable for a veteran New Leftist like myself, but a real one: In our struggle for justice, we must be on the side of justice everywhere, or justice will turn and flee from us, too.

J.D.L., in its narrow-minded yardstick of Jewish defense, perpetuates an ideology of self-defeat and of exile. Though I do not doubt the motives of the leadership, the position is an irresponsible one that comes out sounding reactionary in tone and content. Even if Zionist, the J.D.L. has come closer and closer to identification with the goals and policies of Herut, Israel's right-wing expansionist, antilabor party.

Defense and militancy are acceptable, even necessary, but they should not be practiced for their own sake—rather as a portion of a comprehensive ideology of Jewish liberation, a radical Zionist ideology.

Part Nine

Nine

Voices of the Movement—II

Radicals seem to have an endless capacity to debate, redefine, and sharpen their ideological tools. Contrary to opinion, most radicals are constantly engaging in self-criticism and self-change.

So many areas of American life and Jewish life remain unexplored, so many gaps need to be filled, and so many questions need to be supplied with new facts and new perspectives. American Jewry had, in the 1950's and 1960's, its own "end of ideology" period. So today it is not surprising that radical Jews bring their energies to the exploration of the ideologies of the past in order to develop new perspectives of their own for the future.

The increase in Jewish studies and Jewish "free universities" will result in important resurgencies of Jewish scholarship—one that is both "partisan" and "objective." Jewish history, sociology, literature, and theology, like their black, Chicano, and Amerindian counterparts, are wide open fields for scholars young and old.

Novak takes a critical look at the movement so far, at the response of the Jewish Establishment, and warns against cynicism and parochialism. Ross' anti-Zionism piece is from *The Other Way,* a new journal put out by a new generation of Bundists, inheritors of Yiddish culture, international socialism, and spirited opposition to the Jewish Establishment of another era.

Robbie Skeist's sensitive account of his personal Jewish identity crisis draws an analogy between "coming out" gay and Jewish. And finally, "Oppression and Liberation," a position paper of the Jews for Urban Justice in Washington, dissects the myths of American culture and the impact of the American empire on Jewish life.

The Failure of
Jewish Radicalism

Bill Novak

The newest phase of Jewish radicalism began around 1967.
I say "around 1967" because although there were seeds
planted and developed throughout the Kennedy and Johnson
years, the emergence of our own response was not clear until
1967. The story has been told of how young people who had
been involved in the social activism of the early 1960's, the
civil rights movement, the peace movement, were in many
cases Jewish, although they rarely identified as such. On the
contrary: many saw their own actions as going *against* Jewish
life, at least against the lives and principles of American
Jewry. And the story has been told and retold about how the
civil rights movement changed direction and tone, and became
militant and particularistic, leaving once and for all the age-
worn ideal of the American melting pot, and replacing it with
a new dream of cultural autonomy in a pluralistic society. And
we are also well aware of how these changes left many Jews
politically homeless, and how some are still drifting, still looking. Those who had been politically active in the early 1960's,
in a variety of inherently good and worthwhile causes, found

Bill Novak is editor of *Response,* a member of Boston's Havurat Shalom,
and a graduate of York University and Brandeis University. This article appeared originally in *Genesis 2,* April 8, 1971, and is reprinted by permission of
the author.

themselves radicalized by the expanding war, by America's misguided priorities, by Columbia, Brandeis, Cornell, Berkeley, and especially Chicago. And many of us, in ways which are just now becoming clear, had our Jewish selves radicalized in 1967, in the Six-Day War. For it was then that we learned, more dramatically than in any history class, the tragic lesson which seems to be the paradigm of the Jewish people: When it comes down to the crisis, we have only ourselves.

The experience of American Jewry, and of Jews all over the world, living through the sequence of events in 1967, was fundamentally crucial. The lesson was retaught only three years later, when the Leningrad trials in 1970 proved again that in the end we can rely only upon ourselves.

When the Jewish radical movement, and the larger picture of a Jewish counterculture were being created, when the first indigenous newspapers, the first experiments in community and education were being begun, we talked a great deal about *community,* and about our own situation. We were the people who were going to change the world, who believed that the differences between groups of men could be safely ignored, and they would eventually disappear. But we grew older and wiser, and influenced by the ensuing political developments in American life, we began to think in different terms, and envisaged a pluralistic America, where ethnic and cultural groups could, if they wished, live independently, in control of their own destinies. And we formed free Jewish universities, and read books, and wrote articles, all the time concerned with the Jewish people, quoting Hillel's famous dictum: "If I am not for myself, who will be for me?" And somewhere along the way we forgot about changing the world.

And so we read and we listened and we learned. We absorbed some of the momentum of the Holocaust and of Israel, and we tried to understand what happened in Europe during the 1940's, and what didn't happen in America during those same tragic years. And finally, in 1967, and again in 1970, we learned firsthand about the rest of the world. Except that by then we believed a little less strongly in the rest of the world, and in its great saving power. The New Left? Ah, yes, that dream of a moral politics that would go beyond the corporate liberalism of the Kennedy years. Yes, the New Left would save the Jews, we discovered, like it saved Spain, Greece, Czechoslovakia, and the six million.

And we grew bitter in our disillusionment, and we passed around articles, reprinting them many times over, like M. J. Rosenberg's statement, in which he asserted, in 1969, that from that point on, he would join no movement "that does not accept and support my people's struggle. If I must choose between the Jewish cause and a 'progressive' anti-Israel S.D.S., I shall choose the Jewish cause."

Rosenberg's message, in one form or another, was repeated within the young Jewish community in America for over two years. More recently, this sort of attitude is being adopted by the Jewish Establishment, which is forsaking its traditionally liberal activism for an ostrich-like posture of "taking stock," of "consolidation." *Commentary* magazine, having previously taken to task the American youth culture, now cautions against any Jewish involvement in the Movement. Much more frightening, the usually courageous *Reconstructionist,* generally an island of reason in a sea of hysteria, goes along with and praises *Commentary* because *Commentary* rejects those who separate themselves from the community, and, by implication, regards the survival and internal health of the Jewish community as themselves spiritual goals. This is, indeed, good news, since the large circulation and profound impact of that splendid journal constitute a powerful instrument when utilized for positive Jewish values.

And who, we might ask, are those who "separate" themselves from the community? Apparently, this is a reference to those Jews who have tried to come to terms with their own Jewishness while maintaining political opinions which are no longer popular in organized Jewish life. Of Arthur Waskow's important although admittedly unsuccessful attempt to provide a symbolic language for radical Judaism, the editor of *Commentary* writes glibly that it "might more accurately be considered a contribution to the literature of Jewish anti-Semitism than to the literature of the often overlapping but nonetheless distinct phenomenon of Jewish self-hatred." Pretty harsh words, and pretty harsh times when it is *Commentary* who is identifying the "real" Jews, and pointing out the self-haters, and telling us who apparently ought to be excluded from the Jewish community.

To a large extent, of course, the general inward turning of both older and younger Jews has been necessary and important. But only up to a point. Those who quote the first part of Hillel's saying, mentioned earlier, might remember that he said, right afterwards in the text (*Avot*), "If I am only for myself, then what good am I?" If—as seems to be the case— we have indeed shifted our concerns and priorities from the forest to the trees, from our naive universalism to a more pragmatic particularism, I am afraid we have gone overboard to the point of seeing only the trees, and forgetting all about the forest.

Many of us are outraged when the Prime Minister of Israel sends a telegram of support to Nixon, regarding American foreign policy, or when the Jews of Philadelphia find it necessary to honor a police chief whose record hardly suggests the values we supposedly cherish. But how many of us object when the Jewish Establishment, and sometimes even those who call themselves Jewish radicals, attempt to isolate the National Jewish Organizing Project, or the Jews for Urban Justice, or any of the bolder attempts to combine—however awkwardly at first—political radicalism and Jewish tradition.

There was a hope, the hint of a promise, that things would be different. There were, in the beginning, attempts to synthesize "Jewish" action and "America" action. But now, there seems to be a feeling that we have to choose, that it is an either-or proposition. And so we find ourselves tolerating the Jewish Defense League, because they are Jews, or because the cause they claim to speak for is beyond reproach, or because they are "raising the conscience of the community," or because we dislike their enemies, or because, as it sometimes seems, "at least they are doing something!" And we keep silent about our moral outrage and their open cowardice, and worse, we do nothing ourselves.

If the world has abandoned the Jews, is the proper response in turn for the Jews to abandon the world? If so, what is the point of it all? Israel has shown that she will not be a nation like all other nations, that her code of conduct must conform, as much as possible, to the laws of morality rather than politics. Diaspora Jews must walk the same tightrope, because that is the role of the Jews. We must give up the steady feel of the solid ground beneath our feet. Norman Podhoretz warns American Jews that there is a notion afoot "that the participation of Jews in the Movement, far from constituting a problem to the Jewish community, does honor to that community and is an ornament to its 'idealism.' " We must take that notion and *strengthen* it; we cannot and must not give in to the politics of fear, paranoia, and blackmail.

I do not wish to be mistaken on these matters. I do not take issue with the premise that all Israel is responsible one member for another. It does not end there, however. We have always been a busy people, and we have done many things with our small numbers. The day is short, and there is much to do. Yes, we must continue to act on behalf of Soviet Jewery; we must also not remain silent about other oppressed minorities, in Russia and elsewhere, and in our own backyard.

Several years ago, during the civil rights movement, there were those who said disdainfully, "nobody helped us" and "let them pull themselves up by their bootstraps like we did." These reckless comparisons are being repeated now in new forms, and if we must give the world tit for tat, as if there were no special obligations, no sense of destiny, or of mission, that Jews have always possessed. And long as we are here, it is our duty to make life in America better for all people; and this needn't be at the expense of ourselves. For we must assert it loudly: Mere existence, for Jews, *even in the wake of Hitler,* is simply not enough.

Zionism and the Jewish Radical

Gabriel Ross

Any Jewish movement must be concerned with the problems of insuring a continued Jewish existence. But a radical Jewish movement must go beyond this: it must be concerned with the quality of Jewish life. It must strive for conditions which will allow for the actualization of positive Jewish aspirations; a real possibility only in a liberated world.

Jewish radicalism has this concern with the quality of life in common with all other radical movements and, as is the case with other radical programs, is fiercely opposed by an establishment view of the world. That Zionism is now the philosophy of the Jewish Establishment, its driving force, is incontrovertible.

Yet there are some individuals and groups who consider themselves both Zionist and radical. It may be that they seem radical in their desire for certain immediate changes, but their espousal of a Zionist program should make it clear that their goals are in direct conflict with those of any truly progressive movement.

The program of the so-called radical Zionist may differ

Gabriel Ross, a contributing editor to *The Other Way*, is a Ph.D. candidate at the University of Pennsylvania. This article is reprinted from *The Other Way*, Spring, 1971, which is a publication of the Jewish Labor Bund and the Jewish Students' Bund, by permission of the publisher.

from that of his establishment Zionist counterpart in its militancy, but not in its basic content. This content of Zionism, concepts common to *all* its adherents, can be summarized as follows:

1) The Diaspora has been a totally negative experience marked in its essence only by suffering, and the reason for this suffering, for anti-Semitism, is that the Jews were unlike other people.

2) To become like the other nations and thereby end the suffering, the Jews too must have a country, and Palestine is that country.

3) The creation of the State of Israel has solved the Jewish problem; all that remains is to complete the "ingathering of the exiles," thus further strengthening the state.

What a bleak picture this presents of Jewish history! It would seem that for two thousand years the Jews have merely sought the security of being like other peoples. Nor is its outlook on the Jewish future any brighter; the sponsoring of one tiny state in the Middle East, a state most probably doomed to a condition of perennial belligerency with its neighbors.

* * *

In the process of dealing exclusively with the security of the Jews, Zionism has lost sight of the meaningful content in the Jewish past. The Zionist—even the radical one—tells me that I can live a full Jewish life only in a Jewish state. A full Jew? A good Jew? Then who am I? Who were my parents and their parents?

The Jews, I am patiently told, have acquired a ghetto mentality. Their existence in the Diaspora has been a painful experience. They have been the pawns of more powerful nations. The only point to their credit is that they have persevered through the years so that they can again realize their greatness by reestablishing their long-lost state.

Is my Jewishness merely a ghetto mentality? Is my destiny to bypass the last two thousand years of Jewish history and thus recreate an era of "greatness" with which the Bible-belt Christian is more fully in touch than I?

No! If this were truly my only inheritance, I would rather forego it and assimilate. The Zionist, however, is unperturbed. "You have no choice," he tells me. "Anti-Semitism is the perennial evil which will eventually force you to disintegrate or to seek the security obtainable only in a Jewish state."

Such a Zionist approach to one's Jewish identity no doubt has a great appeal for many, particularly in Amerika. For those to whom their Jewishness is somehow dichotomous with respectability, there is the appeal of a Jewish state, a member in the establishment of nations. For those to whom their Jewishness is barren, there is the pleasure of vicariously reaping the achievements of Israel. For those who feel guilt in having stood by while witnessing the destruction of a third of their people, there is the vision of Jewish armies and retribution. Even for those who are concerned with their Jewishness and have the potential for improving the quality of Jewish life around them, there is the appeal of *aliyah*—leaving the problem behind and thereby, through the logic of Zionism, solving it. For all those who, in effect, fear their Jewish identity, who need to conform, whose lives are constricted by their search for personal security, Zionism does have a great appeal. But surely not for the radical Jew.

* * *

The radical cannot conceive of an isolated Jewish problem, only of a world problem. Through the ages, the Jew has been the wandering hippie expressing his unique life style in the world arena. He did not proselytize others to his particular way of life, but the revolutionary message transmitted by his presence was clearly perceived by those in power: There *are* alternative ways of living and thinking. The destiny of a people is to express its uniqueness. The state is ultimately powerless; it can be repressive, brutal, murderous, but it cannot change the will of a people. Real power, the ability to persist in the striving for self-expression, is always in the possession of the people.

The so-called Jewish problem is the problem of all those who openly show that they *are* different. Its solution must lie in fighting for the fulfillment of the universalistic vision—a liberated world.

How incongruent this vision is with that of the "radical" Zionist who says that he, too, is concerned with liberation, but who, at the same time, views the solution in terms of escape— an armed Jewish state, an enclave in a hostile world. He also says that he is concerned with imperialism, but seems even more concerned with American arms for Israel. He is troubled by injustices imposed on "the Arabs," but cannot come to terms with Palestinian claims for justice. He is critical of Israel's policies, but the leaders of his movement are a part of the ruling coalition government, making him an apologist for Meir-Dayan politics. He is always in a quandary because his Zionism denies the obvious difference between *Israeli nationalism* and *Jewish internationalism;* between the alleged needs of the state and the higher aspirations of the people. He must decide on a direction. If he chooses to be a radical, he must oppose Zionism.

Coming Out Jewish

Robbie Skeist

I'm Jewish. That's important to me. But I have a hard time letting that come out with most people, including a lot of freaks and movement people. Sort of like it was hard a year ago to talk about my emotional and sexual relations with other men. You don't fit in, you're getting carried away with something unimportant, you're making up issues, why don't you talk about dope, why don't you talk about the Third World—you're making me itchy—these are some of the messages I get.

Passover

One thing that recently gave me the excitement to figure out my Jewishness was the spring holiday called Passover. It celebrates the time when the Jews who were slaves in Egypt got up and left. "Why build these stupid pyramids for the Pharaohs? Let's build a new life for ourselves." Last Passover, like every Passover, most of my family got together at Gramma Annie's

Robbie Skeist has lived in Chicago the past six years. He has been active in the draft resistance movement, the Venceremos Brigade in Cuba, and gay liberation movement. This article originally appeared in the *Chicago Seed*, Vol. 7, No. 6, 1971 and is reprinted by permission of the author and the editors of *Chicago Seed*.

to see each other, to read the story of the exodus from Egypt, to eat a lot of food, and to drink a lot of wine.

But it was different from other years. Some of us tried to *really* make it a freedom celebration.

Helen had been in Alabama working for a welfare rights group and a black-controlled board of education. Aunt Sheila was in the radical wing of the teachers union in New York and was helping her students open up to new ideas about school, women's liberation, and the draft. Laurie was working with a women's liberation group and developing new ways to teach little kids. Mom was reading books by Doris Lessing and thinking a lot about herself as a woman. I was working in a bad mental hospital and doing my best to be human with the "patients" and not just follow orders. So . . . "Freedom Celebration" had to mean more than reading the traditional service. Helen got us thinking, and we rewrote some songs and picked out some poems to bring Vietnam, blacks, and Russian Jews into the service.

We borrowed the spiritual "Go Down Moses" and shared in the blacks' understanding that there are still a lot of Pharaohs to be fought. For the last verse, we wrote:

> *This Seder's meaning is not done,*
> *Let my people go.*
> *More fights for freedom to be won,*
> *Let ALL people go.*

We chose the poem *Babi Yar* by Yevgeni Yevtushenko, a Russian, to remind us of the Jews killed by the Nazis and of the problems Jews in Russia have today. And in a Passover service prepared by some radical Jews in Washington, D.C. we found a passage arguing that it's not enough for the United States to provide a comfortable life for some people if the war, racism, poverty, male supremacy, pollution, the isolation of people from each other, and the lack of poetry and joy go on.

That evening when the food was ready and everyone was back from walks, twenty of us crowded around three tables pushed together in Gramma's living room. Uncle Jack started the service, then we went around the table, with everyone taking a turn reading. Those of us who had worked out new ideas for the service used our turns to read poems and statements and sing our songs. Some of the relatives were excited by our approach, others were bored, and a few were angry that we didn't "stick to the tradition."

We *were* within the tradition. Not the tired tradition of doing everything just as it was done before, but the tradition of life and energy, of fighting against oppressors, of arguing, of identifying with Jews of other times and places, loving traditional melodies, or feeling all this with the fresh touch of our lives here and now. I'm getting carried away, carried inside some thoughts and feelings from earlier times in my life.

Looking Back—Grampa Sam

I was just looking for a poem I wrote to Grampa Sam (my father's father) the day after he died. I can't find it but I recall the mood. I felt very close to him and a little in awe. He had an accent; he told stories; he was as comfortable with Yiddish as English. Ever since I was around twelve he and I wrote letters. I wrote about what I was doing, my friends and school, and I asked questions about his life as an immigrant Jew. His letters came with very shaky handwriting and told about his life in Lithuania and his first several years here.

Grampa told me about the little farm he grew up on in the *shtetl*, or Jewish ghetto. His family grew the vegetables they needed there, and his mother had a little bakery.

He went to a Jewish school to learn some prayers and enough Lithuanian and arithmetic to be able to do business with the Christians. Gramma Bertha never went to school. Jewishness was a part of their lives every day, often less as a religion than as a bond between people in an area dominated by Christians who were often hostile.

Grampa Sam used to travel from town to town on horseback

with his father, who was a merchant. When I was fifteen, some kid screamed at me that Jews were always dealing with money. I asked Grampa about his father, and he told me that Jews in Europe weren't allowed to go to the Christian schools, enter professions or certain trades, or farm large areas of land, so being a merchant, tax-collector, or moneylender were some of the few possible ways for a Jew to earn money. Also, in case of an attack on the Jewish ghetto by peasants or by Cossack soldiers, a merchant's family could sometimes pack their money and some possessions, get away on horses and start again in another town. It was useful to the people in power to force Jews into positions dealing with money. It led peasants to blame the Jews instead of the people in power for their poverty.

Gramma Annie

Gramma Annie, my mother's mother, once said a few words about some relatives killed by Nazis in concentration camps. I was about 11. When I was twelve and one-half I read about the concentration camps for a social studies report and was really struck someplace. My twelve-and-one-half-year-old suburban heart wasn't used to being struck. I asked my mother if I could ask Gramma more about the relatives who were killed. She said no. I felt some mystery, sadness, and fear.

Gramma Annie told my mother that the Christians had always treated the Jews bad, and taught her to spit every time she passed a church. Just once or twice when I was little, kids I knew asked me why I killed Christ—but even that once or twice was weird.

Growing Up

In seventh grade I lied to my friends about where I went on Wednesday afternoons. I told them it was a recreation hall but really it was *bar mitzvah* class. *Bar mitzvah* is the religious service celebrating a boy's thirteenth birthday, when he reads from the Torah, the five books of Moses written on parchment in Hebrew. I liked the way Hebrew looked and sounded, and I loved some of the old melodies. Part of the excitement was being wrapped up in something that set me apart from everyday Summit, New Jersey, Republican businessman suburb madras shirt and skirt life.

Even though our town was only three percent Jewish, whenever something good was started, a lot of Jews were involved. The open-housing committee, the kids who refused to salute the flag, the poetry magazine which was attacked for being "atheistic," campaigning for Johnson (because we thought he was the peace candidate). Awareness of pogroms and concentration camps and a Jewish tradition of fighting for freedom made it seem natural to get involved.

Over the last few years, my Jewishness has been way in the background. Sometimes I've listened to people talk about "pushy Jews," or joke about "greedy kikes" without showing any reaction. Sometimes I've avoided letting people know I'm Jewish. (I can "pass.") At two jobs I said I was Polish and Lithuanian and won acceptance by the people I worked with by letting them assume I was Catholic. I have tried to ignore Israel at times, even when it's in the headlines; and when I wore a "Shalom" button some of my radical friends made fun of it. These experiences are not mine alone; many Jews in the movement are "in the closet."

Israel . . .

Israel has been one of the most confusing things to work out for a lot of Jewish radicals. Brought up with a one-sided "Israel is perfect" interpretation in Sunday school, we were disillusioned when we heard of discrimination against Arabs in Israel and the heavy influence of pro-American military people. The movement position became total support for the

Palestinian Arab guerrillas, it was very unfashionable to disagree. I think that radical Jews have a special interest and responsibility in developing a position on Israel that takes into account the needs of *two* oppressed and manipulated peoples: the Jews and the Palestinian Arabs.

There is a Jewish state because Jews had no alternative. At the end of World War II, the Jews who survived the concentration camps needed a place to go. Although the United States and Russia did a lot of talking about how wicked the Nazis were, neither of these countries cared enough about the Jews to offer them homes. Going to Palestine was the only option left open to the Jews and if one result was imposing on Palestinian Arabs, the "great powers" didn't care. In 1948, the United Nations resolved that two states, one Jewish and one Arab, be formed out of Palestine.

Some went to Palestine because it was the "Holy Land," others just because it was a place they could go to. Jews have moved to Israel from all over the world, sometimes just to live in a Jewish country and sometimes to escape from persecution. Often, leftist Jews have hoped that "socialist" movements would insure freedom for Jews, but events like the expulsion of Jews from Poland in 1968 and restrictions on the cultural and religious activities of Russian Jews have proved them wrong. A Jewish state is still necessary.

Still, there are many things wrong with Israel. The permanent readiness for war has given the military a position of great importance and honor, and those who advocate a negotiated peace which recognizes the rights of the Palestinian Arabs are often ignored. Poverty and racism were documented in a study by the Israeli Ministry of Housing, as reported in the American Jewish leftist newspaper, *Freiheit*, on June 6, 1971: ". . . 20 percent of Israel's populace are living in slums. These people are families with many children; 40 percent of Israel's children grow up in these neighborhoods. Over 80 percent of the slum-dwellers belong to the oriental communities . . ." Recently some poor, dark-skinned Jews have formed a group called the Black Panthers to demand equal treatment in jobs, housing, and education. (They are not affiliated with the Panthers in this country; the name was chosen to attract publicity). Another ugly fact about Israel is that recently the Knesset voted *not* to legalize homosexual relations between consenting adults.

... and the Palestinian Arabs

What about the Palestinian Arabs? No one got *their* approval for a Jewish state. Some left their land voluntarily, others were forced out, and to this day many of them live in refugee camps in the Arab nations. Israel has ignored them and the Arab nations have left them in poverty. Some Palestinian Arab groups want to destroy Israel as a Jewish state and establish a socialist state open to Moslems, Jews, and Christians. There has been a lot of fighting between guerrilla groups such as Al Fatah and Israeli troops. Many young radicals in this country support the Arab guerrillas, but I disagree. The Jews are a people, with genetical, historical, cultural, and religious ties. After isolation and oppression in many times and places, they now have a homeland. Many Jews have no plans to ever see Israel, but for those who choose it, it's there. The proposal of Al Fatah for a "secular, democratic, pluralistic state in which Jews and Arabs will live together" denies the right of the Jews to have this Jewish homeland. I am convinced, from listening to Israelis and those who have visited Israel and from reading letters from relatives in Israel, that to destroy Israel as a Jewish state, the Arabs would have to kill most of the Jews.

So there must be another way. One possibility for a solution to this problem would be the creation of a separate state for the Palestinian Arabs. Part of the land for this new state would come from territories now occupied by Israel, and the rest from parts of the old Palestine which are now controlled by Arab nations.

Some Israelis may not want to give up any of the land

they now control, and some of the Palestinians may not want to settle for a separate state on just part of the old Palestine, but this kind of compromise may be the only alternative to these two groups of oppressed people killing each other off.

Reaching Out to Movement Jews

If you don't agree with what I wrote about Israel, what do you believe? It's important to figure out. Each of us needs his/her own identity. Sometimes when dealing with American militarism, racism, or class oppression we have tried to be Viet Cong, blacks, or greasers; it doesn't work. Our commitments have to come from understanding ourselves and our own stake in a new society.

Those of us in the women's and gay liberation movements have a special contribution to make, because we know we get energy by digging into our own lives and fighting for our own freedom. Now we have to figure out our identities and assert ourselves as Jews.

Many Jews will criticize us—the Jewish culture makes women second class and gays invisible, it demands that we all be heterosexual, get and stay married, have smart kids, become professionals, and achieve a certain kind of "success." We don't fit into that pattern and we're still Jews, and we can make the contribution of challenging other people's ways of living. Jewish women have gotten together for discussion groups in New York, and so have gay Jews. We can learn and gain strength by doing the same here.

Together we can decide on a range of actions as radical Jews. Here are some possibilities:

* Protest any discrimination against Jews in this country or in any other countries.

* Educate people about the needs of the Israelis and of the Palestinian Arabs, and set up speaking engagements for Israeli leftists.

* Try to communicate with Jews who own stores or apart-

ments in black ghettos and search for ways to transfer that property to blacks.

* Approach synagogues for space and resources for "serve the people" programs such as medical clinics.

* Look into the policies of Jewish hospitals and try to get them to be responsive to the needs of the patients.

* Talk with Jewish groups about gay and women's liberation.

* Learn about the radical tradition of Jews and share it with other Jews, including temple youth groups and movement Jews.

* Participate as Jews in anti-war demonstrations. We could gather at the Federal Building on Yom Kippur, the Day of Mourning, to mourn the sins of this country in Vietnam.

The Oppression and Liberation of the Jewish People in America

Jews for Urban Justice

There is a Jewish people. It lives and feels its life across state boundaries, drawing sustenance from the Jewish communities of America, the Soviet Union, Israel, Western Europe, and Latin America. It lives and feels its life across millennia, across the rise and fall of several successive civilizations. It is not simply a religious denomination, and its peoplehood is not even chiefly defined by religion. Indeed, its peoplehood is defined chiefly by its refusal, its transcendence, of the conventional categories of peoplehood. The Jewish people is not political, *or* religious, *or* cultural, *or* economic, *or* familial. It is political-religious-cultural-economic-familial.

The Jews for Urban Justice (J.U.J.) was the first of the new Jewish radical groups, being formed in November, 1966. For three and a half years, it published *The Jewish Urban Guerrilla;* today, its major organ is the *Voice of Micah* where this article originally appeared. The J.U.J. is different from most other groups in that its base is not students, but mostly young professional working people and families with children. It is involved in numerous activities: demonstrations, conferences, communal celebrations, a theater group, summer work communes, and the Fabrangen, a multi-faced communal cultural center (see page xlii). This document was written collectively by J.U.J. in the fall of 1970; the present version was reprinted in *Response,* Fall, 1971 issue. Copyright © 1971 by *Response* magazine. At present, the J.U.J.'s most ambitious project is an attempt to focus on the problem of ecocide in Vietnam through the "Trees for Vietnam" program. Our thanks to Mike Tabor for the above information.

What characterized its peoplehood best, at its best moments, was the principle of *halakhah:* the Way, the Path; a wholeness and fusion of body, mind, and spirit; of action and ideology; of person and community.

During the last two centuries, the worst oppression suffered by the Jewish people was, of course, the physical extirpation of its membership by the Nazi genocide, aided or unchecked by many other governments (not least of them the Roosevelt government in America, which failed to open many avenues of action that could have saved millions of lives, hundreds of communities). But in America, during the past fifty years, the Jewish community has also suffered a deep oppression of a totally different kind: an oppression so subtle and so debilitating that it has felt to many Jews like victory.

The oppression of which we speak is precisely the cracking of the community, the splitting of The Path, the isolation and separation of religious Judaism from cultural Judaism from political Judaism from economic Judaism from familial Judaism. The categorization of a people into boxes.

To much of the movement that during the past decade has risen to struggle against the Amerikan empire, defining as "oppression" what we have just described may seem peculiar. There are so many more naked oppressions: the genocide of Vietnam, the subjection of blacks, Chicanos, Indians, and women, the exploitation of workers, the poisoning of the air and water on which all of us depend for our very lives. Yet we believe that in a sense the ultimate oppression, the one that even the most reformist ruling class would boggle at removing, the last-ditch defense of the powerful against the rising tide of popular anger and assertion is the cracking of community, the splitting of The Path into a maze of category boxes.

To understand the depth of our feeling, we ask our radical sisters and brothers to imagine the offer of a bargain from Amerika to the blacks: "Accept Amerika fully, and you're in the club. We'll give you proportional representation or better among the affluent; we'll mix you residentially all 'round; we'll let you celebrate King's birthday; we'll even let you keep political ties with Africa, so long as you disband these trouble-making Panthers that seek socialism here, and forget about community control, and take these jive jobs in our bureaucracies. (See? We'll even add a few of *your* words to *our* language!)"

Perhaps the Amerikan empire cannot do this with the blacks and survive as an empire. *But if it did,* would the bargain be liberation—or oppression? We believe that it would be oppression—and that precisely this has been the status offered the Jewish people.

We are organizing and will organize against that oppression.

This does not mean we seek to restore the Jewish community as it was 200 years ago. The Jewish tradition has incorporated constant transformation, The Path has been a way forward—not a paralysis. There is much in the tradition that was either a corruption of its best sense, or a failure to raise to new possibilities. We shall try to avoid both—knowing, of course, that whatever we create will not be perfect.

We call upon the Jewish people to free itself by joining in alliance with others to abolish the Amerikan empire that now oppresses the Jewish people and many other peoples at home and much of the human race outside. We call upon the Jewish people to join the task of creating a democratic, communitarian, libertarian, and socialist society in America. We believe that a fully socialist society will be one in which many self-governing communities are able to end the alienations of mind and body, of politics from economics, of spirit from work, of individual from collective, and thus to create the new, unalienated person; that these communities will differ freely from each other in the shapes they give to the wholeness they make out of their previously alienated lives; and that among these communities a liberated Jewish people will joyfully take its place.

I—The Jewish Identity: Growing Points

The identity of the Jewish people in America is built out of some specific bricks of Jewish experience. Most of these building blocks can be made to face two ways: they can be, and have been, used either to imprison the Jewish people in fear or smugness, or to provide Jews with a strong fortress from which to sally forth to change the world. The task of a radical Jewish movement is to organize and encourage the development of that side of the Jewish identity, that strand of the Jewish tradition, which would help liberate Jews and transform society. Let us specify some of these building blocks, and how we propose to build upon them:

** The heritage of *Tanach* provides on the one hand a comfortable cocoon for some Jews to rest in pridefully, as the "chosen" people; and on the other hand a constant spur to action by other Jews who take it to require that the Jewish people be a *committed* people (not the, but "a"—one among many). Jews deal in many different ways with the God-focus of *Tanach:* some accept the God-focus, some reject it as anything but a reflection of a transitory historical situation, some reinterpret it. The radical Jewish movement must develop that element of the tradition which sees *Tanach* as an open-ended record of dialogue between the present justice—committed, covenanted, but faltering—and the image or source of a future justice toward which the Jewish people and all humanity must respond and move.

** Almost all Jews perceive their history as one of marginality, persecution, and struggle. This perception includes a legend/history of slavery and liberation in Egypt, captivity and return to Babylon, rebellions against the Syrian-Greek and Roman Empires, pariah treatment and pogroms throughout sojourns in Western societies, the hostility of even some revolutionary movements (such as Russian communism) to Jewish peoplehood and autonomy, and of course the Holocaust. This perception on the one hand provides some Jews with an identity of struggle against the ruling-class institutions of whatever society they live in. On the other hand, it provides other Jews with an identity of fearfulness, retreatism, and sometimes a special fear of mass enmity (rather than of ruling-class oppression), and therefore a willingness to ask the ruling class for protection. The radical Jewish movement must strengthen the latest knowledge that there is no safety for Jews in corrupt bargains with illegitimate authorities: that there is only safety in freedom, and in self-confident and devoted resistance to unfreedom.

** The history, memory, or legend of a fully integral, nonalienated Jewish community, in which elements that are now usually separately known as "religion," "politics," "culture," "ethics," "economics," "family life," etc., were felt, experienced, and lived through as a seamless whole: *halakhah*—not an externalized system of "law" but a "path," a "way" in which the community lived, integrating ideology and action. The triumph of the bourgeoisie in both the economy and ideology (the "Enlightenment"), industrialization and the resulting "rationalization" of Euro-American society brought about the smashing of this seamless community process among the Jewish people in Europe and America, and incorporated Jews there into the ordinary political and economic processes of the industrial capitalist state. "Freedom of religion" as an individual right was exchanged for the former semitolerance of Jewish communities, and many Jews were attracted by what looked like emancipation. But as the lonely individual Jew has felt more and more vulnerable, crushable, in the industrial-capitalist machine, some Jews have more and more clearly harked back to the lost community, or have harked forward to some new version of it. This feeling cannot be said to be anything like a universal in the Jewish people in America, but in semiconscious form is widespread—and is reviving. We must create communities that exemplify a new *halakhah*.

** The culture of Eastern European Jewry—the literature and songs, and especially the religious ceremonials that underline great differences between Jews and all other Americans— are shared so broadly among American Jews, even in dissipated form among the youth who do not know Yiddish or do not take religious ceremonies seriously—that they help unify the Jewish people in America. In addition, there is a growing American Jewish popular (i.e., upper-middlebrow) culture—

Goodbye, Columbus and *Portnoy's Complaint;* Saul Bellow—which, while shared with other Americans, is felt more strongly by Jews. We must revivify the moral-political meaning of such celebrations as Passover and Yom Kippur and encourage a radical Jewish culture.

Memories of the Holocaust are overwhelming among Jews over forty, and persist in unexpected forms among young Jews—for example, in the identification of "genocidal Amerika" with Nazi Germany. These memories stir varied reactions; among some, guilt that they were "making it" in America while their brothers and sisters were being mass-murdered in Europe; among others, indelible fear, leading sometimes to hysterical outbursts; among still others, a quiet, steely determination that genocide against Jews shall not again be permitted; and among some with whom we stand, a belief that future Holocausts are liable to come in new ways, will destroy not only the Jews but also other peoples or all humanity and must be resisted by cracking the kind of institutions that spawned Hitler.

** Identification with the protection of Soviet Jewry and with the survival of the Israeli people is so strong among Americans, that they clearly help form the identity of an American Jewish people. For some Jews this feeling has taken the form of blind and total engagement with the Israeli government; for others it has meant much more skepticism or anger toward certain aspects of Israeli society. But for almost all Jews the "issue of Israel" feels qualitatively different from that of Sweden, Tanzania, Chile, or Rhodesia. We must help to revive the notion of a world-wide Jewish people that resists oppression and does not participate in it.

** The strength of the Jewish family structure has until recently been so great that, explicitly and implicitly, it has contributed to a sense of Jewish peoplehood; explicitly because much of Jewish life and tradition is mediated through the family by such sociologically powerful techniques as the Passover Seder, and implicitly because the resistance of Jewish family structure to the general breakdown of the family in industrial capitalist society has seemed to validate Jewish peoplehood. But this too has had another side: in Eastern Europe there sometimes emerged the Talmudist father and home-preserving mother; men who presumably dealt with "*ultimately serious*" issues of God, *Torah, Talmud* (excluding women), and women who dealt with "immediately vital" issues of emotion, human relations, survival (excluding men). The result in the worst cases was a mutual contempt among men for "unintellectual" women and among women for "ineffectual" men. This syndrome has sometimes turned even more sour under the influence of American individualism and capitalism. It is our task to encourage the emergence of communities in which women, men, and children can be free and the family is a matrix of equality and joy.

So far we have tried to show that even in America, where the "carrot" has been used by the ruling class with perhaps the greatest subtlety in Jewish history to dissolve Jewish peoplehood or render it unthreatening, there remains a Jewish people. But the issue still arises: should this continue? Would it still be desirable for there to be a Jewish people after a democratic transformation of American society? Is it desirable for radicals to identify themselves as Jews and assume the worthwhileness of Jewish peoplehood in the present, when they are organizing for that transformation?

We say yes. We say it for three reasons: one intrinsic to Jewishness, two intrinsic to radicalism.

First: there are some Jews (not all) who not only strongly feel Jewish but strongly want and intend to remain Jewish for Jewish "religious," "cultural," or "political" reasons—that is, for reasons intrinsic to the Jewish "path." This is self-justifying, so far as Jews are concerned; it should carry justification with it so far as radicals are concerned, for a second reason:

Second: so long as any people, any national grouping, desires to be autonomous, radicals outside that grouping should respect and support that desire *so long as it does not involve the oppression of another people.* That is what socialist self-determination means. Some radicals may carelessly call such a desire "racist," and others may put it down as "cultural nationalist." But it is not cultural nationalism *if* the national liberation is linked to the achievement of world liberation, the abolition of empires, and the achievement of democracy. And it is not racist, *if* it (1) is based not on hereditary inclusion or exclusion from the people, but on choice! and, much more important, (2) is *not* based on superior power or wealth—that is, on domination. Black, Jewish, Chicano, Italian, and Appalachian communities could live side by side in a non-racist way *if* none of them controlled another, or had wealth or income superior to another. That is obviously not the present situation in America; but radicals or revolutionaries should be organizing to make it achievable.

Third: we believe (out of both Jewish and general history) that in fact a multi-communitarian society based on real participatory democracy in decentralized institutions is in fact far more likely to involve and reflect real socialism than a unitary society and state embracing more than 200 million people like the present American state. We believe that any aggregation of that many people living under a single all-embracing government (either administrative-political like the one in Washington, or business-bureaucratic like the one in New York) cannot help but become a monster to itself and all other peoples. We believe that a "revolutionary" replica of this monster would still be a monster. We therefore believe that neighborhood, regional, ethnic, and workplace autonomy and participatory democracy are crucial to creating a real people's socialism. We therefore believe that the creation and preservation of autonomous black, Jewish, Chicano, Italian, and Appalachian communities in North America is not a tolerable temporary expedient *but an intrinsically desirable process.*

II—The Specific Oppressions of the Jewish People

In taking up the ways in which the American empire has oppressed the Jewish people, we must address two political issues: First, has the Jewish people been uniquely oppressed, or are some of the oppressions we shall describe identical with those of other peoples? Secondly, has the Jewish people been oppressed from outside by the American empire, or has the Jewish people distorted and oppressed itself?

There is a link between the two issues which arises from the fact that clearly a special kind of oppression has been visited by America upon blacks, Chicanos, and Indians. These peoples were militarily conquered by the empire using naked force, have since been kept under military occupation and/or genocidal conditions—and have carried on guerrilla action against that occupation. Clearly the Jewish people *in America* has not been similarly treated. (It is, however, true that the Roosevelt government acquiesced in the Holocaust, and on many occasions refused aid to the Jewish people as a transnational entity—aid that might have prevented the Holocaust or greatly reduced its genocidal effect.) To the extent that the American empire did not use naked physical force to break and control the Jewish people, is the status of Jews a result of "oppression" that came less from outside, more from within—that came more from self-distortion?

There can be no doubt that in many of the areas we shall mention, the American Jewish Establishment has collaborated with the American empire to control, cajole, and oppress the Jewish people. The interests of the Jewish Establishment have sometimes coincided with the interests of the empire, and so bargains have been struck. The ultimate legal and economic sanctions to enforce these bargains have, however, come from the empire. We predict that an insurgent, autonomous Jewish people would have to face direct governmental and economic pressures from the empire, as well as attempts at repression from the Jewish Establishment. We have already met the latter; we expect to meet the former as the strength of radical Judaism grows. Radical Jews have an obligation to organize *both* for internal democracy within the Jewish people now exercised by a small group of wealthy and powerful Jews; *and* for full democracy in America, and thus the end of the power now exerted by the American ruling class over the Jewish people, over all the peoples and classes that live in America, and over most of the peoples of the world.

Secondly, the question can be raised: Although the oppression of the Jewish people in America is clearly not similar to that of blacks, Chicanos, and Indians, is it similar to that of what might be called the "middle nationalities" in America? If we glance at peoples like Poles, Greeks, Italians, who were on the one hand never militarily smashed and subjugated by the American empire, is it correct to say that on the other hand they were forced into the empire's industrial-capitalist machine and made to abandon their own national identity and self-government? The answer to these questions is that we do not know, and as radical Jews would not presume to say. It may well be so; radical movements from among these peoples will have to analyze and describe their own situations. For what it is worth, we would only say that our hunch—our hypothesis—is that *all* the peoples who work and live in America, even including white Anglo-Saxon Protestants who now live in Appalachia, have been broken to the imperial machine—but in different ways from each other. If that is true, the best we can do is describe our own situation and suggest that other peoples describe theirs.

The most important oppression imposed on the Jewish people by the American empire directly has been the pressure by the empire to split the seamless wholeness of Jewish life-thought-action into fragments.

America has defined Jewishness as "religious," or sometimes as "ethnic"—ruling out the self-governing policy and economy of the traditional Jewish communities. *For self-governing Jewish communities would have been indigestible blocks to the political, ideological, and economic hegemony of the empire at home.* Having defined Judaism as a "religion" which could be isolated from claims to state power or economic self-direction, the empire then acted to subvert any serious, profound spiritual element in even that truncated "religion": it has tried to capitalize the communal, monetize the mysterious, wipe out the sense of wonder. This the empire has done in pursuit of ultra-"rationalized" bureaucratic capitalism, in the attempt to incorporate within "everyday" dimensionality every conceivably threatening intrusion of deep, indigestible, human feeling and spiritual concern. When socialist ideology arose within the Jewish people, the empire encouraged that form of socialism which could be directed away from itself—Zionist socialism—and discouraged that form which was aimed against the empire directly—Bundism.

In addition, certain specific aspects of Jewish peoplehood have been denied, dissolved, or smashed by the empire. The language with which the Jewish people entered America— Yiddish—was practically wiped out by American cultural and economic pressures (who could get jobs; who could have inputs to the mass media, etc.); Hebrew has had similar difficulties, though it is slowly spreading. The celebration of the Sabbath in any profound way as a day of tranquility, contemplation, study, and joy was made extremely difficult— and the price in economic and political terms made high for those who insisted on pursuing the Sabbath. The other Holy Days were stripped of their moral and political meaning and some—such as Chanukah, which began as a radical celebration of a national liberation struggle—were commercialized.

Similarly, the key roles of Jewish life were de-Judaized: the rabbi (a people's teacher and life-long student) was turned into an institutional clergyman; the *schliach tzibur*, "messenger of the people," in the synagogue was turned into a professional "cantor"; the *shochet*, who by slaughtering animals for meat according to a holy process became the joiner of spirit to body, was turned into a butcher. A calendar built around the fusion of humanity into the world of nature was reduced to insignificance in order to fit the business needs of industrial capitalism. The process of *Torah lishma*, studying Torah for its own sake, and even the secularization of this impulse in the study of art and science for their own sakes, was broken by the capitalist ethic, seeking technological advance or social pacification.

In regard to the Jewish family, American society acted in much the same way: it fastened onto the damaging male-female division of roles that we have mentioned above, and worsened it by meshing it with American competitive individualism. Thus the male study of Torah was translated into "making it," the female conflict-resolution role cheapened into manipulation of the family. Thus was created the desanctified family-competition scene typified by the Super *Bar Mitzvah.*

Through both these general and specific mechanisms, the sense of the Jewish people of what is meritorious and who deserves to lead was totally transformed by the empire. The dollar replaced the Book; the manipulator of propaganda media replaced the painstaking seeker after painful truth. "Jewish leaders" were found, named, and given power by the empire—not the Jewish people. And of course they serve the empire, not the Jewish people. Thus Jewish merchants break Jewish law to sell food grown by exploited labor; Jewish scientists break Jewish law to invent new weapons of mass murder and ecocide.

Finally, the warmth and skeptical lovingness which Jewish communities in different places have traditionally felt toward each other has been badly damaged and corrupted by the American empire. The pity and love which most American Jews feel toward Russian Jews who are being stripped by the Soviet government of the cultural identity and history as well as of all political freedom and popular power has been twisted by the American empire into support for that empire's own cold war against the Soviets—a cold war fought not for Jewish or other liberties but solely for American power. The love and concern which most American Jews feel toward the Israeli people has been twisted by the empire into hysterical militarism supporting any alliance on any terms between the American empire and the Israeli government.

This last requires some elaboration. Among a free Jewish people in America, there would almost certainly have developed a wide range of feelings toward the Jewish people in Israel. Some American Jews would have wanted to migrate to Israel, in accord with a belief in "return" to the land of *Tanach*. Some would have wanted to assist the emergence of a healthy, free, democratic, and peaceful Israel, and would at the same time have felt both free and obligated to criticize vigorously the policies or structures of Israel whenever they failed to be free, democratic, or peaceful. Some would have criticized the very existence of the Israeli state, either on orthodox religious grounds or out of a modern commitment to the Diaspora or out of a sensitivity to the Palestinian claims to the same soil or out of a belief that (as the Prophet Samuel said) the Jewish people ought not to have a state "like other nations." *It is a major oppression of the Jewish people in America that this broad range of feelings has been narrowed down almost to one or two that are allowed to be felt by large numbers of Jews.*

There are many ways in which this has been accomplished. In most of them, the Jewish Establishment has acted in concert with the American empire to assert that the only "possible" choices are (a) migration to Israel; (b) total support for Israeli government policy; or (c) dropping out of the Jewish community. But it is also sadly true that some American radicals have responded to this repression by the Jewish Establishment by accepting these false "realities," these restricted choices permitted by the Establishment, acting as if indeed these were the only choices. They have thus been so insensitive to the legitimate range of feelings among the Jewish people as to constrict the choices available to Jewish radicals who wish to view Jewish liberation as a part of world liberation, and to many Jewish radicals this has felt like a real oppression.

Let us take up first the ways in which the Jewish Establishment, in concert with the American empire, has tried to restrict the freedom of the Jewish people on this issue. The empire itself has done its best to define the situation as one in which the cold war against communism is equated with protection of Israel against hostility from some Arab states and peoples, and especially from the most radical ones; in which military support for Israel is the only reasonable way of protecting or improving Israeli society and is also the only legitimate "American" position; and in which that form of support is conditioned (as in blackmail) on support of other imperial objectives.

The Jewish Establishment has been ready—even anxious —to join in this game. It has been "more royal than the king," more militarist than the Israeli generals in divining the goals and nature of Israel. It has scorned the Israeli left, greeted with great pleasure the constantly strengthening alliance between the Israeli government and the American empire, supported the most capitalist elements in Israel. In twenty-five years time it has transformed American Zionism from a movement led by labor unionists and kibbutz-oriented socialists to one dominated by wealthy businessmen. All this was to be expected from a Jewish Establishment that was itself capitalist and that had during the last fifty years tied itself more and more closely to the American empire; in accord with this policy, the Jewish Establishment has put great pressure on Jewish groups and organizations not to take anti-imperial stands on issues of great importance in America—for example, not to oppose the Vietnam War— lest such stands endanger the empire's commitments to the Israeli government. And the Establishment has argued that any criticism whatever of Israeli policy or social structure would weaken political support in America for the empire's alliance with the Israeli government, and would therefore endanger Israel.

Any attempt by the Israeli left or American Jewish left to open up a whole new outlook—to point toward an anti-imperialist Israel at home in the Third World, protected by peace with anti-imperialist neighbors rather than by constantly escalating war against both imperialist client-states and anti-imperialists among her neighbors—any such attempt has been rigorously smashed by the American Jewish Establishment. Thus the Anti-Defamation League of B'nai B'rith pressed all Jewish organizations to avoid sponsoring, assisting, or even debating an independent-left, pro-Third-World member of the Israeli

Knesset who toured America. Thus the Bundist movement—a Jewish socialist, anti-Zionist movement that had great strength in the Jewish communities in Eastern Europe and America before 1940—has been systematically opposed, excluded, and where possible, smashed.

In short, the feelings of solidarity and love—together with constant skeptical reexamination—which we believe would have been widely felt, and legitimately so, within American Jewry toward the Jewish community in Israel, have been warped into blind hysterical support for not only the Israeli state that has been created but for the particular policies of a particular government of that state. The responsibility for this distortion must lie upon the American empire, the American Jewish Establishment, and the Israeli government. Its victim has been the Jewish people in America.

In response to these pressures, however, some radical groups have asserted that the *only* legitimate position for Jewish radicals is total opposition to the existence of an Israeli state. We accept that this is one legitimate position for a committed Jew to take—and some Jews who were fully committed to the Jewish people have, for a number of reasons, taken that position for centuries past.* But we do not believe that it is the *only* legitimate position for radical Jews who are committed to the liberation of the world and the Jewish people. Attempts to insist on it as the only legitimate position stem, we fear, from one of two mistakes in radical or revolutionary feeling or analysis:

Either, in regard to the situation in America, from lack

---

* Some believed that only in the Days of the Messiah can a true Zion living according to Jewish law be rebuilt and that anything less is a travesty, not a fulfillment, of *Tanach;* some, that the Return to Zion will be spiritual, not geographic; some, that a Jewish community should exist in the land of Israel, but by no means a Jewish state; some, that the Diaspora—the dis- than their concentration in Zion; some that Palestine belonged to the Pales- persion of the Jewish people—was politically and spiritually a higher good tinians; some, that all territorial nationalism was obsolete.

of understanding of or hostility to the very notion of a Jewish people in America which would have some special concerns for the Jewish people elsewhere;

Or, in regard to the situation in the Middle East, from an understandable but shortsighted rejection of the deep dilemmas created there by the real emergence, during the past generation, of an Israeli people which is entitled to self-determination and which must at the same time deal justly with a Palestinian people that is also entitled to self-determination.

Our analysis leads us to the following suggestions insofar as radicals outside the Jewish people are concerned:

The word "Zionist" should not be used as equivalent to "oppressor who is a Jew." There are two reasons for this. First, it is quite possible to be a Jewish oppressor without being what most Jews understand to be a Zionist: that is, to be a Jewish oppressor while being uninterested in or even opposing Israel. (Judge Julius Hoffman is just such a person.) Secondly, it is possible to be what in most Jewish contexts is called a "Zionist" without being an exploiter. For example, an American Jewish revolutionary or radical who would like to live in Israel, to organize against the present Israeli social nature, and to press for self-determination for the Palestinian people would be called a Zionist by most Jews. For these reasons we urge that radicals from outside the Jewish people not use terms identifying as "Jewish" or "Zionist" oppressors who happen to be Jewish, any more than radicals outside the black people ought to use terms like "house niggers" to describe oppressors who happen to be black. Such analyses, slogans, and attacks are important *for the Jewish radical movement to work out for itself*. Of course, radicals and revolutionaries generally must work out who is an oppressor, and say so. But ethnic labels should be left to the radicals of that ethnic group.

We will take up below in more detail what we would regard as a legitimate range of behavior on the issue of Israel within a liberated Jewish people who were committed to the liberation of all other peoples as well. Suffice it to say now that the alternatives now "permitted" among Jews must be enormously expanded in some directions.

III—The Oppressions Jews and Others Share

Of course there are many aspects of their lives in which American Jews are oppressed not because they are Jews, nor in their Jewish peoplehood—but as workers and consumers and residents in the same ways that their non-Jewish co-workers and coconsumers and neighbors are oppressed. It is important for a radical Jewish movement to be clear about this, and to raise these issues at the same time it is raising issues of particularly Jewish oppression. To do otherwise would be to retreat into the worst forms of a more cultural pluralism—which would not in fact liberate the Jewish people. (What good would Shabbat be if for six days of work our lives were utterly alienated and exploited? Indeed, would Shabbat be Shabbat?)

On the other hand, to abandon the particularly Jewish issues would ignore the nature of the American empire, would sell out our own belief that liberation must happen in and through real communities—not merely some abstract "human" identity—and would crush our own deep knowledge that one of those communities is Jewish.

The crucial fact about America that we must keep in mind is this: *The empire has acted so as partly to homogenize and integrate all communities into an atomistic, easily-governed mass; and partly so as to preserve just enough differences and separations between various communities as to make it difficult for everyone to move together.* Thus, for example, the empire has not, on the one hand, forced all women into the modern industrialized work force on a totally "equal" basis; but it has also not kept all women as separated slaves at home.

Similarly with blacks and Chicanos: they are not *purely* internal colonies, and not *simply* members of the same exploited working class as other workers.

In order to organize effectively and liberate all Americans, we must grasp this doubleness and organize through it, not reject it or pretend it isn't there.

What then are the "non-specific" oppressions it is important for a Jewish radical movement to address—the oppressions that large numbers of the Jewish people suffer as workers, consumers, residents? First, a swift examination of the class distribution of American Jews reveals that they are chiefly in two classes: the old middle class of small businessmen or self-employed professionals (grocers, physicians, etc.) or the new working class of hired professionals (teachers, civil servants, social workers). There has been a great shift in the last fifteen years in the direction of the new working class.

In the small-business role and in some of the hired-professional roles, Jews (as well as other "middle nationalities" like Italians, and often together with the black bourgeoisie) have been used by the empire as the ill-paid-front-line exploiters or controllers of the poor. Thus Jewish grocers and Jewish teachers have been both pressed by the ruling class—as grocers and teachers, not as Jews—to exploit and control black communities. For example, banks, wholesalers, and great real-estate owners have through high interest rates, high wholesale prices, and high rents pushed small grocers into charging high prices for marginal goods. Basically the same mechanism is used by the empire when it assigns Jewish teachers to be front-line controllers of black children, and tries to break any effort by Jewish teachers to mutiny against this role. The result has been deep antagonism between the blacks and the Jews who were forced by the ruling class into this deadly embrace—and sometimes the emergence of anti-Semitism on the one side and anti-black racism on the other.

Radicals must of course reject both these responses and work toward an understanding in both groups of how both are being trapped (in different ways and with different levels of suffering) by the American ruling class. Obviously, a Jewish radical movement should be organizing Jewish businessmen and teachers to turn against the empire; Jewish grocers to join with other grocers in like situations to resist the banks and serve the people; Jewish teachers to join with other teachers in like situations to resist the public-school administrations and serve the students.

There are ways in which the whole Jewish community as part of the whole American community suffers from forms of exploitation and oppression that are imposed upon the whole society by the corporate empire:

The destruction of the environment: All of us are subjected to poisonous air and water and to the danger of a total collapse of a life-supporting environment of plants, animals, and planet Earth. The danger is universal and the oppression increasingly imposed on all (though the in-workplace pollution of mines and factories is still worse than general environmental pollution). Most of this environmental degradation is done for corporate profit; a great deal is linked to the high-energy, low-labor technology of the war machine. Many elements of the Jewish tradition support far more life-affirming, life-protecting politics; it would be urgent for a radical Jewish movement to draw on *and expand on* these elements of the tradition and to ally itself closely with all other movements prepared to resist the corporate-military rape of earth. It should be made clear to Jews that individual responsibility in this matter requires *political* responsibility; not just that each family decide to use lead-free gasoline, but that the whole structure of the oil-auto-highway complex be remade, and transportation put under the direct control of its users and workers so that transportation can serve life, not destroy it.

Militarism, imperialism, and the danger of thermonuclear holocaust: Again, all are endangered. The fact that the Jewish people would not be singled out for destruction by a nuclear war should not blind us to the fact that general thermonuclear war would almost certainly destroy the Jewish people while decimating humanity. On behalf of ourselves and the whole human race, we have an obligation *as a Jewish movement,* not simply as people who happen to be Jews, to end the militarism that is clearly moving toward that result. In the "meantime," while preparing for the Holocaust, modern American militarism saps the freedoms essential to the Jewish people and all other peoples living in America. It provides the physical and political technology and the political back-up for the internal militarism we call repression or a police state. It also provides the technology and back-up for imperialism in the Third World. To all these dangers Jews are especially sensitive; we should organize against the root institutions that feed these dangers.

The destructiveness of the "educational" system: Because of the Jewish past, disproportionate numbers of American teachers and students are Jewish. Jews thus suffer disproportionately from the new forms of oppression placed by the American educational system upon all its students and teachers. The schools and colleges do not teach, they train. They do not liberate, they dull the mind. They create not citizens but job holders; they encourage not spontaneity but regularity. Teachers and students are taught to police each other. Radical Jews should be drawing anew upon both the Jewish tradition and the radical vision to break the bonds of present schooling and recreate a free interplay of knowledge and moral reason—as exemplified in the Talmud, itself a kind of seminar notes from a free university.

The collapse of public services: All Americans, though not to an equal degree, now suffer from the generation-long failure to invest in such crucial needs and services as health facilities, sewage systems, schools, transport, housing, etc. We should be pressing not only for reallocation of resources to these areas, but for a tax system that requires the rich to pay for them, relieving the poor and the semi-poor working- and middle-class from the burdens of much of the present regressive tax system. In addition, we should be trying to achieve direct democratic control over these services, to be exercised jointly by those who work in them and those intended to be served by them rather than by a corporate or political or administrative elite. Thus we should be creating worker-and-community-controlled co-op groceries, not assisting capitalist merchants; starting teacher-and-student-controlled schools, not helping the downtown educational administrators. *The Jewish hospital system should be one major focus of our energies in this area.* In all this the Jewish tradition is clear. We should be organizing in and through it, and developing its obvious public-oriented thrust in new emphatic ways.

The exploitation of consumers: The distinction between recipients of "public" services ("clients") and recipients of "private" services ("consumers") must be reexamined by a radical Jewish movement. Why is food not a public service? Should, for example, whole milk and vitamin-enriched soy bread be absolutely free to all Americans? But wherever, and for however long some form of "private" provision of food, furniture, clothing, etc., is considered desirable, every effort should be made to establish direct public controls to end and prevent the present corporate exploitation of consumers. Direct controls should include local neighborhood, workplace, and ethnic-group control, not the present process of Federal commission review, which constantly falls under the control of the corporations being "regulated."

No seriously radical Jewish movement can ignore these areas in which Jews are oppressed, along with other people, while focusing solely on arenas in which Jews are oppressed as Jews or in special "Jewish" ways. To do so would not only leave Jews unliberated in crucial aspects of their lives, but would also mean adopting for our movement a new version of the slogan "Jews at home, citizens outside." We utterly reject any such idea, believing as we do that Jewishness is adequately expressed only through wholeness, and therefore that our movement—as well as fully liberated individual Jews—must be Jewish both "at home" and "outside"; both on "Jewish" and on "general" problems.

IV—The Vision and the Way

The Jewish experience is replete with injunctions, commandments, and urgings, all directed at the ideal of universal brotherhood built on the concept of absolute equality. However, more than mere expressions of brotherhood are the commandments to seek justice and provide charity to all those in need. More than statements of social justice, these ideals were meant to reflect a desirable condition of human interaction.

The modern kibbutz movement of Israel, for example, was built on such principles, and we of the radical Jewish movement of America reject the notion that only in a Jewish state can such ideals be attained by the Jewish people. At least a portion of us will continue to give priority to building socialist communes, both rural and urban, *here*. That is not to advocate, however, a dropping out from the struggle. On the contrary, any communitarian movement which is to present a serious alternative to the individualistic life style upon which capitalism feeds will of necessity, we believe, become political. For if the prophetic vision of a time when men and women "shall beat their swords into plowshares and their spears into pruning hooks"—a time when "nation shall not lift up sword against nation, neither shall they study war anymore"—is ever to become a reality, it will necessitate the smashing of the power which stands in the way—the power of the American empire.

Our tradition tells us that the vision of the Messianic age is always before us, but the power to move toward it is within each human being. Long ago Judaism evolved a body of principles and rules called the *Halakhah* (the Way) whose purpose it was to help each human being to unite all aspects of his existence into an organic whole directed at the realization of the Vision. In addition to regulations concerning ritual, the *Halakhah* dealt with business relations, social obligations, the provison of charity, and the insuring of justice, as well as the celebration of the beautiful mysteries of life. To follow the

Halakhah, in principles as well as in letter, was to engage in the Messianic process. Today, the following of the traditional *Halakhah* is automatically to put oneself in opposition to the capitalist superstate; to oppose the exploitation of labor, the destruction of life, and the profit of the few at the expense of the many. As Jews we declare our intention to participate in the revolutionary process by synthesizing and following a new *Halakhah.*

Our new way will consist of the same elements as the old; i.e., the love of life, respect for all of Nature, the encouragement of individual development within a communal context, an active passion for social justice and human equality, a recognition of human potentiality. However, it will also be framed in the context of the realities of our day; i.e., an expanding technology, imperialism, racism, sexism, ecological disaster. We recognize the oppression caused by a system characterized by materialism and an overcentralized technology. We recognize our obligation to denounce evil everywhere it appears and work in a united community to hasten its disappearance. We dedicate ourselves to the creation of a decentralized socialist order, for that is the only way in which we can end our own oppression and that of all peoples. We will destroy the system that oppresses us by liberating its institutions.

The new Jewish community that we foresee will be one organized along many different lines. Some will form themselves into *havurot* (fellowships) of maybe 50-100 each; each *avurah* will be unique, but all will practice in some degree of communality as well as strong participation in the expanding Jewish culture. Others will form American-style kibbutzim where the collective will work as a unit and live as a unit. Others will form larger new communities (one of which might be the home of a new Jewish university) that will engage in a full range of activities and living experiments. Others will live within the larger community but still involve themseves in the cultural life through participation in the educational and celebrational activities. The entire community will, in keeping with its mission, work closely with other individuals and cultural groupings to further the revolutionary process in America. The people will liberate the schools to serve their communities; they will force the hospitals, clinics, and other medical institutions to serve their needs, and they will build new institutions; and they will form collectives and cooperatives independent of, and in direct opposition to, the capitalist system.

We dedicate ourselves to the struggle for the achievement of our vision; a society where people will be able to develop their highest potential as unique human beings, with full awareness of the total commitment that struggle will entail.

Epilogue

No historian of the New Left can ignore the muckraking influence of *Ramparts* magazine. Sol Stern is a leading figure of this radical journalism. As a graduate student at Berkeley, he witnessed, participated in, and reported the Free Speech movements and edited *Root and Branch* magazine. It was Stern who wrote the *Ramparts* article which exposed the involvement of the C.I.A. in the National Student Association.

It is fitting, then, that our anthology end with the insights of one at the very heart of the New Left, describing his disillusionment with the movement's Middle East stance and his conversion from a Jewish radical to a radical Jew.

It is important to note that Stern has not abandoned his own radicalism, but rather broadened its purview to include Jewish liberation alongside the liberation of other groups. Stern dissects the inconsistencies and obscurantism of "movement hip"—a code language of shallow rhetoric and angry slogans which often passes as radical analysis.

He challenges both the New Left and the Jewish Establishment to join in the struggle for peace in the Middle East. Perhaps Stern's words will contribute to a more healthy trialogue among Jewish radicals, radical Jews, and the Jewish Establishment, both in America and Israel.

That, in fact, is the purpose of this book. In republishing Stern's article and the other pieces, we hope to add to the discussion and debate—a proud tradition for generations of radicals.

My Jewish Problem–and Ours
Israel, the Left, and the Jewish Establishment

Sol Stern

There are all these strange Bob Dylan stories passing around New York these days: that he is studying Hebrew with a hip, radical rabbi out on Long Island; that he attended the debate between Meir Kahane and Abbie Hoffman and offered to give some money to the Jewish Defense League; that he told Huey Newton he couldn't support the Panthers because of their stand on Israel; and lastly that he didn't come out to attend the spontaneous birthday demonstration organized outside his East Village apartment on May 24th, because he was turning 30 in Tel Aviv.

Is there a Jewish Bob Dylan, a reincarnated Robert Zimmerman? Is the poet of rebelliousness and universal liberation of the 1960's who was *bar mitzvahed* in the 1950's now trying to bear witness to a lost Jewish identity? It happened to Moses Hess, to Herzl, Freud, Chagall, and countless others. And if Bob Dylan has a Jewish problem, there are a lot of Jewish radicals newly concerned about their Jewishness and its relation to revolutionary politics who could be sympathetic.

My own Jewish problem first surfaced at a meeting I at-

Sol Stern is a contributing editor of *Ramparts* and is working on a book about Israel and Zionism. This article is reprinted from *Ramparts*, August, 1971, by permission of the author.

tended about a year ago at one of Berkeley's political communes. I had gone to hear a report from members of San Francisco Newsreel about their trip to Palestine guerrilla camps in Jordan and Lebanon. The principal speaker was a leather-jacketed, hip-talking, thirtyish radical named Chuck, who was Jewish, had graduated from the City College of New York, and called himself a Marxist-Leninist and a revolutionary internationalist. Chuck told a livingroom full of Berkeley radicals that he had originally been "up-tight" about meeting the guerrillas because he was Jewish. When he got to Jordan, however, he discovered that the guerrilla struggle was aimed only at the Zionists, not the Jews—and he was welcomed as a "revolutionary brother."

"The program of Al Fatah," said Chuck, "is to create a democratic socialist Palestine where Jews and Arabs can live together, and where Jews will enjoy full civil and political rights. They are not fighting the Jews—only the Zionists, and the Zionist political structure." Chuck didn't have much more to say about the moral and political aspects of the Palestinian conflict; the rest of his talk was a rhapsodic account of the military aims of the guerrilla program, delivered in "movement hip," a self-conscious vernacular picturing the guerrilla cadres as "heavy dudes" and "brothers off the block," and describing the Fatah program as "right on."

To my question about the rights of the Jews to self-determination, Chuck answered, "The Jews are not a nation. They ought to fight for progress in whatever country they happen to live." The Jews "ripped off the land," and the Jewish state was racist and imperialist; therefore Israel was illegitimate and Fatah was correct in calling for its destruction. Later on he added another of the charges often levelled by movement people, a gem apparently picked up in the guerrilla camps as the gospel truth: that the Zionists had been in cahoots with the Nazis. "Don't you know," I was asked, "that Theodore Herzl had discussions with Hitler?"

Newsreel had also brought back a pro-Fatah propaganda film that for sheer falsification of recent history has to rival the House Unamerican Activities Committee's classic of the early 1960's, *Operation Abolition*. The film depicted the creation of the State of Israel as entirely the work of British imperialism, which dumped all the Jewish immigrants into Palestine to set them up as a colonial bulwark against the Arab masses. It didn't mention the British white paper of 1939 which restricted and then cut off Jewish immigration. Nor did it mention the British sea blockade of boats bearing escapees from Nazi-occupied Europe which resulted in ship-loads of Jews going to the bottom of the Mediterranean. Also omitted was any reference to British opposition to the U.N. partition of Palestine, nor the subsequent British support for the five Arab armies which attacked the State of Israel. Most flagrant of all, it ignored the Jewish underground struggle against 100,000 British occupation troops which lasted from 1944 to 1947.

I went away from that meeting stunned by this crude and infantile approach to the complex moral and political issues underlying the Arab-Israeli dispute. But it was part of a trend, not an isolated case; and in subsequent months underground and movement publications were filled with material on the Middle East that was hardly more sophisticated. When I engaged in several debates on the issue with people on the left I was derisively labeled a "Zionist," as if this epithet placed my arguments beyond the pale of legitimacy.

All this put me in an unusual position. Though I was born in Israel, my family emigrated to this country when I was three years old. I never considered myself a Zionist, nor did I feel any special attachment to Israel. My father had come to Palestine in the 1920's as a revolutionary socialist and a Zion-ist. But his radicalism soon conflicted with the Zionist estab-lishment and a political split forced him to leave his kibbutz. As a worker in Tel Aviv in the 1930's, he joined other Jewish socialists in protesting the Histadrut (the Zionist labor feder-ation) policy of excluding Arab workers. As a result, he was blacklisted by the Jewish Agency and harassed by the British mandatory authority. At the same time he was forced to pick up the gun in self-defense against Arab attacks on Jewish settlements. Then, as now, it was not easy to be a Jewish radical in the Holy Land.

Though he came to reject organized Zionism, my father later regarded the creation of the State of Israel as a progressive step and a necessary solution for the remnants of European Jewry. I grew up sharing those views. Most of my college arguments about Israel were with Zionist kids from Hillel who regarded any criticisms of Israeli government policy as treason, especially from one who was a Sabra. To me, on the other hand, they were middle-class hypocrites who wore their Jewishness on their sleeves. My heroes at that time were those whom Isaac Deutscher called the "NonJewish Jews" —Spinoza, Marx, Trotsky, Rosa Luxemburg—the internationalists who, in the prophetic tradition of Judaism, spoke for the emancipation of all humanity.

In 1967, as an editor of this magazine, I wrote a major part of our editorial on the Six-Day War, which got us into trouble —not with the left, but with some pro-Israeli Jews who had been financing the magazine. The editorial clearly affirmed the legitimacy of the Jewish state, but was nevertheless critical of the general foreign policy of the Israeli government. It was a position that seemed reasonable enough in those days.

Today that same editorial would be attacked by many on the left (including more than a few who once saw it as forthright and principled) as a simple-minded, perhaps a "fascist," apology for Zionism. This turnabout raises some serious questions, questions which remain largely unanswered by the quality of the dialogue on Israel today. Have the issues changed that much, or is it the people?

The ideological conflict between Marxism and Zionism is nothing new. To Marx, the Jews were a "people-class" whose historical survival, as well as the centuries of anti-Semitism directed against them, could be explained by their economic function in different historical epochs. Marx believed socialism would solve the "Jewish question" by eliminating the economic roots of anti-Semitism and permit the Jews to become fully assimilated. And it was Moses Hess, a political comrade of Marx's (they were both sentenced to death during the 1848 revolution) who wrote the first political Zionist tract in response to him.

Lenin made significant revisions in Marxist theory on the national question when he argued that socialism must extend to all national minorities the right to secede and form their own republics. He, of course, remained adamantly anti-Zionist, because the Zionism of the time tended to make deals with the imperialists, and because it distracted Jewish workers from the task of making European revolution. Trotsky, however, who lived to see the use of crude anti-Semitism against him and his followers by a "socialist" regime in Russia, became convinced towards the end of his life that socialism itself would not eliminate the Jewish question; that after the revolution Jews must be given the choice of living in a national homeland of their own. Although he regarded Zionism as an inappropriate solution for the Jewish problem, because he could not conceive of any way of transferring millions of Jews to Palestine and because of the conflict with the Arabs it was engendering, he clearly conceived of the possibility of a "Jewish state."

Events in Europe and Palestine in the 1940's made the Marxist-Zionist debate about the solution of the "Jewish question" somewhat academic. By 1948 there was a Jewish nation numbering one-half million in existence in Palestine—in fact, if not legally—and it was struggling for its independence against both British imperialism and Arab reaction. Several hundred thousand more Jews who wanted to go to Palestine were rotting in the camps for displaced persons of post-war Europe. Ironically enough, the Soviet Union was the first nation to extend diplomatic recognition to the State of Israel. Andrei Gromyko gave the most pro-Zionist speech the U.N. had ever heard when he argued for the partition of Palestine into a Jewish and an Arab state.

These circumstances explain why in 1948 Marxists and the rest of the Western left supported the existence of Israel. In 1954, Isaac Deutscher eloquently expressed the revision of old Marxist assumptions that history had forced upon him:

"Israelis who have known me as an anti-Zionist of long standing are curious to hear what I think about Zionism. I have of course long since abandoned my anti-Zionism, which was based on a confidence in the European labor movement, or, more broadly, in European society and civilization, which that society and civilization have not justified. If, instead of arguing against Zionism in the 1920's and 1930's I had urged European Jews to go to Palestine, I might have helped to save some of the lives that were later extinguished in Hitler's gas chambers."

Even in 1967, in an article bitterly attacking Israel for its actions in the Six-Day War, Deutscher said, "Arab nationalism will be incomparably more effective as a liberating force if it is disciplined and rationalized by an element of internationalism that will enable the Arabs to approach the problem of Israel more realistically than hitherto. They cannot go on denying Israel's right to exist and indulging in bloodthirsty rhetoric." At about the same time, Fidel Castro said, "True revolutionaries never threaten a whole country with extermination. We have spoken out clearly against Israel's policy, but we don't deny her right to exist."

Only a few years later however, "true revolutionaries," including Fidel himself, are once again, in the name of Marxism, denying the right of a Jewish state to exist in the Middle East. Jewish national consciousness now is being portrayed as incompatible with revolutionary internationalism. The images of the contestants in the Middle East conflict have been reversed from what they were in 1948, and the truce between Marxism and Zionism has been shattered. Now it is the Arab side that has the aura of being a national liberation struggle and a people's war, with the attention of the internaional left being focused on Palestinian guerrillas, not on the reactionary Arab governments. Coincidentally, in Israel there has been a clear shift to the right. The socialist sector of the economy is relatively less important than it was, and Israel's foreign policy, once genuinely neutralist, has become increasingly wedded to that of the United States, with the world Zionist movement equating Jewish interests with those of bankrupt American imperialism.

These are perplexing developments. They shattered for me the unspoken assumption that there was no conflict between being a Jew and a radical. That is my "Jewish problem." But it is also the movement's problem because its knee-jerk approach to the Middle East and the question of Jewish nationalism is not only leaving the field to a conservative Jewish Establishment, but is also alienating many young radical Jews who want to be part of the solution, rather than part of the problem.

*　*　*

If the problem is an anguishing one for Americans, it is doubly so for Israeli leftists who have lived with it longer and more intimately than we have. We might consider their pleas, for Israel was, after all, made of a revolution in the streets against a colonial occupying power.

Before it happened anywhere else in the Third World, a Jewish underground army in Palestine had defeated and expelled a sizeable British occupying army in a fight conducted for the most part, not by the official Zionist agency's military arm, the Haganah, but by two underground military organizations, the Irgun and its smaller offshoot, the Stern Group. The Sternists, who never numbered more than 200, specialized in assassinations of British officers and dynamiting British military installations, and justified their revolt with an anti-imperialist ideology. They were the Weathermen of their day, self-sacrificing young revolutionary fanatics who believed that exemplary violence by a small disciplined group could be a catalyst in setting off a broader national liberation struggle.

Two Stern group martyrs, 17-year-old Eliahu Hakim and
21-year-old Eliahu Bet Zouri, went to a British gallows in
Cairo in 1944 after assassinating Lord Moyne, the highest
ranking British political officer in the Middle East. During
their trial, they eloquently appealed to the Arabs for a joint
anti-imperialist struggle against the British, and nationalist
Egyptian students demonstrated their support in the streets of
Cairo.

Today the man who was the military commander of the
Stern Group is still giving the official Zionists hell. His name is
Nathan Yalin Mor, and he writes for Israel's leading news-
paper, *Haaretz*, calling for radical changes in the govern-
ment's policies towards the Arabs. Recently he referred to
Golda Meir as a "vindictive old lady."

Yalin Mor made a tour of the United States and western
Europe last year talking to left groups. Everywhere he went he
denounced the policies of the Israeli government on the occupied territories, while reminding his audience that both as a
leftist and as a Jew he could give no support to the program
of Fatah, for they would merely replace Israeli occupation
with the total suppression of Jewish nationalism.

Another of Israel's most widely read left-wing journalists,
Amos Kenan (see page 55), is also a veteran of the Stern
Group. Last year in Israel he described his underground organization to me as a "mixture of religious mystics and coldblooded,
revolutionary communists. We were a disciplined revolutionary
party that believed in the right of a revolutionary minority to
disobey and go its own way even if it meant precipitating a civil
war." Kenan read to me from old Stern Group leaflets that were
distributed to the Arabs in 1947, calling for a joint Jewish-Arab
struggle against the British imperialists. One of them said,
"Let us prevent a Jewish-Arab war. Jewish and Arab blood is
shed in Tel Aviv and Jaffa. Who is responsible for that
bloodshed? The occupying forces and the imperialist in-
triguers. A Jewish-Arab war is necessary to the British to
prove that the British are needed. A Jewish-Arab war is the

last justification for British occupation here. We want no war against our Arab neighbors. To attack Arabs in the streets is to help the British—it is also a crime against the Hebrew nation."

Kenan scoffs at the much-discussed distinction which Fatah makes between Zionists and Jews. "A few years ago they called me a Jew and wanted to kill me, now they call me a Zionist and they still want to kill me. I'm still the same person and I still want to live—and if they force me to I will fight as a Zionist. I also can use the same trick. I can go around killing Arabs and call them Fatah. They tell me they just fight against the 'Zionist structure,' not the Jews, but what they call the 'Zionist structure' is my self-determination. They say they will respect the rights of Jews to practice their religion in the new Democratic Palestine. Do you think I will give back statehood for the right to belong to a religious sect? If there is no other way for us to stay alive and preserve ourselves as a people, then the Jews have the same rights as Algerians and Black Panthers—we have to organize self-defense and fight back."

Younger left-wing Israelis express their political frustration in the same manner. Take the particular case of Ron Cohen, a 32-year-old kibbutznik who digs the Cuban revolution, supports the National Liberation Front of Vietnam, admires the Black Panthers, and calls himself a Marxist-Leninist. ("I think Mao Tse-Tung has the most correct interpretation of Marxism today," he told me). Ron also happens to be a captain in the paratroopers who saw combat in the Sinai during the Six-Day War and has since spent about a month of every year in the occupied territories patrolling against the guerrillas.

Ron helped organize Siach, the New Israeli Left, with ex-members of Mapam, after Mapam decided to enter the coalition government. They have gone into the streets several times in American movement-style demonstrations. They blocked traffic in Jerusalem, tried to march on Hebron to protest the government's plan to settle 250 Jewish families there, and even invaded Golda Meir's garden, where they clashed with the police, and where Ron Cohen had his head bloodied by a police club.

I discussed all this with Ron and several of his Siach comrades at his kibbutz, Gan Shmuel. On the walls of the kibbutz cottage where we met were American anti-war and Black Panther posters. Everyone was in a somber mood—just a few days before one of the kibbutz kids had been killed on the Syrian front. All of them had fought in the Six-Day War, which they saw as a war for salvation and survival, and they all spoke bitterly about the politics in the Arab world that had led up to it. "All my life I had fought for peace with the Arabs, and tried to speak to them and then suddenly I was forced to kill them," said Cohen. "The War changed everything. Before 1967 things were much easier for the left. We could talk about real issues, about Vietnam and imperialism and what was happening to socialism in this country. Now the mood here is incredibly chauvinistic. We can't talk about Vietnam anymore."

Siach is always confronted with a typical response in its attempts to proselytize. It goes something like this: "O.K., let's say we accept your argument. We must recognize the Palestinian Arabs as a national entity; we must take back refugees; we must make initiatives and compromises. But where is the equivalent compromise on the other side? Where is the Arab Siach which calls for recognition of the Jewish nation?" The Siach kids admitted that they can't answer these questions very well.

"Al Fatah uses the money it gets from the Saudi Arabian government to send its representatives around the world and print up its propaganda in several languages," says Cohen. "The Israeli government also does this but we don't have the money or the resources to get our position across. And even when we speak to European leftists, they can't understand our struggle. Because of the war with the Arabs, which threatens our very national existence, we on the left here are at a lower level of struggle. This is our problem—we are in a national struggle instead of a class struggle. There can be no deepening of the class or social contradictions within Israel as long as every Israeli feels that there is a dire security problem. We try to explain this to New Left people in Europe—but they don't understand."

*   *   *

The question of whether there is an "Arab Siach" is more than a rhetorical point. I have heard left-wing Israelis say openly that if the Palestinian movement were willing to come to terms with the existence of Israel and the Israeli government still obstructed the creation of a Palestinian state, the Palestinians would then find allies inside Israel, even "armed allies." As long as the Palestinians insist on "liberating" all of Palestine, however, they will succeed only in uniting all Israelis, including those on the left, behind the government.

This is where the left's confusion begins. Al Fatah's periodic assertions that they are now for a "democratic secular state of Palestine," where all Jews, Moslems, and Christians will have equal rights, have led many people on the left to honestly believe that the Palestinians have gone through a remarkable political transformation on their attitudes towards relations with the Israeli Jews. Some believe that Fatah's position opens up the possibility of working toward a binational state as a solution to the conflict, and that it is Israel which unreasonably insists on an exclusive Jewish state. But such assumptions are contradicted by almost every official statement put out by Fatah. Fatah's official seven-point program, for example, refers to the future Palestine as "part of the Arab Fatherland." And when an interviewer asked Yaser Arafat how he reconciled the idea of a progressive democratic state for all peoples with the Fatah slogan, "Long live Palestine, Arab and free," he answered, "A democratic progressive state in Palestine is not in contradiction to that state being Arab . . . the word Arab implies a common culture, a common language and a common background. The majority of the inhabitants of any future state of Palestine will be Arab . . . ."

Israeli leaders are described by Fatah as "diehard racist Zionists who obviously do not qualify for a Palestinian status." Other Jews will be allowed to remain, "provided, of course, that they reject Zionist racist chauvinism and fully accept to live as Palestinians in the New Palestine."

Here is another suggestion from *Fatah,* published in Beirut, of how the Jewish problem in the new Palestine might be solved: "Early last year, we officially declared the adoption of the unitary, nonsectarian and democratic Palestine state as a humane solution to the Palestine problem. In line with this objective, Fatah has contacted a number of Arab countries urging them to receive back their Jewish nationals who have emigrated to occupied Palestine and to accept their return as full-fledged citizens as they were before. Some Arab countries have accepted this proposal."

Such statements make it clear that the Palestine which Fatah envisions is one of an Arab state which "tolerates" a Jewish religious minority. Zionism, which by Fatah's criteria is simply Jewish nationalism, would be considered a crime. No concession of any kind is made to the idea of Jewish national self-determination, nor is there to be any legitimate binationalism, as Fatah's most recent official statement on the question emphasizes: "The call for a nonsectarian Palestine should not be confused with a multireligious, a polyreligious, or a binational state. The new Palestine is not to be built around three state religions or two nationalities."

Those who believe that Fatah's pronouncement on relations with the Jews are a great step forward ought to ponder the fact that even the discredited reactionary Palestinian leadership of the 1940's (including the Grand Mufti, who spent the war years alongside Hitler in Berlin) always said they would tolerate a Jewish minority in an Arab Palestine. They often offered guarantees that the Jews would be treated with justice as long as they had no Zionist aspirations; that is, if they gave up their desire for political sovereignty. If the Jews had been willing to accept minority status, there could have been a settlement with the Arabs 30 years ago. But then, what was the point of returning to Palestine in the first place? It was the desire for self-determination and autonomy that was at the heart of Zionism and still is the common denominator uniting virtually all Israelis.

Some Marxist-Leninists in the West—groups such as those congregating around the *New Left Review* in England and the International Socialists in the United States—understand the weakness of Fatah on the national question. They base their support of the Palestine Liberation movement on the theory that Marxist-Leninists in the Palestinian Democratic Popular Front (who are critical of Fatah for its nationalism and its support of bourgeois Arab regimes) will someday wage a joint struggle with the Marxist-Leninists in Matzpen (the Israeli Socialist Organization), and that this revolutionary union will result in the overthrow of Zionism as well as the reactionary Arab governments, leading to the creation of a unified, revolutionary-socialist Middle East in which the de-Zionized Jews will enjoy their national rights.

But Matzpen is a tiny Trotskyist sect which is even less significant on the Israeli left than the Democratic front is among the Palestinians. When I was in Israel last year, they claimed a membership of about eighty; since then they have split three ways. But since they claim to be the only truly "anti-Zionist" group in Israel, it does not really matter if they have two thousand members or two; they would still be the living proof, for those who need to believe it, that the distinction which the Palestinians make between Zionists and Jews has some kind of meaning for the millions of Israelis.

But what Matzpen's "anti-Zionism" comes down to is the demand that Israelis give up the protection of their state in return for the eventual prospect of self-determination offered by one tiny fraction of the guerrilla movement—a fraction which, judging by the lessons of recent national liberation struggles in Algeria, Syria, and Iraq, will probably be eliminated after the revolution. Matzpen asks Jews to embark on a course which entails a very high probability of committing national and cultural suicide, in return for the very small possibility that by doing so they will usher in a new socialist Utopia in the Middle East. Is it any wonder that most Matzpen people eventually wind up leaving the country and that their main activities are not in Tel Aviv or Jerusalem, but London, Paris, and New York, where they find more respectful (and naive) audiences?

Of course, most of the people on the left who have taken a position on the Middle East conflict couldn't be bothered by this kind of ideological eyewash. Mostly we are confronted by clodhoppers shouting "right on" for Fatah and damn the consequences. I have heard some of them say that they don't support Matzpen because they regard them as Trotskyist sectarians who are too hung up on the question of self-determination. These people can't think of a single group on the Israeli left that deserves support. The implication is clear: the only thing any Israeli can do to qualify for revolutionary credentials is to pick up the gun and fight alongside the Fatah commandos.

That such a political line is approved by some Jews in the movement should hardly be shocking by now. But it is equally clear that this kind of perverted internationalism (an internationalism that would make Marx and Lenin wince) is partly creating its own counterreaction. For what else but nationalism is an appropriate response to the kind of "revolutionary internationalism" that makes Moshe Dayan and Itzchak Rabin out to be pigs and bandits who should be hunted down and killed, but is quiet about the Pakistani generals who direct the slaughter of the civilian population of East Bengal because the Chinese have given it their O.K.; that makes Yaser Arafat out to be a hero even though his movement is non-Marxist and non-socialist, while considering Israeli socialists non-persons?

The movement gets into such absurd positions because of its considerable confusion on the role of nationalism. Since the left is committed ideologically to an internationalist perspective, it follows that there is something reactionary about nationalism. The contradiction is that some militant nationalisms are seen as a prelude to anticolonialist and anti-imperialist struggles. Thus the left has fallen into the trap of approving selectively only those nationalisms which engage loudly in anti-imperialist rhetoric, whatever the reality. There is considerable sympathy on the left for various black nationalist movements in this country and in Africa. But the Southern Sudanese blacks who have been waging a struggle for years for their self-determination against a dominant and imperious majority in the north are practically ignored, because the Sudanese Arabs have laid claim to membership in the anti-imperialist camp.

In the same way, because Palestinian nationalism is now rhetorically associated with anti-imperialism, it is "right on," while Israeli nationalism, which once played a real, anti-imperialist role in the Middle East, has become intrinsically evil. Thus, instead of seeing the Palestine-Israel struggle as a tragic and destructive struggle between two nations fighting over the same turf, a collision that requires healing by compromise and mutual recognition, the left applies models that have no relevance. And how futile it seems to try to point out the obvious: that Amman is not Hanoi, and the P.L.O. is not the N.L.F., and that Tel Aviv is not Saigon.

The glib notion that the way to solve the problem is to create a democratic secular state of Palestine where Arabs and Jews live in peace ignores the obvious fact that Fatah hasn't geared up just to go out of business after a secular Palestinian state is created. It has not tried to create a Palestine national renaissance to merely usher in some universalist homogenized society, but one which serves the very special needs and aspirations of the Arab Palestinian people.

Even in the very best of worlds the prospects of a binational state working are not very good. And in the most basic conditions of the Arab-Israel dispute—two intensely nationalistic peoples who have lived in armed confrontation with each other for half a century, facing each other over hair triggers—

it is less likely. What is needed is an accommodation that allows for separation into two national entities. To suggest any other course is to ignore the countless disasters that have occurred in recent years as a result of the attempt to force two peoples into one single-state structure—in Iraq, where Arabs slaughtered Kurds; in Chad, where blacks oppressed and warred against separatist Arabs; in Sudan, where Arabs waged a war of extermination against blacks who want their independence.

*   *   *

If the solutions proposed by Fatah and its left supporters are unworkable at best, are not the accusations against Israel nonetheless based on real injustices? And is not the animus against Israel justified? Well, yes and no. The problem is the failure to make proper distinctions between government actions which should be opposed (in conjunction with the Israeli left) and the notion that the whole national enterprise is therefore tainted and illegitimate.

Take the simple-minded accusation heard more and more commonly on the left—that Israel is "imperialist." The notion that Israel, a tiny country of three million people with no heavy industry, is an imperialist power is on its face a grotesque absurdity. Israel has no access to the oil or raw materials in the Arab world. It has no exploitative trade with the Arabs, nor a class of local exploiters which it uses to extract its profits. It is true that Israel has often made unscrupulous alliances with imperialist powers like the U.S. when it has been in her interest, but this should hardly justify the call for the elimination of Israel as a society. There are at least a dozen African states far more compromised, but no one on the left calls for their elimination. If one were looking for "imperialist lackey" states, a good place to begin might be Nigeria which is penetrated, supported, and manipulated by no less than three imperialist powers—Britain, America, and the Soviet Union. Yet the left which now calls for the elimination of Israel, not only did not apply that remedy to

Nigeria but a good part of it applauded the war of extermination waged against the Biafrans.

And what about the refugees? There is no doubt that much of the blame for the plight of the Palestinian refugees must fall on Israel's shoulders. Her refusal to take back substantial numbers of refugees and her insistence on seeing the problem totally in political and not in human terms for twenty years is one of the most serious blights on Israel's record. But there is another side to the coin. It cannot be forgotten that the refugees were created as a byproduct of a brutal civil war in which atrocities and terror were committed by both sides. If the Arabs at least bear a share of responsibility for that civil war, by their refusal to accept a compromise solution based on partition of the land and by their unwillingness in twenty years to call off the civil war, then they too must share the responsibility for the consequences—including the refugees.

It is misunderstanding the issue today to see the "refugee" problem as synonymous with the Palestinian national liberation struggle. Solving the refugee problem is not the same as giving the Palestinians their national rights. Indeed it may be the other way around. For, if the refugee problem were solved on the basis of the humanitarian concern for peoples returning to their original lands, that is, if Israel took back all of the 700,000 refugees that left in 1948, they would still be a minority within a Jewish state, whereas the Palestinian national movement, whose very base is now in the refugee camps, would be dealt a crippling and perhaps final blow with its population spread between Israel and Hussein's Jordan. Thus, to use the tragedy of the refugees to justify support for a program of the elimination of the State of Israel is outrageous and cynical. There are any number of solutions which could resettle refugees in a Palestinian Arab state and still allow for the existence of a Jewish state. Even if the Israeli government should unilaterally offer to take back every single refugee tomorrow, there would be no change in Fatah's program or in the left's support for it; for the program and that support is based on the elevation of one nationalism to total superiority over another.

* * *

One cannot help suspecting that the basis of the anti-Israel position, especially among the large number of Jews in the movement, is not necessarily based on an objective analysis of the situation in the Middle East. It has, I am convinced, many psychological roots. It is no accident that most anti-Israel Jews in the movement grew up in the upper middle-class, assimilated Jewish homes where they experienced a Jewishness that was on the whole reactionary, decadent, and antiseptic. If they went to synagogues, it was to do meaningless exercises in what one Jewish publication recently called "haunted echo chambers." If they learned about Israel, it was not about its revolutionary tradition, but an image passed on by Leon Uris and the Zionist Organization of America. No wonder these kids grew up feeling no qualms when the international left called for the destruction of Israel, and regard Jewishness itself as intrinsically reactionary.

But to explain such a phenomenon is not to excuse it. If the insensitivity to the real historical experience and needs of the Jewish people, and of Israel, is merely an irrational reaction to Beverly Hills and Miami Beach Jewishness, then someone ought to correct it. One of its consequences is that it continues to play right into the hands of the reactionary American Jewish Establishment, which wants to consolidate its image as the only defenders of the legitimate aspirations of the Jewish people. In the exertions of the Jewish Establishment, one sees the left's arguments merely stood on their head. Where the left has said to young Jews, "to be for the survival of Israel is to betray the world revolution," the Jewish Establishment seems to be saying, "if you are for the world revolution, you betray your people." All this makes for strange bedfellows, with the left and the Jewish Establishment cooperating in the polarization of the Jewish community between pro-Israel warriors and simple-minded, anti-Jewish revolutionaries.

The ideological justification for the Jewish Establishment's role was spelled out by *Commentary* magazine in a recent issue devoted to the proper relationship between Jewishness and radicalism. The title *Commentary* put on its cover was "Revolutionism & the Jews." It would have been more accurate to call it "Revolutionism *or* the Jews." Thus historian Walter Laqueur unabashedly tells us that, on the question of the Middle East, "the thought of the movement has a certain logic and consistency; once one accepts the basic premises, one cannot stop short where Israel is concerned." In Laqueur's analysis, any action which weakens American foreign policy must weaken Israel, since Israel's survival is now based on American power to counterbalance the Russian military presence in the Arab countries. "The anti-Israel faction of the New Left is thus absolutely correct in its criticism of the pro-Israel radicals. Once one accepts the basic assumption that the American Establishment is totally evil, that its foreign policy is simply a function of its imperialist, antirevolutionary characer, and that the defeat of America is in the interests of world revolution, one cannot logically make an exception of American policy in the Middle East."

Laqueur's argument is, of course, precisely as inane and one-dimensional as the New Left argument which he perverts for his own purposes. Israel survived in 1948 without any American weapons, and is dependent ultimately not on big-power support, but on its own willingness to fight for its survival. As the Vietnamese have proved, small nations can and do win their independence from superpowers. Laqueur's real purpose in all of this is not to caution about Israel's demise but to underplay the significance of a self-conscious and growing Jewish radical movement both in Israel and the United States. Thus he lumps Siach together with Matzpen and dismisses them both, and predicts that Jewish radicals in the United States, to the extent that they remain preoccupied with radical causes such as Indochina, women's liberation, and pollution, will become more estranged from Jewish concerns. "This may be all to the good, for the present stance of the Jewish radical is a half-way house, morally and intellectually inconsistent, and thus untenable in the long run."

In another of the *Commentary* articles, sociologist Nathan Glazer develops the theme of separating the radical chaff from the Jewish wheat. One of Glazer's specialties is his theory of the right-wing backlash, which he uses as an hysterical whip to discourage any kind of radicalism at all. Now he argues that the end of the war in Vietnam may bring "the rise of a stab-in-the-back myth, in which it will not only be students and professors and intellectuals who will be attacked, not only Jews in their role as members of this general community, but conceivably Jews *as* Jews." How do we head off this imminent pogrom? According to Glazer, all the Jewish intellectuals should stop mucking about with radicalism, should be more moderate and balanced, should swim more securely in the mainstream, and stop finding so much fault with America.

This is of course more than sociology. It is *Commentary's* own form of Jewish self-hatred, with Glazer coming on like the classic old Jewish *bubba* who trembles in fear of a pogrom every time she hears of a Jew getting into some troubles with the gentiles.

Commentary's monthly fulminations against every movement for social change from women's liberation to the counterculture might be dismissed as the sour grapes of a bunch of West Side New York intellectuals hankering for the golden age of the 1950's when they were *de rigeuer* and traveled around the world on C.I.A. credit cards. On the questions of Jews, however, their combination of Sammy Glick and Spiro Agnew homilies ("listen kid, don't knock this country, its been good to us") reflect a widespread sense of fear and isolation.

Commentary has always been a bellwether for the thinking of the Jewish Establishment—the rich, assimilated Jews who run the major Jewish organizations and make the "Jewish opinion" that the mass media picks up. In the 1950's the magazine was the focus of the lobotomized American celebration, the end of ideology, and the notion that America was the "good society." Anyone who suggested that there might be a crisis lurking somewhere beneath the surface was an old-fashioned "ideologist." In those years *Commentary* was a complete apologist for America's cold war policies, as well as for the anticommunist hysteria that swept the country (though they preferred a more subtle and intellectually rigorous one than vintage McCarthyism). Then as now they hated Jewish radicals particularly since, as they often argued in their pages, Jews had it made in America as nowhere else in history, and any Jew who questioned America's munificence was being traitorous to all Jews as well.

In the early 1960's *Commentary* timorously rode the New Frontier bandwagon. The style of that period was one of questioning old assumptions, asking for apparently imaginative programs. After all, many of the *Commentary* writers were now going to the White House. Ever the slave of fashion, the magazine was "for" civil rights, concerned about blacks, talking about disarmament. But, as the mood of liberal reexamination changed into a deeper and more fundamental radicalism and as the questions began to grapple with an imperialism and racism structurally inherent in American society, *Commentary* pulled in the reins and warned the intellectuals they were going too far.

In all this, *Commentary* reflected deep currents running through the entire American Jewish community. American Jews, living almost entirely in the huge urban caldrons that were rocked by the liberation struggles of the late 1960's, were largely represented in the professions that came into direct physical contact with the black revolt—they were the teachers, the social workers, the lawyers, the doctors.

There were two reactions to this contact with the American crisis. Many lower-middle-class and working-class Jews became rednecks. Their fear of blacks and social change resulted in votes for unabashed reactionaries like Mario Procaccino in New York in 1969 and Sam Yorty in Los Angeles. The upper-class Jews continued to mouth the old liberal platitudes, but isolated themselves into the suburbs and began to blame the deepening crisis on the radicals. They were afraid, suddenly feeling isolated and marginal as Jews, and they desperately wanted to believe that if the radicals, and particularly the Jewish radicals, could be stopped, then things would get better. Instead of trying to understand what there is about official Judaism and Zionism that is turning off the young, and trying to do something about it, they reacted by placing certain political ideas beyond the pale of respectability.

Thus *Commentary* Editor Norman Podhoretz says quite frankly that Jewish radicals should be boycotted by the organized Jewish community. Podhoretz is upset that some Jewish organizations have seen fit to dribble a few pennies to Jewish radical groups and have even tried to have a dialogue with the New Left. In response to the interest shown by a few rabbis and organizations in Arthur Waskow's Freedom Seder (see page 25), *Commentary* stigmatizes the whole effort as nothing less than "a document of self-loathing and self-abasement masquerading as a document of self-affirmation." No, it is more than Jewish self-hatred. It is, says Podhoretz, actually "anti-Semitism," which he newly defines as anything against the interests of those Jews whose patronage he receives and whose neuroses he expresses.

There is a special irony in Podhoretz's appointment of himself as the policeman of the Jewish community and the protector of Jewish rights and interests. For the fact is that the people who pay Podhoretz, the American Jewish Committee that publishes *Commentary*, are like most Establishment Jews who have made it in America in that they do not have a very strong record of courage when it comes to actually doing something for Jews in trouble.

There is of course the notorious and shameful story of how most American Jewish leaders did nothing to protest against the Roosevelt administration when it turned its back on the doomed Jews of Europe. Here is the verdict of the journalist Dorothy Thompson (no self-hating Jewish radical she) on the organization that publishes *Commentary*:

"The American Jewish Committee tried to soft peddle things. It advised watchful waiting. It refused to participate in parades, demonstrations, protest meetings. It tried to get the government to do something but very, very quietly. Hush, hush was the word."

A generation later, Hannah Arendt wrote the brilliant book, *Eichmann in Jerusalem,* which asked some penetrating questions about just what Jewish leaders in Europe and Palestine were doing anyway. Norman Podhoretz took to the pages of his magazine to suggest, again in the name of the interests of the Jews, that there was something obscene and indecent in the very questions Miss Arendt raised. It was still "hush, hush."

Even on the question of Israel there is reason to wonder about these defenders of the Jewish interest. In 1948, when many left-wing Jews were risking their necks to break the American embargo on guns to Israel, the American Jewish Committee was again advising a policy of caution and moderation. And in the early 1950's, when Israel was much closer to the ideals of an egalitarian society than it is today and was also in more trouble, *Commentary* was much more lukewarm than it is today. A frequent theme of the articles *Commentary* was running in those days was the fear that Israel might go Stalinist.

All of which forces one to wonder just whom *Commentary* is thinking of when it claims to speak for the interests of the Jews. Is it all the Jews of the world and their right to live their lives in a decent world order, exploiting no one and being exploited by no one? Or is it a much smaller group of American Jews who have it made here in America and don't want anyone rocking the boat?

* * *

Commentary's prediction and hope for a severing of all relations between radicalism and the Jewish community could become a reality, especially with a little help from the left. It could create a situation in which the entire organized Jewish community shuns Jewish radicals like the plague, while the

radical community declares all expressions of Jewish consciousness to be objectively counterrevolutionary. Such a
development would, of course, be a tragedy for both parties.
It is hard to imagine a healthy radical movement that has no
distinctively Jewish element in it or that sets itself against the
national and cultural aspirations of the Jewish people, just as
it is hard to imagine a decent Jewish community that does not
find some common ground with the movement.

One of the few hopeful signs in all of this is the rapid
growth of a self-conscious Jewish radical movement despite
the best efforts of *Commentary* and the Jewish Establishment
to undercut it. It may well be one of the fastest growing movements on the campuses. By conservative estimates there are
Jewish radical groups of one kind or another now on close to
100 campuses, and they turn out 35 separate newspapers.
They are a varied collection—some are radical Zionists;
others are Diaspora-centered and more critical of Zionism,
though affirming the legitimacy of Israel; some work exclusively on Soviet Jewry, while others concentrate on trying to
radicalize traditional Jewish organizations. But their common
denominator is a widespread sense that it is legitimately in the
Jewish tradition to work for universal liberation, while it is
part of the radical tradition to be true to one's own roots.
While traditional campus Jewish organizations such as Hillel
are expiring at a rapid rate, the Jewish radicals are creating
political space where problems that divide Jews and the movement might begin to be worked out.

As for Israel, it too will get a little leavening from these
new Jewish radicals. The big *machers* of the World Zionist
Organization are going to see a lot of hell-raising from young
radical Zionists this winter at their quadrennial Congress in
Jerusalem. And anyone who doubts that Israel needs a full-
scale cultural revolution for its full health and survival might
recall the recent spectacle put on by the Israeli Minister of
Housing. He called a press conference to announce and defend the start of construction of a new Jewish housing project
on the outskirts of Jerusalem which required the demolition

of Arab houses and the removal of their occupants, some at the point of a gun. The housing plan for Jerusalem on which this brutal action was based had been condemned by a committee of distinguished international architects as a civic monstrosity. If the Israeli bureaucrats have their way, they may yet have as their epitaph that, after 2000 years of Jewish history, they managed to turn Jerusalem into a giant, all-Jewish shopping center.

The fight over the dimensions of the Jewish consciousness, however, is not over. Social conditions in Israel are ripe for the growth of a radical movement that might restore the revolutionary tradition of Israel, as witnessed by the recent violent street demonstrations by young oriental Jews who call themselves Black Panthers. But it is no accident that those demonstrations erupted at a time when the war front was almost totally quiet. For, if an opposition movement is to blossom, there must be a real peace and a settlement of the national question. Thus, Israeli radicals need some help from the Palestinian radicals, and the international left could help in this reconstruction by establishing ties with *both* the Palestinian and the Israeli left on the basis of mutual respect for both national liberation movements.

Even if some of these things started to happen tomorrow, it wouldn't mean instant socialism and revolution in the Middle East. It wouldn't mean the immediate end to imperialism and exploitation there. But it could begin a process where socialists and radicals on both sides talked to each other.

And that would also go a long way toward solving my Jewish problem—and ours.

A Listing of Radical Jewish Movement Groups, Newspapers, and Journals and Bibliography

A Listing of Radical Jewish Movement Groups, Newspapers, and Journals

The radical Jewish movement is a new movement, constantly changing and innovating. To help the reader, the following index has been developed. An excellent source of information of local as well as national groups is *A Guide to Jewish Student Groups,* compiled and edited by Ann Rothstein and designed by David Kaufman. It can be obtained from the "umbrella" organization for the movement in North America: North American Jewish Students' Network, 4th Floor, 154 West 27th Street, New York, New York, 10001. They are great people. The reader could also write to the editors of this book in care of the publisher.

For information on groups in Europe, Israel, and elsewhere, the international "umbrella" organization is the World Union of Jewish Students (W.U.J.S.), 247 Grays Inn Road, London WC1, England.

There are, in addition, two news services: for North America, the Jewish Student Press Service, 4th Floor, 154 West 27th Street, New York, New York, 10001, and in Israel, the Jewish Liberation Information Service, P.O. Box 7557, Jerusalem, Israel.

For those interested in films and tapes, which can be rented at nominal fees, about the movement and related issues, contact Bernard M. Timberg, 2715 Ellsworth, Berkeley, California, 94705.

LISTING 379

The following is a list of various national and local groups, along with the city where their main headquarters is located.

National Groups

American Zionists Youth Council (New York City)
American Zionist Youth Foundation (New York City)
Atid-Conservative Judaism (New York City)
B'nai Akiva—Religious Zionists (New York City)
Hamagshimim—Zionist (New York City)
Hashomer Hatzair—Socialist Zionist (New York City)
Ichud Habonim—Socialist Zionist (New York City)
Israeli Student Organization (New York City)
Lubavitch Youth Organization—Orthodox (New York City)
Masada (New York City)
National Jewish Liberation Movement (New York City)
North American Jewish Youth Council (New York City)
Radical Zionist Alliance (New York City)
Student Struggles for Soviet Jewry (New York City)
Student Zionist Organization (Montreal)
Yavneh—Religious Students Association (New York City)
Youth Mobilization for Israel (New York City)
Yugundtruf—Youth for Yiddish (New York City)

Major High School and College Groups

B'nai B'rith Hillel Foundation (Washington, D.C.)
B'nai B'rith Youth Organizations (Washington, D.C.)
Canadian Young Judea (Toronto)
Jewish Defense League (New York City)
National Conference of Synagogue Youth (New York City)
National Federation of Temple Youth (New York City)

Noar Mizrahi (New York City)
United Synagogue Youth (New York City)

Campus and Community Based Groups

Action Committee for Soviet Jewry (Toronto)
Am Chai (Chicago)
American Students for Israel (Philadelphia)
Berkeley Union of Jewish Students (Berkeley)
Brandeis Yiddish Theater (Boston area)
Chavurot Aliyah (Chicago)
Chevrei (Beloit, Wisconsin)
Council of Jewish Organizations [Columbia University] (New
    York City)
Étudiants juifs francophones (Montreal)
Fabrangen (Washington, D.C.)
Havurat Shalom (New York City)
Havurat Shalom Community Seminary (Boston area)
Hebrew House (Oberlin, Ohio)
House of Love and Prayer (San Francisco)
Institute for Creative Jewish Living (New York City)
Jewish Activist League (Boston)
Jewish Liberation Project (New York City)
Jewish Liberation Project (Durham, North Carolina)
Jewish Peace Fellowship (New York City)
Jewish Radical Community (Los Angeles)
Jews for Urban Justice (Washington, D.C.)
Mippies—Messianic International Party (Boston)
Progressive Students for Israel (Toronto)
Radical Jewish Student Union (Seattle)
Radical Zionist Caucus (Vancouver)
Students for Israel (Chicago)
Zamir Chorale of Boston (Boston)
Zamir Chorale Foundation (New York City)
    Plus many, many others.

LISTING 381

Europe

Organisation des sionistes révolutionnaires (Brussels)
Organisation des jeunes juifs révolutionnaires (Paris)
Young Mapam (London)
Revolutionär zionistich Jugendgruppe (Vienna)
Sozialistisch zionistich Bund (Frankfurt)
Progressive Zionists (Scandinavia)
Revolutionary Israeli Students (Oxford)
Israel-Palestine Socialist Action Group (London)
Union of Jewish Students in Germany (Munich)

South America

Izquierda judío universitario (Caracas)
Frente de izquierda sionista (Chile)
Neuve sion (Buenos Aires)
Amos (Buenos Aires)
Hativa Mordechai Anilevich (Uruguay)
Negued Hazerem (Mexico City)

Plus other groups, many clandestine, in Morocco and Algeria.

Israel

Siach (New Left)
Matzpen (Compass)
Black Panthers
Movement for Peace and Security

Journals and Newspapers

United States

Davka (Los Angeles)
Genesis 2 (Boston)
The Jewish Radical (Berkeley)
The Jewish Liberation Journal (New York City)
Response (Boston)
ACIID (St. Louis)
Voice of Micah (Washington, D.C.)
Chutzpah (Chicago)
Columbia Jewish Free Press (New York City)
Ha Am (Norman, Oklahoma)
Hashofar, (Cleveland)
Doreinu (Washington, D.C.)
Hayom (Philadelphia)
Nefesh (Ann Arbor, Michigan)
Out of the Desert (Albuquerque, New Mexico)
Youth and Nation (New York City)
Herut (New York City)
The Other Way (New York City)
University Jewish Voice (Austin, Texas)
Attah (Madison, Wisconsin)
Rock of Ages Review (Chicago)

Canada

Strobe (Montreal)
Masada (Downsview)
Or (Toronto)

Europe

Israël-Palestine (Paris, Brussels)
Turtle (London)

LISTING   383

W.U.J.S. Journal (London)
Jewish Student Review (Oxford)
Co-existence (London)
Dialog (Germany)
Pressespiegel (Germany)
Hatikva (Rome)

Israel

Lillit (Hebrew University, Jerusalem)
Pi-Ha'aton (Hebrew University, Jerusalem)
Para K'dosha (Tel Aviv University)
Israel International (Jerusalem)
Haolam Hazeh (Tel Aviv)
Israeleft News Service (Jerusalem)

Bibliography

This list of books and articles should spur the reader to seek out new/old paths. The references cover a broad area: Jews and radicalism, the religious roots of Jewish radicals, the sources of student protest, and the identity of Jewish youth today. Reference is also made to the ideological and religious foundation of Jewish radicalism in the works of Ber Borochov, Martin Buber, Moses Hess, Bernard Lazare, and Nachman Syrkin.

There are a few books that readers should be aware of: Arthur Waskow, *The Freedom Seder* and *The Bush is Burning;* James A. Sleeper and Alan Mintz, *The New Jews;* Mordechai Chertoff, *The New Left and the Jews;* Bruce Goldman, *Up Against the Wailing Wall* (forthcoming); Uri Avnery, *Israel Without Zionists;* plus the works of Albert Memmi, *Portrait of a Jew* and *The Liberation of the Jew,* Isaac Deutscher, *The Non-Jewish Jew,* and the works of Elie Wiesel. These books are all a good beginning: go, study, teach, learn . . . and organize.

Alter, Robert, "Revolutionism and the Jews: Appropriating the Religious Tradition," *Commentary,* 51, 2, February, 1971, 47–54.

American Zionist Youth Council, "Movement in Search: Zionism Reconsidered," New York, n.d.

Astor, Gerald, "The Agonized American Jew," *Look,* 35, 8, April 20, 1971, 17–19.

Avneri, Shlomo, "Palestinians and Israel," *Commentary,* Vol. 49, June, 1970, 31–44.

Avneri, Uri, *Israel Without Zionists.* New York: Macmillan, 1968.

Axelrad, Albert, Robert Goldburg, Huey Newton, Morris U. Schappes, and George Wald, "The Black Panthers, Jews, and Israel," *Jewish Currents,* February, 1971. Available in reprint from *Jewish Currents.*

Ber Borochov, *Nationalism and the Class Struggle: A Marxian Approach to the Jewish Problem.* New York: Poalei Zion-Zeirei Zion of America, 1937. This is a hard to get translation, long out of print. An adequate English translation of Borochov's major work, called *Nationalism and Class Struggle: Essays in Zionism and Socialism,* has been published by the Radical Zionist Alliance, New York.

————, "The National Question and the Class Struggle," in Arthur Hertzberg, *The Zionist Idea.* New York: Harper and Row (Torch Books), 1959, 353–366.

Bikel, Theodore, "Report on Jewish Campus Youth," *Congress Bi-Weekly,* 35, October 28, 1969, 10–16.

Braiterman, Kenneth, "The Micro-Generation Gap," *Midstream,* XVI, 3, March, 1970, 31–36.

————, "The Jewish Defense League: What Safety in Karate?" *Midstream,* XVI, 4, April, 1970, 3–15.

Braun, Jonathan, "The Student Revolt and the Jewish Student," *Midstream,* XVI, 3, March, 1970, 41–44.

Buber, Martin, *Between Man and Man.* New York: Macmillan, 1965.

————, *Hasidism and Modern Man,* trans. and ed. by Maurice Friedman. New York: Harper and Row, 1966.

————, *Paths in Utopia.* Boston: Beacon Press, 1971.

Buch, Peter, "The Palestinian Revolution and Zionism," *International Socialist Review,* 32, 1, January, 1971, 8–13, 24–26.

Chertoff, Mordechai (ed.), *The New Left and the Jews.* New York: Pitman, 1971.

Deutscher, Issac, *The Non-Jewish Jew and Other Essays.* New York: Oxford University Press, 1968.

Dworkin, Susan, "Zionist Radicals on Campus, Part One," *Pioneer Woman,* 45, September-October, 1970.

————, "Zionist Radicals on Campus, Part Two," *Pioneer Woman,* 45, November–December, 1970.

Fein, Leonard, "Dilemmas of Jewish Identity on the College Campus," *Judaism,* 17, Winter, 1968, 10–21.

Feinstein, Sara, "A New Jewish Voice on Campus," *Dimensions in American Judaism,* 4, Winter, 1970, 4–11.

Feldstein, Donald, "Campus Jews and Jewish Institutions," *Midstream,* XVI, 4, April, 1970, 58–64.

Flacks, Richard, "The Liberated Generation: An Exploration of the Roots of Student Protest," *Journal of Social Issues,* 23, 3, July, 1967, 52–75.

————, "Who Protests: The Social Bases of the Student Movement," in Julian Foster and Durward Long (eds.), *Protest: Student Activism in America.* New York: Morrow, 1970, 134–157.

Friedman, Norman L., "The Problem of the 'Runaway Intellectual': Social Definition and Sociological Perspective," *Jewish Social Studies,* 31, January, 1969.

Friedmann, Georges, *The End of the Jewish People?* Garden City: Doubleday, 1967.

Glazer, Nathan, "The Jewish Role in Student Activism," *Fortune,* 79, January, 1969, 112–113 *et seq.*

————, "Revolutionism and the Jews: The Role of Intellectuals," *Commentary,* 51, 2, February, 1971, 55–61.

Greenberg, Irving, "Jewish Survival and the College Campus," *Judaism,* 17, Summer, 1968, 259–281.

Guttmann, Allen, *The Jewish Writer in America.* New York: Oxford University Press, 1971.

Hertzberg, Arthur, *The Zionist Idea.* New York: Harper and Row (Torch Books), 1959.

Hess, Moses, "Selections from Rome and Jerusalem (1862)," in Arthur Hertzberg, *The Zionist Idea.* New York: Harper and Row, 1959, 116–139.

Hirsch, Tannah, "The J.D.L.: Heroes or Hooligans?" *The Jerusalem Post,* Wednesday, March 4, 1970, 5.

Horowitz, Irving Louis, "The Student as Jew," *The Antioch Review,* XXIX, 4, Winter, 1969–70, 537–546.

Kahane, Meir, Joseph Churba, and Michael King, *The Jewish Stake in Vietnam.* New York: Crossroads Publications, n.d.

————, *Never Again!* Los Angeles: Nash Publishing Company, 1971.

Kaye, J. M., "On the Campus," *Jewish Frontier,* 36, December, 1969, 14–17.

Keniston, Kenneth, "The Sources of Student Dissent," *Journal of Social Issues,* 23, 3, July, 1967, 108–137.

———, *Young Radicals.* New York: Harcourt, Brace and World, 1968.

———, "Notes on Young Radicals," *Change in Higher Education,* I, November–December, 1969, 25–33.

———, *The Uncommitted: Alienated Youth in American Society.* New York: Dell (Laurel Edition), 1970.

Lamm, Zvi, "The New Left and Jewish Identity," *Dispersion and Unity,* 10, 1970, 64–65.

Laqueur, Walter, "Revolutionism and the Jews: New York and Jerusalem," *Commentary,* 51, 2, February, 1971, 38–46.

Lazare, Bernard, "Jewish Nationalism and Emancipation (1897)," in Arthur Hertzberg, *The Zionist Idea.* New York: Harper and Row, 1959, 469–476.

Levin, Morris, "A Survey of Research and Program Developments Involving Jewish Adolescents and their Implications for Center Service," *Journal of Jewish Communal Service,* Spring, 1971, pp. 208–228.

Levy, Henry W., "Jewish Youth in Revolt," *Pioneer Woman,* 44, September–October, 1969, 3–5. (Parts II and III appeared in later issues).

Lipset, Seymour M., "The Left, the Jews, and Israel," in *Revolution and Counter-Revolution.* Garden City: Doubleday (Anchor Books), 1970, 375–400.

———, "The Socialism of Fools," *The New York Times Magazine,* January 3, 1971, 6–7, 26–37, 34.

Lukas, Anthony J., "The Making of a Yippie . . . Take One Midwestern Kid, for Example," *Esquire,* 72, November, 1969, 126–141.

Marx, Karl, *A World Without Jews,* D. D. Runes, ed. New York: Philosophical Library, 1959.

McGee, John, "Vigilante Karate," *Black Belt,* August, 1971, 46–49.

Memmi, Albert, *Portrait of a Jew.* New York: Orion Press, 1962.

———, *The Colonizer and the Colonized.* New York: Orion Press, 1965.

————, *The Liberation of the Jew*. New York: Orion Press, 1966.

————, *Dominated Man*. Boston: Beacon Press, 1969.

Mintz, Alan, "Notes on a Point of Departure," *Midstream*, XVI, 3, March, 1970, 45–50.

Newsweek, "The American Jew: New Pride, New Problems," March 1, 1971, 56–64.

Novack, George, *How Can the Jews Survive? A Socialist Answer to Zionism*. New York: Pathfinder Press (Merit Pamphlet), 1969.

Orenstein, Eugene, *et al.*, "The Jewish Youth Scene: Main Issues and Problems," *Jewish Currents*, 24, October, 1970, 4–15, 18–23, 28–35.

Porter, Jack Nusan, "Jewish Student Activism, *Jewish Currents*, 24, May, 1970, 28–34. Also reprinted in Caroline Rose (ed.), *Minority Problems*. New York: Harper and Row, 1972.

————, "The Activist Student," *Jewish Frontier*, 37, May, 1970, 19–23.

————, "The Jewish Student: A Comparative Analysis of Religious and Secular Attitudes," *YIVO Annual of Jewish Social Science* (forthcoming).

Rogowsky, Edward T., "Intergroup Relations and Tensions in the United States," *American Jewish Year Book—1969*, 70, 1969, 71–100.

Rose, Peter I., *The Ghetto and Beyond*. New York: Random House, 1969.

Rosenberg, M. J., "My Evolution as a Jew," *Midstream*, August–September, 1970, 50–53.

Rosenfield, Geraldine, *Interim Report on the New Left and Alienated Youth*. New York: American Jewish Committee, December, 1967 (mimeographed).

Ross, Benjamin, "Jewish Radicals and the Jewish Community," *Midstream*, XVI, 3, March, 1970, 51–60.

Rubenstein, Richard I., *Israel, Zionism, and the New Left*. New York: Zionist Organization of America, 1969.

Ruchames, Louis, "Jewish Radicalism in the United States," in Peter I. Rose, *The Ghetto and Beyond*. New York: Random House, 1969, 228–252.

Schappes, Morris U., "The Jewish Question and the Left—Old and New," *Jewish Currents*, 24, June, 1970, 4–13, 29–37.

Schub, Louis (ed.), *The New Left and Israel*. Los Angeles: Center for the Study of Contemporary Jewish Life—University of Judaism, 1971.

Segal, Bernard E., "Status Orientation and Ethnic Sentiment Among Undergraduates," *American Journal of Sociology*, 71, July, 1965, 60–67.

Siegel, Danny, "The Essence of My Commitment," *Midstream*, XVI, 3, March, 1970, 37–40.

Sleeper, James A., and Alan L. Mintz (eds.), *The New Jews*. New York: Random House (Vintage Books), 1971.

Sokol, Moshe, "The Jewish Radical," *The Jewish Observer*, 7, 4, February, 1971, 7–9.

Syrkin, Nachman, "The Jewish Problem and the Socialist Jewish State," in Arthur Hertzberg, *The Zionist Idea*. New York: Harper and Row (Torch Books), 1959, 329–350.

Triebwasser, Marc A., "The Jewish Activist Youth Movement," *Congress Bi-Weekly*, 37, March 6, 1970, 15–19.

Trotsky, Leon, *On the Jewish Question*. New York: Pathfinder Press (Merit Pamphlet), 1970.

Van den Haag, Ernest, *The Jewish Mystique*. New York: Dell, 1971, especially pp. 95–104.

Waskow, Arthur, *The Freedom Seder*. New York: Holt, Rinehart, and Winston, 1970.

———, *The Bush is Burning*. New York: Macmillan, 1971.

Wiesel, Elie, *The Jews of Silence*. New York: Random House, 1969.

———, *Souls on Fire: Hasidic Portraits and Tales*. New York: Random House, 1972.

Woodward, Kenneth, Phyllis Malamud, *et al.*, "The American Jew," *Newsweek*, March 1, 1971, 56–64.

World Union of Jewish Students, "Comparative Study of the Attitudes Among Jewish Students Before and After the Six-Day War." London: W.U.J.S., February, 1970 (mimeographed).

Yaffe, James, *The American Jews: Portrait of a Split Personality*. New York: Paperback Library, 1969, particularly 274–292.

Ziegler, Mel, "The Jewish Defense League and Its Invisible Constituency," *New York*, 1971, 28–36.

Jack Nusan Porter, born in the Ukraine during World War II where his father was a commander of Russian partisans, and educated in America, received his Ph.D. in sociology from Northwestern University in 1971. He has taught at Northwestern, De Paul University, the Passavant-Wesley Nursing Schools, and most recently as Assistant Professor of Sociology at the State University of New York—College at Cortland. He was co-founder of the Radical Jewish Student Movement in Chicago. His articles and reviews have appeared in *Jewish Currents, Congress Bi-Weekly, American Journal of Sociology, Jewish Frontier, Commonweal*, and the *International Review of Sociology*. He is presently at work on two books: *The Jewish Rebel* and *The Sociological Imagination of Film*. He is also editorial consultant in sociology to the Dushkin Publishing Group.

Peter Dreier is a native of Plainfield, New Jersey. He graduated from Syracuse University with degrees in sociology and journalism. He spent his junior year at the University of London and has worked as a newspaper reporter and as a community worker in Israel, Puerto Rico, and Guatemala. He presently teaches sociology at Roosevelt University, is a Ph.D. candidate at the University of Chicago, and is a member of the Am Chai community in Chicago. He has also taught at Chicago State University. When not with others he keeps to himself.